D1598724

The Psychology of Personality

Critical Assessments of Contemporary Psychology
A Series of Columbia University Press
Daniel N. Robinson, Series Editor

The Psychology of Personality

An Epistemological Inquiry

James T. Lamiell

Columbia University Press   New York   1987

Columbia University Press
New York   Guildford, Surrey
Copyright © 1987 Columbia University Press
All rights reserved

Printed in the United States of America

Library of Congress Cataloging-in-Publication Data

Lamiell, James T.
  The psychology of personality.

  (Critical assessments of contemporary psychology)
  Bibliography: p.
  Includes index.
  1. Personality.   2. Personality assessment.
I. Title.   II. Series.   [DNLM: 1. Personality.
2. Personality Assessment.   3. Psychological Theory.
BF 698 L231p]
BF698.L3716   1987   155.2'01   86-29878
ISBN 0-231-06020-3

This book is Smyth-sewn.

Book design by J.S. Roberts

To my Mother
Rita Jacobs Lamiell
and to the memory of my Father
Thomas Joseph Lamiell
(1916–1969)

Contents

Acknowledgments

There are many individuals who in a variety of ways contributed mightily if indirectly to the accomplishment of this work. Speaking chronologically, I would first like to thank E. Jerry Phares, Franz Samelson, and Leon Rappoport, who during my graduate training at Kansas State University both taught me much and gave me the liberty to make what I would of what I had learned. For countless hours of stimulating discussion at the University of Illinois, I am grateful to many, but most especially to Gerald L. Clore, William F. Chaplin, Mark A. Foss, and Steven J. Trierweiler. To colleagues and students at Georgetown University as well, I extend my thanks, both for your intellectual vigor and for your patience through my two years of assurances that I would dispatch some or another duty of mine "as soon as I finish the book."

Among the many others who have informed my thinking and encouraged my efforts, I owe the greatest of thanks to Frank J. Landy, Rom Harré, Jean-Pierre DeWaele, Joseph F. Rychlak, and my Georgetown University colleague Daniel N. Robinson. While I know that no one of them could embrace without qualification everything that I have written, I also know that each of them will find here ample evidence of their influence on my thinking.

There is last, though for this only by virtue of reasons standing above and beyond all others, to thank my wife Leslie, my son Kevin, and my daughter Erika. Speaking to you and not of you, I say that for more than you gave in patience, encouragement, and understanding, I would not have the temerity to ask.

Preface

Over a decade has now passed since, as a graduate student frustrated by the utter failure of a master's thesis research project, I resolved to abandon the psychology of personality, and to seek another domain in which to make whatever contribution I might to our understanding of human behavior. With many others during the early and mid-1970s, no doubt, I had concluded that personality research was a fruitless endeavor. In the face of evidence marshaled by others that there was precious little if any consistency in the behavior of individuals over time and across situations, it had become increasingly difficult to defend the notion that "personality" even existed. Moreover, the results of my own research to that point had offered, so far as I could tell, nothing to contradict this conclusion.

On the other hand, there was also mounting evidence that laypersons' intuitive beliefs in the existence of personality remained intact. Following the lead of investigators who had offered "illusory correlation" as an explanation for these rather curious intuitive beliefs, I decided to direct my research efforts toward a further exploration thereof. Little did I then suspect that those efforts would eventually lead me back to the psychology of personality—if indeed I ever really left it, which I now doubt—with a vastly different perspective.

In a concise interpretation of the evidence that he had accumulated relevant to the so-called "illusory correlation" phenomenon, Shweder argued as follows:

Respondents on interpersonal inventories and questionnaire interviews are shown to unwittingly substitute a theory of conceptual likenesses for a description of behavioral co-occurrences. Considerations about similarity are confounded with judgments about probability to such an extent that *items alike in concept are inferred to be behaviorally characteristic of the same person* even when, as is typically the case, conceptual relationships among items do not correspond with the actual behavioral relationships among the items. (Sweder 1975:481–82; emphasis added)

To make a long, technically burdensome story short and to the point, my own studies of illusory correlation led me to the conclusion that it was the phenomenon itself that was the illusion. I arrived at this conclusion not from evidence that in formulating subjectively meaningful characterizations of themselves and others the thinking of laypersons is grounded in "valid" correlational beliefs, but on the basis of evidence that laypersons' subjective personality judgments are not grounded in *correlational* beliefs at all. What is more—and of much greater significance in the long run—the evidence showed that laypersons' subjective characterizations of self and others are not even grounded in the normative considerations of individual differences that would by definition underlie correlational beliefs (the interested reader will find a detailed explication of these views in articles by Lamiell, Foss, and Cavenee 1980, and by Lamiell 1980; see also Shweder 1980).

With what I took to be strong empirical evidence to this effect in hand, I began to suspect that there was a great deal more at stake here than the "illusory correlation" (non)phenomenon. For it has long been held that one's personality is properly defined in terms of the qualities, attributes, or characteristics that distinguish him/her from others, and consequently that one judges others by normative, individual differences considerations. But if it is true that subjective personality judgments are not based on such considerations, the question naturally arises as to what sorts of considerations they are based on. Another question that arises is: if subjective conceptions of personality cannot be understood in terms of the logic and analytic methods of the traditional individual differences paradigm, then why should personality investigators insist on framing "objective" conceptions of personality in those terms? The answer, I have concluded, is that *they shouldn't*, and I take it as my chief burden in this book to defend this conclusion. By so doing, I hope to contribute to the redirection of basic personality research away from technically sophisticated but theoretically uninformative studies of individual differences, and toward *the study of individuals* in ways that are at least formally suited to the task of advancing personality theory.

We will be revisiting in this book, not surprisingly, what has come to be known as the "nomothetic vs. idiographic" controversy, a controversy that has dogged the field for several decades now. Indeed, much of chapter 1 is focused on that controversy, particularly as it was fueled by the writings of Gordon Allport.

However, as I am at pains to point out in chapter 1, the thesis to be developed in this book deviates importantly from that articulated by previous critics of the so-called "nomothetic" paradigm. More specifically, I am not arguing that personality investigators are in need of a viable alternative to conventional "nomothetic" inquiry because the knowledge yielded by such inquiry is not "idiographic." Instead—and contrary to an assumption that has been shared by disputants on both sides of the controversy—the position I am going to defend here is that personality investigators are in need of a viable alternative because the knowledge yielded by "nomothetic" inquiry *is in fact not nomothetic* in any sense that a *personality theorist* would be compelled to take seriously.

At no point in the history of the nomothetic-vs.-idiographic controversy has anyone seriously contested the notion that a theory of personality—any theory of personality—is in its very essence a framework for conceptualizing the behavior and/or psychological functioning of individuals. Hence, the historic hegemony of ersatz "nomotheticism" is properly attributed to the long-standing and widespread belief that the empirical knowledge about *variables* with respect to which individuals have been differentiated constitutes empirical knowledge about the *individuals* who have been so differentiated. Unfortunately, this belief is as thoroughly false as it is firmly entrenched, and it is in just that belief where the problem lies. For knowledge that is interpretable *for no individual* cannot possibly constitute knowledge about *individuals in general*, and the latter is the only interpretation of the term "nomothetic" to which a personality theorist can logically be bound.

      I would contend that unless and until those who animate the field of scientific personality psychology arrive in large numbers at an understanding of the points just made, genuine advances in our theoretical conceptions of personality, and of the role played by personality in human action, simply will not be possible. Moreover, of this much some five years of experience as an associate editor of the *Journal of Personality* has persuaded me beyond whatever faint doubt I might otherwise have had: the thinking of most contemporary personality investigators is so thoroughly dominated by the techniques and technical concepts of individual differences research that it cannot successfully be countered on any terms other than its own.

      I mention all the above not only to help the reader to anticipate what is to come, but to forewarn that some of what follows is fairly technical in nature. I have sought to simplify the technical aspects of the material wherever possible, but in many instances I have encountered limits to simplification which I felt I could not transgress without compromising my arguments. My hope is that through an analysis of the logic and methods of conventional "nomotheticism" that is as "hard-nosed" as conventional nomotheticism itself, a not insignificant number of current and future personality investigators can be persuaded that individual differences research is in fact fundamentally ill-suited to the purposes of a science of personality.

      To this end, my treatment in chapter 1 of the nomothetic-vs.-idiographic controversy and other relevant matters is followed by a discussion of conventional "nomotheticism's" basic tenets (chapter 2), and of the legacy thereof throughout the various schools of thought that can be identified in contemporary personality psychology (chapter 3). With all this as relevant background, I try to explain in chapter 4 why the knowledge yielded by individual differences research—in any of its various forms—has always been inherently inadequate to the task of advancing personality theory.

In chapter 5, I begin what I regard as an attempt to constructively redirect basic research in the psychology of personality. In a fashion that might initially perplex many readers, however, I do not abruptly distance the discussion from individual differences research but instead analyze further the nature of the measurement operations on which the characterization of persons has traditionally been and might alternatively be predicated. Central to this discussion is a comparison of normative and interactive models for psychological measurement. While conventional "nomothetic" inquiry has always been based on the logic of normative measurement, I try to show in chapter 5 that normative measurement is itself based on the logic of interactive measurement.

Now as it happens, it is also in the logic of interactive measurement where I have been finding an answer to the question to which I was led by my earlier researches on "illusory correlation." Specifically, subsequent research has yielded strong evidence that subjective judgments concerning one's own and others' personality characteristics are grounded in essentially dialectical rather than normative considerations, whereby *what is relevant is what differentiates a person from the person s/he is not but might otherwise be.* Chapter 6 is devoted largely to a discussion of empirical research relevant to this point. However the reader might choose to regard that research from a substantive standpoint, I believe that for its purely formal aspects it offers one concrete illustration of the manner in which methodologically rigorous inquiry yielding knowledge that is interpretable at the level of the individual can be conducted without in any way compromising the quest for nomothetic principles.

Of course, I also believe that the relevance of the material presented in chapter 6 extends beyond the purely formal, and it is this point around which chapter 7 is centered. There I defend the recent calls by some contemporary personality investigators for renewed attention to cognitive phenomena, and reject the contention of others that such constitutes a deviation from the traditional concerns of personality theory. I argue that because every theory of personality either is or necessarily invokes a conception of human cognition, the latter is a phenomenon of central relevance to theoretically driven research in the field. If this is so, then the question of how persons frame subjective conceptions of themselves and others is pertinent not only—or, perhaps, even primarily—for what it tells us about subjective conceptions, but for what it tells us about the *reasoning process* that underlies them. The latter, I believe has far-reaching implications for the conduct of personality research broadly defined.

There is one point that I would encourage the reader to keep in mind as s/he proceeds through this book: while much of what I have written concerns, for reasons I have sought to explain, matters methodological, the subject matter is not, in my own mind, methodology. The subject matter is *epistemology*. The guiding questions here are: with what sort of knowledge is a theory of personality concerned? What sort of knowledge does individual differences research actually yield? In what sorts of knowledge are subjective conceptions of self and others rooted? To what sorts of questions ought basic, theoretically driven research in the psychology of personality be aimed?

I am certain that for many who will chance to read this book, it will not read comfortably. Beyond the technicalities, much of what I have to say is wholly antithetical to what are, at least among those who answer to the appellation "personality psychologist," deeply entrenched beliefs. Nevertheless, I have written what I have written on the assumption that the reader both can and will consider carefully the arguments developed, agreeing with me, at the very least, that a psychology of personality that is *epistemologically* unsound is *unsound*, and that from the standpoint of a would-be scientific discipline, such a state of affairs is simply unacceptable.

1 Epistemology and the Psychology of Personality

In his discussion of publication trends in contemporary personality psychology, Hogan (1983) noted that 1985; Harré 1981; Rorer and Widiger 1983; Rychlak 1976a; Tyler Individual Differences section of the *Journal of Personality and Social Psychology* would place that section—by itself—among the top five or six of all journals published by the American Psychological Association. On these grounds, Hogan was pleased to announce "the good news . . . that personality psychology is alive and well" (p. 4).

Given the historical context in which it was offered, this rather sanguine perspective is not altogether groundless, and there are undoubtedly many who share it. For those familiar with the discipline's recent past are well aware that it has been a troubled one. Never the darling of academic psychology to begin with,[1] personality psychology came to be viewed with still greater disdain by specialists in other areas, even as it was being torn by dissension and doubt from within.

Unquestionably, a watershed here was the publication, in 1968, of Walter Mischel's *Personality and Assessment*. In that

---

1. Hall and Lindzey (1978:4) note that "personality theory has occupied a dissident role in the development of psychology. Personality theorists in their own times have been rebels. Rebels in medicine and in experimental science, rebels against typical methods and respected techniques of research, and most of all rebels against accepted theory and normative problems."

work, Mischel mounted a serious challenge to a "critical assumption" that was—and remains—widely regarded as inherent within the concept of personality itself, i.e., the assumption of the "consistency of particular predispositions within any individual" (Mischel 1968:9). The putatively relevant empirical evidence available at the time seemed to provide precious little support for this assumption, and thus raised doubts in many circles about the very concept of personality as an instrument of psychological theory. Under the weight of such doubts, many investigators simply left the psychology of personality for dead, and of those who did not follow suit immediately, a good number were soon enough persuaded to do so. For some, the *coup de grâce* was mounting evidence that enduring beliefs in the existence of relatively stable, coherent behavior patterns—i.e., "personality" in the only form recognizable to empiricism—could themselves be explained as the (stable and coherent) illusions of perceivers, born, unwittingly, of the biasing influence of their own preexisting conceptual schemes (see, e.g., Shweder 1975, 1982; see also Lamiell 1980; Lamiell, Foss, and Cavenee 1980; Shweder 1980).

For a great many investigators, then, the major conclusion to be drawn from all this was that with respect to the objectives of scientific psychology, the study of "personality" was at best superfluous and at worst counterproductive. To the stubborn souls who endured fell the task of somehow defending the concept of personality against long odds, and we scarcely oversimplify matters to say that the literature of the past two decades or so has been singularly devoted to this task.

It is against this backdrop, I think, that the trend cited by Hogan can be seen as encouraging. It constitutes, if nothing else, clear evidence of a conviction—sustained among some and even renewed among others—that a scientific psychology bent on defining away personality and related concepts (self, identity, etc.) is ultimately vacant, however incorrigible those concepts have been, and however satisfactorily the discipline might seem to be getting along without them. In this sense, therefore, we may readily (and gratefully) acknowledge that the psychology of personality is "alive."

Yet a scholarly discipline can hardly be regarded as "well" simply because it is "alive," and searching analyses undertaken in recent years have led to the conclusion that the field is anything but well, its manuscript-submission behavior notwithstanding. Consider, for example, the remarks with which Sechrest concluded his contribution to the 1976 edition of the *Annual Review of Psychology*:

The reader, along with this writer, may think that many of the |studies that have been reviewed| are individually interesting. Many of the findings are fascinating, and some are bound to prove seminal to a series of fairly integrated efforts. But most are likely, however dazzling they may be, to have little longer life and impact than the rockets of the Fourth of July. The individual studies lack direction and staying power, and they suggest a status for the field of personality that puts one in mind of the apocryphal jet pilot who assured his passengers that while the plane was lost, it was at least making good time. (Sechrest 1976:22)

Some two years after Sechrest's article appeared, Donald W. Fiske introduced his book *Strategies for Personality Research* as follows:

A thorough reexamination of the personality field is imperative. The need is evident not only from an unprejudiced appraisal of the limited progress made in recent decades and of the nature of that progress. The assumptions underlying the study of personality must be made explicit and critically reviewed. What have we been doing? Where are we? What can we do about our situation? (Fiske 1978a:3)

One who would dismiss the above as idiosyncratic crankiness will find little solace in analyses provided by numerous other authors (see, e.g., Carlson 1971; Conley 1983; DeWaele 1985; Harré 1981; Rorer and Widiger 1983; Rychlak 1976a; Tyler 1978). And while those authors clearly disagree with one another (and I with them) in many important respects, they converge on at least one point: the vast bulk of empirical research that has been conducted in the name of "personality" over the past several decades has failed to advance personality *theory* in any enduring way.

The present book emerges from the conviction that

this problem remains very real—the best efforts of previous critics notwithstanding—and that it cannot be ignored any longer.
For the naive optimism of "dustbowl empiricists" aside, informed
scholars in every scientific discipline have always recognized that
where there are no advances in theory, there are no genuine advances in understanding. It follows that unless personality investigators are prepared to inhabit a discipline wherein the objective
of understanding personality and the role that it plays in the production of human behavior is completely abrogated in deference
to what now passes for "behavioral prediction," the problem is
going to have to be addressed satisfactorily. Moreover, to the degree that renewed busyness among contemporary personality investigators is diverting attention from the problem—and this much
is at least implicit in the critiques of the field that have already
appeared—it is entirely conceivable that that very busyness will
only guarantee the result it now seems for all the world to belie:
the demise of the discipline.

Whether a compelling case for any of this can be made
is naturally a matter on which the critical reader will wish to reserve judgment. Of this much we can be certain from the start,
however: any informed appraisal of personality psychology's current health—or lack of it—will rest ultimately on considerations
rather more penetrating than the rate at which manuscripts are
being submitted to its journals. The question is not *how much* is
being done in the name of personality. Rather, Fiske suggested,
the questions are: *what* is being done? and where is it all leading?

Personality Psychology's Epistemological Problem

Framing the Issue

In contemporary textbook discussions of the psychol-
ogy of personality, it has become virtually *de rigueur* to begin by
posing some variant of the discipline's most basic ontological
question: what is personality? Routinely, however, authors move

rapidly to a discussion of the fact that, as useful as the concept seems to be in everyday discourse, psychologists have yet to settle on any definition of personality that is at once substantive, precise, and generally agreed upon. Consider that personality has been variously defined as

the dynamic organization within the individual of those psychophysical systems that determine his [her] characteristic behavior and thought. (Allport 1961:28)

the person in the situation, and only what is not accounted for in terms of focal, contextual, and background stimuli may be ascribed to personal or inner factors. (Helson 1964:541)

that which permits a prediction of what a person will do in a given situation. (Cattell 1950:2)

the process of living. (Angyal 1941:374).

In the face of such divergence, one can well appreciate the position taken by Hall and Lindzey (1957), who, in the first edition of their now-classic text, *Theories of Personality*, argued that

[no] *substantive definition of personality can be applied with any generality.* By this we simply mean that the way in which a given individual will define personality will depend completely upon his particular theoretical preference. . . . Once the individual has created or adopted a given theory of personality, his definition of personality will be rather clearly implied by the theory. (Hall and Lindzey 1957:9)

In the three decades that have elapsed since this passage first appeared in print, nothing has transpired that would render it anachronistic. On the contrary, it seems as true now as ever that, in the last analysis, defining personality is itself a matter of personality. It is significant, however, that despite personality investigators' continuing inability to agree on exactly what it is that they are studying, they have had little trouble maintaining broad consensus on how to go about studying it. Dating at least to 1918, when R. S. Woodworth formally imposed the techniques of intelligence testing on the systematic assessment of (other?)

personality characteristics, it has been generally understood—indeed adamantly insisted—that "the study of personality is essentially the study of *individual differences*" (Wiggins et al. 1976:4; emphasis added).

A major thesis to be developed in this book is that whatever other difficulties the psychology of personality might have, this unwavering commitment to individual differences research constitutes the discipline's most fundamental problem. Indeed, I will argue below that vis-à-vis our overriding pantheoretical objectives, the individual differences paradigm is, in all its various guises, a "mind-forged manacle"[2] of the most insidious type. For in its alluring combination of sophisticated quantitative techniques and simple intuitive appeal, that paradigm has repeatedly confounded the most dedicated efforts to advance our scientific understanding of personality, and it has done so without betraying in any large measure the fact that it is inherently ill-suited to the task.

The reason is that while the critical assertions of personality theory—any personality theory—concern the behavior or psychological functioning of *individuals*, individuals differences research quite literally focuses attention on the *spaces between* individuals, and there is simply no logically valid way in which to claim knowledge about the former on the basis of evidence concerning the latter. Unfortunately, the illusion that matters are otherwise is as compelling as it is pervasive, and it is therefore likely to endure for as long as the subtle but critical errors of reasoning in which it subsists elude our grasp.

It is in consideration of just these points that I identify the discipline's most fundamental problem as *epistemological* in nature. It is rooted in a failure to appreciate the utter, irreconcilable disconnectedness between the kind of knowledge about human behavior sought by a personality theorist on the one hand and the kind actually provided by individual differences research on the other hand. Once this disconnectedness is brought into

2. My apologies to William Barrett, who in using this phrase to entitle the prologue of his marvelous book *The Illusion of Technique* (1979) noted that he himself had borrowed the phrase from William Blake.

focus, it becomes apparent that there are *no* refinements of the traditional paradigm—be they purely technical, based on a more "enlightened" selection of variables, or both—that could possibly salvage that paradigm as a methodological framework within which to advance personality theory. The problem will not be resolved by tinkering *within* the paradigm because the problem *is* the paradigm, or, more precisely, the way in which it has been (mis)used by investigators conducting empirical research.

Some Historical Perceptive

Readers already familiar with the literature of personality psychology will undoubtedly detect in what has just been said traces of a controversy that has been festering within the discipline for 50 years, since Gordon Allport (1937) formally introduced the so-called "nomothetic vs. idiographic" distinction to the field. Since to many this controversy has never seemed terribly fruitful, I should mention that the arguments to be developed in this work deviate substantially from those thus far mounted on either side of the dispute. Because of this, however, some historical perspective is perhaps in order.

Unquestionably, my assertion concerning the discipline's epistemological problem is rooted firmly in Henry A. Murray's (1938) contention that "The objects of study [in personality psychology] are *individual organisms, not aggregates of organisms*" (p. 127; emphasis added). While my adoption of this thesis will immediately be interpreted by some as an explicit endorsement of the "idiographic" point of view, one would be hard-pressed to identify any personality theorist—contemporary or "ancestral"—who has ever rejected Murray's thesis in principle. For where but at the level of the individual organism would one expect to explore personality, however conceived, as an instrument of psychological theory? Thus, if to be "idiographic" simply means to concern oneself with the behavior or psychological functions of individuals, then all personality theorists are ultimately "idiographic" in their outlook. And yet if this is so, then we are compelled to wonder, as Holt (1962) did nearly two decades ago, what

(if any) genuine substance the interminable nomothetic-vs.- idiographic controversy could have embodied to begin with.

Rather than constituting a debate over metatheoreti-
cal ends, this dispute has actually centered around the question
of how to pursue those ends scientifically, i.e., in a fashion that
is at once

> (a) methodologically rigorous;
> (b) logically compatible with the objective of under-
> standing individual behavior/psychological function-
> ing; and
> (c) consonant with scientific psychology's larger ob-
> jective of establishing general principles or laws.

The individual differences paradigm continues to dominate empirical personality psychology simply because the vast majority
of investigators remain convinced of that paradigm's unique capacity to embrace all three of these desiderata simultaneously.

As it happens, only the first of the three, methodological rigor, can be claimed with any legitimacy at all, for reasons
that will be developed in later chapters. For the moment, we shall
focus on the basic assumptions from which commitment to the
individual differences paradigm emerged, for there lie the initial
ontological, epistemological, and metaphysical foundations of the
enterprise. Those assumptions can be summarized as follows (see
Beck 1953; Eysenck 1954; Falk 1956; Harris 1980):

> 1. That "the" human personality is structured in terms
> of a finite number of underlying qualities (or attributes, charac-
> teristics, predispositions, traits) in some amount of which every
> individual is endowed by nature and/or by nurture.
> 2. That through programmatic studies of individual
> differences in behavior, the components of this generic structure
> can be discovered scientifically and defined operationally as vari-
> ables of a dimensional and/or categorical nature.
> 3. That once the presumed generic structure has been
> discovered and operationalized, the substantive features of any
> given individual's personality can be specified comprehensively

in terms of that personality's measured coordinates or "location" within the structure.

4. That the empirically established relationships between and among the component variables of the generic structure and measures of overt behavior across a wide variety of settings will embody the general principles or laws under which personality factors (operating alone, in combination, or in interaction with external factors) influence, determine, or cause a given individual's behavior.

By no means did the pioneers in this venture begin in agreement as to just what the components of "the" generic human personality would prove to be, nor can the mass of empirical findings accumulated during some sixty years of painstaking research be taken to have resolved much of anything (see Fiske 1973, 1974, 1978a, 1978b, 1979). Still, the belief persists that the scientific study of personality cannot advance significantly without some viable taxonomic foundation of the sort just described (see Gleitman 1981), and various programmatic efforts to achieve the same persist to this day (e.g., Bem 1983; Buss and Craik 1983a, 1983b, 1984a; Golding 1978; Mehrabian and O'Reilly 1980; Wiggins 1979).

Were he with us now, Allport would hardly be surprised by the failure thus far to establish what would amount to a periodic table of personality elements. For it was his abiding doubt about this notion that led him to introduce the distinction between "nomothetic" and "idiographic" approaches, and to admonish his colleagues of the ever-present need to supplement the former with the latter. The operative word here is "supplement," because Allport did not reject the possibility that some general—i.e., universally applicable—dimensions/categories of personality existed. Nor did he reject the notion that conventional individual differences research was logically suited to their discovery and operational specification. What Allport steadfastly resisted was the assumption that any given individual's personality could be *comprehensively* specified or understood solely in these terms.

Allport believed that every individual's personality consists partly or entirely of traits not found in the personality of every—or perhaps even any—other person. He also believed that within each personality these "noncommon" elements somehow combine with the "common" or "universal" elements in ways so as to produce unique personalities; i.e., personalities that could not be fully understood as mere quantitative variations on a singular generic structure. Since in Allport's view these theoretical possibilities could not be accommodated by the assumptions underlying the traditional individual differences research paradigm, he concluded that assertions about individual personalities based on findings generated within that paradigm—i.e., assertions based on knowledge of the sort he labeled "nomothetic"—would inevitably have to be supplemented by knowledge gained in some other ways, through knowledge of the sort he labeled "idiographic."

Unfortunately, the arguments that Allport mounted in defense of his position, though brilliant in some respects, were in other respects inconsistent, incomplete, and/or ambiguous (see Franck 1982). It is partly for this reason that his arguments have never substantially influenced the praxis of empirical personality psychology. Nor was this fact lost on Allport himself, who concluded one of his final contributions to the psychological literature as follows:

Nevitt Sanford (1963) has written that by and large psychologists are "unimpressed" by my insisting on [the nomothetic-idiographic] distinction. Well, if this is so in spite of 4 decades of labor on my part, and in spite of my efforts in the present paper—I suppose I should in all decency cry "uncle" and retire to my corner. (Allport 1966:107)

With the most persistent critic of strict adherence to the "nomothetic" paradigm thus dispatched, we should not be surprised to find that paradigm continuing to dominate the thinking of contemporary personality investigators. As Sechrest (1976) and Rorer and Widiger (1983) have pointed out, and as no one familiar with the field's current literature could fail to see, the study of individual differences remains the *sine qua non* of empirical personality research.

It is possible that if Allport's arguments had been developed more thoroughly and/or if those that he did develop had been attended to more closely, both he and contemporary personality psychology would have enjoyed better fates. Whether or not this is true, nothing is going to be changed simply by revisiting Allport's views here. Instead, it would appear that if personality psychology is ever to benefit from the insights Allport did have, it will be necessary to explore some of those areas in which his incisiveness was lacking.

Further Historical Consideration

In his use of the terms "nomothetic" and "idiographic," the German philosopher Wilhelm Windelband (1921) sought to distinguish between two kinds of knowledge, that attainable through scientific methods on the one hand, and through nonscientific (essentially historico-analytical) methods on the other hand. In borrowing Windelband's terms, therefore, Allport seemed to be suggesting that at least some of the knowledge sought by personality investigators would lie beyond the pale not only of individual differences research but of scientific methodology in general. If the message he intended to convey was other than this (and I believe that in fact it was; see below), efforts to so persuade his critics could not have been aided by passages such as the following:

The individual, whatever else he may be, is an internally consistent and unique organization of bodily and mental processes. But since he is unique, science finds him an embarrassment. Science, it is said, deals only with broad, preferably universal, laws. Thus science is a *nomothetic* discipline. Individuality cannot be studied by science, but only by history, art, or biography, whose methods are not nomothetic (seeking universal laws), but *idiographic*. (Allport 1961:9)

Nunnally may well have had this passage in mind when, in a text entitled *Psychometric Theory*, he said of the nomothetic-idiographic controversy:

The idiographists |e.g., Allport| may be entirely correct, but if they are it is a sad day for psychology. Idiography is an antiscience point of view:

it discourages the search for general laws and instead encourages the description of particular phenomena (people) . . . Efforts to measure personality traits are based on the hypothesis that the idiographists are not entirely correct, that there are some general traits of human personality. The nomothetic point of view should be tested to the limit; otherwise, to accept an idiographic point of view in advance is to postulate that only chaos prevails in the description of human personalities. (Nunnally 1967:472)

Insofar as these remarks reflect the broader antipathy with which Allport's views were received by his contemporaries, it is not terribly surprising to find him eventually "crying uncle." What is more relevant to our present concerns, however, is the fact that well before this *dénoument*, Allport recognized the growing perception of his position as antiscientific, and he actively sought to counter it. For example, in a 1962 contribution to the *Journal of Personality*, Allport urged that the term "idiographic" be dropped as a referent for his views, and that the term "morphogenic" be used instead. Thus he sought to disassociate himself from a term he had borrowed from philosophy, and to relabel his position with a term borrowed from a scientifically respectable discipline: biology. Moreover, the remainder of the article in which Allport suggested this new terminology (which was never widely embraced) was devoted primarily to a discussion of various methods of inquiry which he felt could be made to pass muster as scientific (see Runyan 1982).

In addition, and consistent with a point made earlier, there are places in Allport's writings where he disavows any categorical rejection of "nomothetic" methods. Thus, later in the same text in which the seemingly antiscientific passage appeared we find Allport admonishing the reader to

bear in mind that we are not condemning the common trait approach. Far from it. When we wish to compare people with one another, it is the only approach possible. Furthermore, the resulting scores, and profiles, are up to a point illuminating. We are simply saying that there is a second, more accurate way, of viewing personality: namely, the internal patterning [the morphogenesis] of the life considered as a unique product of nature and society. (Allport 1961:360)

Personality exists only at a postelementary state; it exists only when the common features of human nature have already interacted with one another and produced unique, self-continuing and evolving systems. This is not to say that the search for common elements or common human functions is undesirable. For the most part the science of psychology does this and nothing else. I insist only that if we are interested in *personality*, we must go beyond the elementaristic and reach into the morphogenic realm. (Ibid.:361; emphasis in original)

In the light of such maneuvers, it seems clear to me that Allport was trying to convince his critics that whatever else he might be advocating, it was not an antiscience point of view. But in direct proportion to his (limited) success with these maneuvers, Allport merely traded one set of problems for another. For in passages such as the one just cited, doctrinaire "nomotheticists" have found little that is irreconcilable with their own views, and what remains seems unamenable to scientific inquiry.

In particular, adherents of the traditional individual differences paradigm have never viewed themselves as foreclosing in principle the need to explore how the universal elements of personality function "morphogenically" in causing an individual's behavior to take on a particular pattern or style. Indeed, the last of the four assumptions said earlier to constitute the foundation for that paradigm can be seen as an endorsement of this very notion; previous authors seeking to incorporate Allport's thesis into the mainstream have emphasized just this point (Beck 1953; Falk 1956). But on this account, Allport's desire to move beyond the search for common elements reduces to mere impatience, born of his unwillingness to accept the fact that morphogenic inquiry while ultimately necessary, would be premature in the absence of a viable "nomothetic" foundation. And as for Allport's suggestion that the style a particular person's behavior does assume in a "postelementary state" might literally be unique—as opposed to *individual* in the sense of being *one's own*—the response within the mainstream has always been that there is no scientific way to resolve the question of uniqueness one way or the other, and so it is simply moot (Levy 1970; Sanford 1963).

When all is said and done therefore, it would appear that the difficulties Allport encountered in carrying his message to mainstream personality investigators can be summed up as follows: he could never alter the collective perception among his intellectual adversaries that an "idiographic" approach to the study of personality was and is either (a) wholly compatible with and subsumable by traditional "nomothetic" methods after all, and hence valid but superfluous, or (b) ultimately incompatible with prevailing methods, but in that event non- or antiscientific. Either way, Allport ends up in his corner.

Transcending the Nomothetic vs. Idiographic Controversy

As unlikely as it might seem given what has been said thus far, the continuing domination of empirical personality psychology by individual differences research is not primarily attributable to Allport's lack of persuasiveness in areas where he deviated from the mainstream. Instead, the resilience of the traditional paradigm has much more to do with an assumption that Allport granted—indeed shared with—his adversaries, namely, that individual differences research is logically suited to the discovery of whatever universal principles personality psychology might ever have to offer. In challenging this assumption, we find at last the grounds on which to transcend the nomothetic vs. idiographic controversy as it has materialized historically within the field.

The term "nomothetic" is rooted in the Greek *nomos* plus *thetikos*, which translate as "lawful thesis" or "dogma." Accordingly, this term has come to refer to universal principles or general laws. Now whenever the issue of establishing such principles or laws is raised, one of the most fundamental questions is: *What are the entities over which generality/universality is being sought or asserted?* For as concerns the epistemology of scientific inquiry, the answer to this question specifies the level of analysis at which theoretically relevant hypotheses must be tested, and at which putatively relevant empirical evidence must be interpretable.

As indicated earlier, personality theorists have always recognized with Murray that "the objects of study are individual organisms, not aggregates of organisms." This being the case, it is perhaps apparent that individual persons constitute the entities over which generality must be sought in the search for nomothetic principles of personality. That is, a general principle of personality would properly be thought of as one that has been found to hold, within the limits of induction that characterize all scientific inquiry, *for each of many individuals.* It follows that research devoted to the search for such principles must be conducted—and its empirical findings must be interpretable—at the level of the individual.

Until he was finally relegated to his corner, what Allport maintained—against all odds, but quite properly as it turns out—was that the knowledge generated by research conducted within the individual differences paradigm would never be sufficiently individualized or "idiographic" in nature. What Allport failed to see clearly is that the knowledge generated by research conducted within that paradigm would never be nomothetic in nature either, at least not in any sense that a personality theorist would be compelled to take seriously. It is because Allport's appreciation for this point scarcely outpaced that of his adversaries that the latter have always seemed able to dismiss him—then and now—as a renegade who was at best impatient for a kind of knowledge that traditional methods would eventually provide anyway, and at worst antiscientific.

But on the view to be defended here, traditional individual differences research is flawed in substantially greater measure than even Allport realized. The reason is that *the empirical evidence generated by individual differences research has no legitimate interpretation whatsoever at the level of the individual.* Because such research does exactly what its name suggests, its yield is singularly uninformative about any one of the individuals the differences between whom have been studied. This being the case, we are entitled to wonder just how such research manages to carry the name "nomothetic." For how can findings that are uninterpretable at the level of the individual possibly be regarded as advancing the quest for general principles of individual psychological functioning? And if the individual differences paradigm cannot advance this quest, then in what sense is it suited at all—let alone "uniquely"—to personality psychology's nomothetic objectives?

The answers to these questions reside, of course, in the fact that the empirical findings generated by individual differences research are not recognized as being uninterpretable at the level of the individual. Instead, knowledge about variables in terms of which individuals are compared is routinely translated as if it somehow constituted or conveyed knowledge about each of the individuals so compared. As long as the errors of reasoning that inevitably infect the translation process remain obscured, the entire enterprise seems reasonable, and the illusion that individual differences research logically serves the quest for general principles of personality is maintained.

A Case in Point

An excellent illustration of the epistemological problems to which I have been alluding is provided by the dispute over temporal and transsituational (in)consistency in behavior, which has occupied center stage in the literature of the field for well over a decade.

That dispute was sparked by the work of Mischel (1968) who, it will be recalled, was concerned to evaluate empirically a "critical assumption" supposedly inherent within the concept of personality, i.e., the assumption of "consistency of particular predispositions within any given individual." Mischel discovered in his archival inquiry that correlations were routinely quite low between measures of individual differences in personality characteristics and the behavioral differences that in theory should have been predictable from such measures. He concluded that the assumption of any appreciable degree of behavioral consistency was, at the very best, in need of serious reexamination.

Now given the tenets of the generic-structure conception of personality, it is not surprising that this suggestion was widely regarded as a challenge to the very concept of personality. Once a commitment to generic structuralism had been made, the most fundamental task for empirical personality research was obviously that of identifying the component variables of the presumed structure. Variables qualifying for inclusion would be those for which correlations of the sort Mischel inspected were found to be high, for these would be the variables in terms of which to account for the observable manifestation of personality, i.e., consistency in the behavior of individuals over time and across situations. By the same token, a low correlation presumably constitutes evidence that individuals have not been consistent with respect to the measured attribute over time or across situations. Such an attribute would not qualify as a personality variable, and therefore would not be included in any model of "the" personality's generic structure.

Under the terms of this conception, it should be apparent that insofar as empirical research on individual differences variables repeatedly yields low correlations, the sought-after set of personality "elements" remains null, and one is at some point led to question the existence of personality itself. This is precisely the challenge that Mischel's evidence was widely perceived to embody. Nor, in this light, is it difficult to understand the diligence with which other investigators have sought to meet that challenge with empirical evidence of their own. Such evidence has been adduced in the form of demonstrations that correlations of the sort inspected by Mischel can be and often are quite high, provided that one secures them properly (see, e.g., Block 1977; Epstein 1979, 1980; Gormly 1984; McGowan and Gormly 1976).

For all the time, effort, and journal space that has been devoted to the consistency-vs.-inconsistency controversy, it is unfortunate that the empirical evidence over which it has been waged has been completely misinterpreted by disputants on all sides. More specifically, as concerns the question of the "consistency of particular predispositions within any given individual," the simple fact of the matter is that both the "low" correlations cited by Mischel and the "high" correlations that have since been produced by others mean exactly the same thing: that the individuals assessed were *not equally* (in)consistent in their respective manifestations of the measured "predispositions." Given any such correlation, therefore, there is no assertion about the degree of consistency with which a particular predisposition has been manifested by individuals *in general* that could possibly be valid. The only exception to this view occurs when the correlation in question is perfect, because that is the one instance in which what has been found to hold for persons *in the aggregate*, i.e., as a group, can also be said to hold for persons *in general*, in this case for each of the individuals in the group. Unfortunately, the distinction between what is truly general and what is merely aggregate has been thoroughly mangled by conventional "nomotheticism"—the best efforts of such as Bakan (1966) notwithstanding—and it is just here where the consistency-vs.-inconsistency debate has foundered epistemologically.

The erroneous reasoning here consists in the notion that if a perfect correlation means that in general the individuals studied were perfectly consistent in their relative manifestations of the measured attribute—which is true—then "high" correlations must mean that in general the individuals were "highly" consistent in this regard—which is not true—and "low" correlations must mean that in general the individuals were inconsistent in this regard—which is not true either (a graphic illustration of these facts will be provided in chapter 4).

It is not irrelevant that although Mischel's highly influential findings were published after Allport had died, evidence and conclusions virtually identical to Mischel's had been published several decades earlier (Hartshorne, May, and Shuttleworth 1930; Lehman and Witty 1934; Symonds 1931). Moreover, Allport was both aware of this earlier work and aware of the fact that the low correlations reported therein did not establish that "in general" people were inconsistent, but only that they were not consistent in the same ways, or in ways that an investigator could expect to discern simply by imposing his/her own trait concepts on all of them simultaneously (see Bem and Allen 1974, on whose work I will comment more extensively in chapter 3). Unfortunately, Allport either failed to see or chose not to pursue the logical fact that even if the investigators had obtained "high" correlations, the same conclusions would have been mandated.

What is so ironic about this is that if Allport had pursued this latter point, he might actually have come closer to achieving his larger objective of drawing personality investigators out of the individual differences paradigm. In any event, and in light of the rebukes that have been heaped upon Allport over the years, it seems only fair to point out this much: if with respect to the specific theoretical issue Mischel (1968) raised, his findings had been properly interpreted at the time either by himself or by the field at large, then his book *Personality and Assessment* would have been written and/or received as the massive empirical vindication of Allport's views that in fact it is, rather than as a challenge to the concept of personality that it neither was nor ever will be. The same holds for all the empirical evidence that has since been brought to bear on the consistency vs. inconsistency controversy, including, I should note, the omega-square ratios and coefficients of generalizability that are sometimes reported instead of conventional correlation coefficients (see Golding 1975).

If we can state with confidence only that no personality theorist worthy of the name has ever been strongly committed to a thesis of "predispositional consistency" within individuals, we can state with absolute certainty that none need ever pause for empirical evidence that does not test that thesis anyway. Still, it is hoped that a useful purpose has been served by drawing attention to the consistency-vs.-inconsistency controversy here, because in my own view it illustrates with alarming clarity the central problem with which I am concerned in this book, namely, the gulf that has developed over the years in personality psychology between its theoretical concerns and its prevailing methodological practices. If the substance of the debate can be dismissed as a red herring, the faulty epistemology in terms of which it has been waged cannot.

From Individual Differences Research to a Psychology of Personal Knowledge

While my critique of the individual differences paradigm necessarily involves a close analysis of issues that would normally be classified under the heading "methodology," the problem with which I am concerned, as I said earlier, is not fundamentally methodological but epistemological in nature. Thus advances in our understanding of personality are not going to be achieved merely by adopting some new research technique(s). Of course, insofar as the problem is partly methodological—and any epistemological problem is—we have every reason to expect that its solution will entail methodological adjustments of one sort of another. But the other side of any epistemological problem is theoretical, and it is in this domain that our quest for an alternative to the conventional paradigm must be firmly rooted. We must seek to clarify the kind of knowledge about human behavior sought within personality theory, and then embrace—or if necessary create—a methodological framework that is both rigorous and formally suited to the specified concerns.

Attempting to articulate one pantheoretical agenda for the psychology of personality is, of course, a hazardous (if not presumptuous) undertaking. As noted earlier, there has never been any broad consensus within the discipline on just what personality "is," and one could argue that the overriding objectives of the field are likely to remain as diverse as the definitions of personality yielded by its extant theories. Nonetheless, I believe that it is both possible and necessary to transcend this pluralism without distorting or destroying it. On the other hand, I do not see how this can be accomplished without taking seriously Levy's (1970) insight that "the concept of personality owes its existence to man's [sic] psychological tendency to seek meaning in his experience" (p. 19). In the final analysis, a theory of personality is concerned not with behavior per se—and certainly not with individual differences in behavior—but rather with the *meaning* of behavior as framed, consciously or otherwise, within the mind of the behaving individual.

Levy's assertion does not deny the clear and substantial differences that do exist between the various schools of thought within personality theory (psychoanalytic, cognitive–social learning, phenomenological, existential, humanistic, etc.). It merely suggests that those differences are best viewed as the reflection of divergent assumptions about *how* individuals frame meaningful ideas, rather than disagreements over whether such ideas are framed, or whether they are embodied in an individual's behavior. When personality psychology's pantheoretical agenda is viewed this way, one is led inexorably to the conclusion that basic research must be addressed ultimately to questions concerning (a) the grounds on and reasoning processes by which individuals frame those meaningful ideas that constitute their own knowledge, broadly defined, and (b) the nature of the relationships between such knowledge and overt action. In effect, this view asserts that personality psychology's core concern is subjective or *personal knowledge*.

Consistent with this general orientation, several years ago I proposed something I chose to call an "idiothetic" approach to the study of personality as an alternative to the "nomothetic" paradigm (Lamiell 1981, 1982). At that time, I coined the neologism "idiothetic" in a somewhat offhand attempt to highlight the possibility and the necessity of reconciling the study of individuals—the discipline's "idiographic" concern—with the search for general principles of human psychological functioning—the "nomothetic" aim. However factitious this particular usage might have been, there is a legitimate translation of the term, one suggestive of its formal compatibility with the views outlined above. Defined with reference to its linguistic roots, the term "idiothetic" literally means "of or pertaining to *one's own* (idio-) point of view, knowledge, or *thesis* (-thetic)," and it is this definition that reflects the approach I envision; an approach whereby the substantive individuality of personal knowledge is respected without negating the possibility of extracting nomothetic principles. The latter would be sought through studies of the processes by which personal knowledge is framed within the mind and extended into behavior.

These views will be expounded in more detail in later chapters. Meanwhile, it will be useful to keep in mind that although there is substantial compatibility between these views and recent calls for a heightened emphasis on cognitive matters, my own views differ in some important respects from much of what is currently recognized as "cognitive personality psychology" (e.g., Cantor and Kihlstrom 1981; Cantor and Mischel 1977; Forgus and

Shulman 1979; Higgins, Kuiper, and Olson 1981; Mischel 1978; Shaver 1985).

For one thing, my conception of what is entailed by a cognitive personality psychology is much better captured by the term *human judgment*—and all that might imply—than by the term "information processing." What is "information" anyway? On what grounds does information become information to a person? How is that which one knows, consciously or otherwise, related to that which one does and does not do? What sorts of explanations must personality psychologists invoke in order to discuss behavior in these terms? All these questions are of central relevance to a viable psychology of personality, and if I do not pretend to answer them all here, nor do I believe that we can afford to look past them.

Equally important is the fact that, increasingly, the individual differences research paradigm is influencing cognitive personality psychology no less than it has historically dominated research on more conventional topics. As a result, this still burgeoning movement is in danger of being undermined by the same epistemological problems that plague what some critics of the movement continue to regard as "the study of personality itself" (Bem 1983:547). For just this reason, however, I take with utmost seriousness Mischel's (1979) assertion that "an adequate analysis of behavior cannot proceed without serious attention to the cognitive processes of both the actors and the observers, the subjects and the scientists of our field" (p. 752). Indeed, this book can be regarded as an attempt to follow up on that suggestion directly, paying no less attention to the cognitive processes of the scientists than to those of the subjects.

Concluding Remarks

Sechrest (1976) argued that

to too great an extent the field of personality has been dominated, at least in terms of salience, by psychologists pursuing the ubiquitous but elusive, and maybe even chimerical, differences between persons. Paradoxically, these psychologists have operated more often than not from a theory that posits not differences but universals. Freud's developmental states, Adler's striving for superiority, Jung's animus-anima, Maslow's need hierarchy, and many other concepts were meant to apply to everyone everywhere, but psychologists became bogged down in studying differences in a way that has never been very productive. . . . [This] is not to deny the importance of individual differences; but until we know more about basic processes of personality, it is difficult to know how to fit the differences in. (Sechrest 1976:4)

As is surely apparent at this point, my own views are in substantial accord with Sechrest's, and hence discordant with the dominant view in the field for over sixty years. Not the least of the reasons for this hegemony is the fact that individuals' personalities do, after all, differ. The problem is that while our respective personalities may be different, it does not follow that the study of variables investigators have chosen to characterize those differences will illuminate anyone's personality or the role that it plays in the production of his/her actions.

Just why so many have for so long believed otherwise is a matter that requires painstaking appraisal, and the appropriate place to begin is with a discussion of the logic and methods of individual differences research itself.

2 Methodological Foundations of Conventional "Nomotheticism"

I noted in chapter 1 that the long-standing commitment of personality investigators to the study of individual differences has been nurtured by and in turn has nurtured what was termed the "generic structure" conception of personality. The essence of that conception is that any given individual's personality can be described, and its effects on behavior understood, in terms of the level at which it is endowed with certain basic attributes present to one degree or another in all personalities.

From the classical "nomothetic" point of view, then, the overriding objectives of programmatic personality research have always been to: (a) identify the basic attributes comprising the generic structure; (b) derive valid empirical indicators thereof, i.e., faithful measures of the levels at which the attributes exist within any given personality; and (c) establish empirically the relationships between the attributes and overt behavior, i.e., the "laws" of personality functioning.

The focus of this chapter is on the methodological concepts and principles on which personality investigators have based their pursuit of these objectives, for it is here that we find the epistemological core of conventional "nomotheticism."

The Mechanics of Personality Assessment

Figure 2.1 conveys some sense of the symbiotic relationship that exists between "generic structuralism" as a theoretical conception of personality and conventional "nomotheticism" as a research paradigm (see Loevinger 1966). The boxes shown in region I of the figure represent individuals, P_1, P_2, P_p, . . . P_n, each of whose personality is thought to be definable in terms of the level at which it is endowed with certain basic attributes. These attributes are represented as the A's within each box.

The B's, shown in region II of the figure, signify overt behaviors manifested by each of the n persons depicted in region I. Under the terms of the generic structure conception it is assumed that there are "enduring and consequential" between-person differences in the patterns that these overt behaviors take on over time and across situations (see Block 1977). It is further assumed that such differences result from and are thus explainable in terms of between-person differences in the levels of the attributes. Note that the arrows connecting regions I and II are dashed rather than solid; because the precise nature of the relationship between underlying personality characteristics and overt behavior is unknown.

Quite obviously, an investigator does not and cannot directly measure the levels of the respective attributes within an individual's personality. However, on the assumption that those attribute levels do exert a systematic influence on one's overt behavior, the possibility exists of estimating the former on the basis of observations of the latter. For such purposes, the overt behaviors represented in region II of figure 2.1 become, from the perspective of the personality investigator, the observational variables, the OV's, shown in region III of the figure.

From a strictly methodological standpoint, then, it can be said that conventional "nomothetic" personality research begins with the assignment by an investigator of numerical values or scores to individuals, in such a way as to represent empirically the degree to which various underlying attributes are manifested

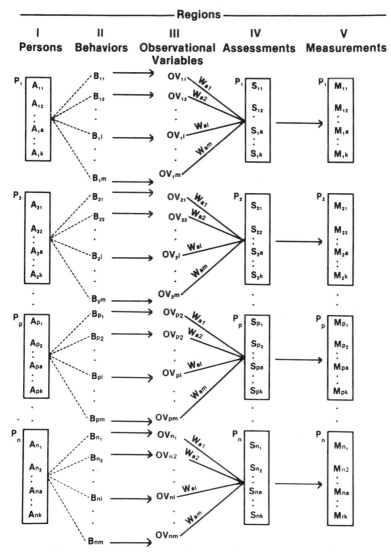

Figure 2.1 Schematic for Conventional Personality Assessment and Measurement

in certain observations that have been made of each of those individuals. The assignment of such scores is the essence of formal personality assessment, and the process by which this is typically accomplished can be explained in terms of the following general equation:

$$S_{pao} = \Sigma_{i=1}^{m} (OV_{pio}) (W_{iao}) \qquad (2.1)$$

where the symbols are defined as follows:

S_{pao} = *the assessment made of person p* with respect to attribute *a* on occasion *o*,

OV_{pio} = an item of information obtained on occasion *o* concerning the behavior of person *p*, expressed as a value of observational variable *i*,

W_{iao} = *the weight or importance attached to observational variable i* as a reflection or instantiation of underlying attribute *a* on occasion *o*, and

$\Sigma_{i=1}^{m}$ = the additive combination rule under which the $[(OV_{pio})(W_{iao})]$ units, of which there are *m*, are combined into an overall assessment, S_{pao} (see Nunnally 1967).

In words, equation (2.1) simply states that an assessment of person *p* with respect to underlying attribute *a* on occasion *o* is an additive combination of *m* items of information concerning the behavior of person *p* on occasion *o*, with each item of information being "weighted" according to the degree to which it is seen by the investigator to reflect or "betray" that underlying attribute.

The observational variables depicted in region III of the figure 2.1, and represented by the OV component of the equation, may or may not be rooted in actual observations of behavior. To be sure, such is the case in some instances (see Goldfried and Kent 1972). However, for ethical, practical, and in some cases even theoretical reasons, observational variables are usually defined on the basis of verbal statements about behavior [see Cattell's (1950) discussion of L-, T-, and Q-data as bases for personality description and measurement; see also Fiske 1978a].

In so-called "projective" tests of personality, for example, observational variables are generated on the basis of individuals' verbal responses to intentionally ambiguous "stimuli" such as the Rorschach ink blots or thematic apperception test (TAT) pictures (see Murray 1938; McClelland 1951). The rationale underlying such tests is that in the face of ambiguity, an individual will project certain aspects of his/her personality into various statements about the "stimulus." A properly trained and sufficiently experienced test administrator therefore should be able to detect and codify those statements in a way that reveals at least some aspects of the individual's underlying personality structure. While projective testing has at times been criticized by mainstream "nomotheticists" on the ground that it is not sufficiently objective, insofar as the detection/codification process employed by the test administrator can be made explicit, projective testing can be understood in terms of equation (2.1) no less than other, more "objective" approaches.

Perhaps the most commonly employed personality assessment procedures -are those referred to under the general heading of "paper-and-pencil" techniques. In such procedures, the OV component of equation (2.1) might be defined on the basis of (a) a subject's statements about his/her own behaviors, formulated as responses to the items of a self-report questionnaire, or (b) memory-based ratings of the subject's behaviors provided by others presumed to have knowledge thereof (e.g., parents, teachers, peers, etc.). Within these two broad categories there are, of course, many extant variations, and investigators have awakened to numerous controversies over the years concerning the fidelity of verbal statements about behavior as indicators of actual behavior (see, e.g., Nicholls, Licht, and Pearl 1982). For our present purposes, however, the important conceptual point lies in what is methodologically common to all formal personality assessment procedures, namely, the engagement of some technique(s) whose function is to secure items of information concerning the behavioral tendencies of the subjects under investigation. However they are secured, these items of information constitute the observational variables depicted in region III of figure 2.1 and represented by the OV component of equation (2.1).

As that equation indicates, the formal assessment of individuals with respect to their underlying personality characteristics also entails some specification of the weight or importance to be assigned to each observational variable in determining the total score, S (see Bem and Allen 1974; Hase and Goldberg 1967). Ideally, of course, these weights would be defined in proportion to degree to which various behaviors are actually influenced by that attribute, although, as was mentioned earlier, the relationships are in fact unknown.

In the very earliest stages of a research program, it is common for an investigator to rely on intuition as a basis for determining the weights. To use a rather stark example, if one wished to assess junior executives with respect to the underlying attribute of achievement motivation, it might seem intuitively reasonable to attach considerable importance (and thus to assign a high weight) to an observational variable conveying information about the amount of overtime voluntarily invested in company business. In contrast, information concerning the extent to which vegetables are consumed as part of one's daily diet might seem, intuitively, irrelevant to the assessment of achievement motivation. If so, then an observational variable conveying information on this matter would be given a weight of zero in the computation of achievement motivation scores.

As helpful and perhaps even necessary as intuition can be in the early phases of research, most contemporary investigators would argue that questions concerning the weight to be attached to discrete observational variables should ultimately be settled on empirical grounds. We will return to this point later on. For the moment, it may be helpful to consolidate what has been said thus far through a simple but concrete example.[1]

1. Here and in subsequent chapters, the examples to be used are indeed quite simple. Hence the reader should keep firmly in mind the fact that my objective is to clarify certain basic methodological points relevant to an epistemological analysis of conventional "nomotheticism," and not to defend any particular "test" or assessment procedure.

An Illustration

Several years ago, I conducted an informal survey to identify a set of activities representative of those in which students enrolled at a large midwestern university might be expected to engage in varying degrees. From the results of this survey, I selected 18 different activities, and then asked individual subjects to indicate the frequency with which they "typically" engaged in each activity. The responses obtained from one of those subjects, who will be referred to hereafter as "Smith," are shown in figure 2.2.

For the sake of illustration, let us suppose that these responses are veridical, i.e., that the X's shown in the figure faithfully indicate the frequency with which Smith "typically" engages in each of the activities listed. Let us further suppose that for theoretical reasons, we wish to assess Smith's behavior pattern with respect to the personality attribute "sociable vs. unsociable." From the standpoint of assessment methodology, then, the problem here is to generate a score that indicates the degree to which available information concerning Smith's "typical" behavior manifests the underlying attribute in question.

To solve this problem, the individual differences investigator would begin by imposing some numerical coding scheme onto the activity frequencies shown in figure 2.2. For example, an integer scale ranging from 0 to 9 might be employed arbitrarily, keyed to the obtained responses in such a way that 0 would be the numerical code assigned to "never" responses, 9 would be used to code "very frequently" responses, and values 1 through 8 would be used to code responses falling between these extremes. It should be apparent that in imposing this (or any other) scoring scheme onto the information contained in figure 2.2, one is, in effect, defining the observational variables depicted in region III of figure 2.1 and represented by the OV component of the equation.

Now as we have already seen, any formal assessment of Smith's behavior pattern requires, in addition to the above, some specification of the importance to be assigned to each ob-

Self-reported Frequency

M _x_ F ___

Activity		Never or almost never	Seldom	Occasionally	Frequently	As often as possible
1. Studying or reading intellectual material	(0)				X	
2. Participating in artistic or creative activities	(+1)		X			
3. Casual dating	(+3)			X		
4. Engaging in pre-marital sex	(0)	X				
5. Participating in athletic activities	(+4)				X	
6. Reading/viewing pornographic materials	(−3)		X			
7. Watching television	(+1)				X	
8. Listening to music	(−2)				X	
9. Working at a part time job	(+1)				X	
10. Playing cards	(+4)			X		
11. Partying	(+4)			X		
12. Attending live entertainment or movies	(+3)				X	
13. Participating in outdoor activities (camping, hiking, etc.)	(+2)				X	
14. Participating in events of a religious nature	(+2)			X		
15. Cutting classes	(0)		X			
16. Getting high on alcohol and/or marijuana	(0)			X		
17. Using drug other than alcohol or marijuana	(−1)	X				
18. Lectures/seminars (outside of coursework)	(+1)			X		

Figure 2.2 An Illustrative Self-Reported Activity Pattern

SOURCE: Adapted from J. T. Lamiell, M. A. Foss, R. J. Larsen, and A. Hempel, Studies in intuitive personology from an idiothetic point of view: Implications for personality theory, Journal of Personality 51:438–67. © 1983 by Duke University Press. Reprinted by permission of the publisher.

servational variable in determining his total score. Since this discussion is purely illustrative, let us assume that this question has been settled previously on empirical grounds, and that the weights are as indicated in parentheses to the right of each activity listed in figure 2.2.

The (arbitrarily selected) scale of measurement for these weights ranges from −5, signifying extreme unsociability, through 0 to +5, signifying extreme sociability. Thus, activities 5 ("participating in athletic activities") and 11 ("partying") are being viewed as important indicators of sociability, as evidenced by the fact that each of those observational variables has been assigned a weight of +4 on a scale where +5 indicates extreme sociability. In contrast, activities 6 ("reading/viewing pornographic materials") and 8 ("listening to music") are being viewed as rather unsociable activities, as they have been assigned weights of −3 and −2, respectively, on a scale where −5 indicates extreme unsociability. Finally, note that activities 1, 4, 15, and 16 (studying or reading intellectual materials, engaging in premarital sex, cutting classes, and getting high on alcohol and/or marijuana, respectively) have been assigned weights of 0, indicating that information concerning degree of involvement in those activities is being viewed as irrelevant to determining sociability/unsociability.

Having thus defined the OV and W components of equation (2.1), the computation of S is a simple matter of cross-multiplying each activity frequency value by its corresponding weight, and then summing the 18 cross-products. In this instance, the application of equation (2.1) yields a value of +114. This value, then, constitutes an assessment of Smith with respect to the underlying attribute "sociable vs. unsociable."

From Assessment to Measurement

The question that arises at this point, of course, is: what does the numerical value +114 mean? Just how sociable/unsociable does does a score of +114 "make" a person, and how is this matter to be decided? The fact that the question arises at all bears testimony to a crucial distinction between personality *assessment*, on the one hand, and personality *measurement* on the other. Were the distinction superfluous, then a satisfactory—indeed obvious—answer would be given directly by the assessment +114.

What is lacking is a frame of reference: any inference concerning the meaning of a given assessment with respect to an underlying attribute requires that the former be viewed within some context of comparable entities. Precisely this function is served by personality measurement. That is, personality measurement can be viewed as nothing more or less than a formal procedure for "locating" discrete assessments within context, or relative to specified reference points. In terms of figure 2.1, personality measurement can be defined as that operation by which the S assessments in region IV are transformed into their corresponding measurements as depicted in region V. The latter values—not the former—are the desired empirical indicators of the levels at which an individual's personality is endowed with specified attributes.

In 1944, Raymond B. Cattell, one of the most skilled psychometricians in the history of personality psychology, argued in an important but apparently little-known article that there are three basic rationales for psychological measurement: *normative, ipsative,* and *interactive.* In normative measurement, the meaning of the assessment made of a given person with respect to a given underlying attribute (e.g., +114 in the above example) is discerned by placing it within the context of assessments made of other persons with respect to the same underlying attribute. In ipsative measurement, context is defined in terms of other assessments made of the same individual, either for other attributes or for the same attribute at other points in time. In interactive measurement, context is specified not in terms of other actual assessments but in terms of the properties of the assessment procedure or "test" itself (e.g., with reference to the highest and lowest scores that are in principle obtainable under the procedure used to generate the assessment in question). Of ipsative and interactive measurement more will be said in chapter 5. For now we shall focus on normative measurement, simply because that is the rationale in terms of which conventional "nomothetic" inquiry proceeds.

In *Personality Measurement: An Introduction*, Kleinmuntz (1967) states flatly that "all meaning for a given score of a person derives from comparing his score with those of other persons" (p. 47). Now as Cattell discussed no less than two other rationales for psychological measurement, it should be understood that Kleinmuntz's assertion is simply not true. It should also be apparent, however, that a normative measurement rationale meshes perfectly with the theoretical assumptions underlying the generic-structure conception of personality.

Perhaps the simplest procedure for transforming "raw" assessments into normatively meaningful measurements is to re-define the former in terms of rank order. For example, a measure of 1 might be assigned to the individual with the highest obtained assessment, a measure of 2 to the individual with the next highest assessment, and so on. However, the vast bulk of individual differences research proceeds on the assumption that personality assessments can legitimately be transformed into normative measurements conveying interval as well as ordinal information. That is, the transformation procedure most commonly adopted is one whereby the resulting numerical values are taken to reflect not only the relative rankings of individuals but also the magnitudes of the distances between individuals along the underlying dimension of interest.

To illustrate what is involved here, let us consider the data in table 2.1. Column I begins with Smith's assessment, +114. The remaining entries in the column represent assessments of 30 other individuals regarding the attribute "sociable vs. unsociable," made in exact accordance with the procedure used to derive the assessment of Smith. Collectively, then, the 31 "raw" assessments shown in column I provide a context with reference to which each assessment can be transformed into a normatively meaningful measurement.

Table 2.1 Some Illustrative Data

	I	II	III	IV	V
Subject	"Raw" Assessments	Deviations from Mean	Squared Deviations from Mean	First-Obtained Z-score	Second-Obtained Z-score
1.	114	8.26	68.23	+ .41	+ .54
2.	87	−18.74	351.19	− .92	− .92
3.	59	−46.74	2,184.63	−2.30	−2.23
4.	87	−18.74	351.19	− .92	− .92
5.	97	− 8.74	76.39	− .43	− .26
6.	83	−22.74	517.11	−1.12	−1.10
7.	87	−18.74	351.19	− .92	− .73
8.	95	−10.74	115.35	− .53	− .54
9.	150	44.26	1,958.95	+2.17	+2.23
10.	140	34.26	1,173.75	+1.68	+1.57
11.	121	15.26	232.87	+ .75	+1.90
12.	132	26.26	689.59	+1.29	+1.20
13.	145	39.26	1,541.35	+1.93	+ .87
14.	140	34.26	1,173.75	+1.68	+1.57
15.	92	−13.74	188.79	− .67	− .49
16.	108	2.26	5.11	+ .11	+ .07
17.	98	− 7.74	59.91	− .38	− .21
18.	100	− 5.74	32.95	− .28	−1.38
19.	99	− 6.74	45.43	− .33	− .16
20.	87	−18.74	351.19	− .92	− .92
21.	96	− 9.74	94.87	− .48	− .30
22.	88	−17.74	314.71	− .87	− .87
23.	117	11.25	126.79	+ .55	+ .68
24.	103	− 2.74	7.51	− .13	− .16
25.	90	−15.74	247.75	− .77	− .59
26.	119	13.26	175.83	+ .65	+ .58
27.	101	− 4.74	22.47	− .23	+ .91
28.	102	− 3.74	13.99	− .18	− .21
29.	103	− 2.74	7.51	− .13	+ .02
30.	116	10.26	105.27	+ .50	+ .44
31.	122	16.26	264.39	+ .80	− .40
Sum	3,278.00	0.00	12,849.94	0.00	0.00
Mean	34.74		414.51	0.00	0.00
SD	20.36			1.00	1.00
Var	414.51			1.00	1.00

Under the terms of the normative measurement operations most commonly employed by individual differences investigators, two basic "points of reference" would be derived from an array of assessments such as shown in column I of table 2.1. The first is the arithmetic mean or average, defined as the sum of the assessments divided by the number of assessments. In our example, the mean is equal to 3,278/31 = 34.74.

The second basic point of reference, the standard deviation, indexes the spread of scores around the group mean. Arithmetically, the standard deviation is defined as the square root of the average of the squared deviations of the scores from their mean. Using the data in table 2.1, this arithmetic is illustrated in columns II and III. The value shown at the bottom of column III, 414.51, is the average of the squared deviation scores. Thus, the square root of this value, 20.36, defines the standard deviation of the values displayed in column I.

Once the mean and standard deviation of an array of "raw" assessments have been determined, the process of transforming the latter into normatively meaningful measurements is quite straightforward mathematically, and is defined by the following equation:

$$Z_{pao} = (S_{pao} - \bar{S}._{ao})/SD._{ao} \tag{2.2}$$

where the symbols are defined as follows:

Z_{pao} = the sought-after normative measurement of person p with respect to attribute a on occasion o,

S_{pao} = the "raw" assessment of person p with respect to attribute a on occasion o, as defined by equation (2.1),

$\bar{S}._{ao}$ = the mean of the S-values within a group of individuals on occasion o, and

$SD._{ao}$ = the standard deviation of those same S-values, computed in the manner just illustrated.

Continuing with our example, a normative measurement of Smith with respect to the underlying attribute "sociable vs. unsociable" would be defined as follows:

$$Z = (114 - 34.74)/20.36$$
$$= +.41$$

This value tells us two important things about Smith's status with respect to the underlying attribute. First, the absolute value of the Z-score, .41, expresses the ratio of Smith's *individual* deviation from the group mean to the *standard* deviation around the group mean. Second, the sign of the Z-score, which in this case is positive, indicates the direction of Smith's deviation from the group mean. When this sign is considered in the light of the arbitrary scoring conventions used to generate the original "raw" assessments—and hence the group mean—it indicates that Smith deviates from the group mean in the direction of "sociability," In the language of conventional personality measurement, therefore, Smith's Z-score of +.41 specifies his status along the underlying personality dimension "sociable vs. unsociable" as 41/100 of one standard deviation above (i.e., in the "sociable" direction away from) the group mean.[2]

In the case of person 2 in the table, a "raw" assessment of +87 was obtained. Thus, a normative measurement of this individual with respect to the attribute "sociable vs. unsociable" would be defined as $Z = (87 - 34.74)/20.36 = -.92$, specifying his/her status as 92/100 of one standard deviation below (i.e., in the "unsociable" direction away from) the group mean. Proceeding in this fashion, a normative measurement can be defined for each of the remaining individuals, with results as displayed in column IV of the table.

These values constitute the measurements depicted in region V of figure 2.1, and are taken as empirical indicators of the levels of the corresponding attributes depicted in region I. The mean and standard deviation of the measurements arrayed in column IV are, respectively, 0.00 and 1.00. This is always the

---

2. Note that there is nothing in a Z-score itself that will yield knowledge about the attribute with respect to which an individual has been normatively measured. To endow such a measurement with a psychological—as opposed to merely mathematical—interpretation, one must invoke the presumed meanings of the observations on which the "raw" assessment was based. From an epistemological standpoint, this matter is not at all trivial, as we will see in chapter 5.

case for any set of measurements defined in the above fashion, whatever the original assessments. It is an inherent feature of what are known as *standardized measurements*.

Determining the Temporal Reliability of Personality Measurements

Of course, the mere fact that numerical values have been assigned to individuals is no guarantee that a personality variable has actually been tapped in the process. Before any claim to this effect can be pressed, it has traditionally been held, a measure must be shown to have certain psychometric properties, foremost among which is temporal reliability.

Under the generic structure conception of personality, it is assumed that the level of a given attribute within an individual's personality remains more or less constant over time. Thus ceteris paribus, trustworthy measurements of individuals with respect to that attribute will also remain constant (or very nearly so) when taken at different points in time. If evidence to this effect fails to obtain, one possible interpretation is that the assumption of constancy is invalid for the attribute in question, in which case its status as a personality attribute is rendered dubious. Another possibility, however, is that the attribute *is* one with respect to which individuals differ in enduring and consequential ways, but that the measurements being obtained are too insensitive or error-laden to detect this fact. The failure to demonstrate reliability is then framed as a technical rather than theoretical problem mandating a return to the beginning of the assessment process.

By way of illustration, let us extend the above example. Suppose that one month after obtaining the measurements shown in column IV of table 2.1, the same 31 subjects are measured with respect to the same attribute, and in exact accordance with all the same procedures. Let us further suppose that the measurements obtained this second time are as displayed in column V of the table. Here again, the mean and standard deviation of these measurements are, respectively, 0.00 and 1.00.

Technically speaking, the task here is to derive a single quantitative expression of the degree of similarity between the two sets of measurements. As Cronbach and Gleser (1953) showed, the most generally viable approach to this problem would be to compute (a) the arithmetic difference for each matched pair of measurements (Z-scores), (b) the square of each difference value thus obtained, (c) the sum of these squared difference values, and finally (d) the square root of this sum. The resulting numerical value would constitute an index of dissimilarity. It should be intuitively apparent that its value would be zero—indicating no dissimilarity and hence identity between the two sets of measurements—if and only if the two measurements obtained were identical for each individual in the sample. Under these hypothetical circumstances, the derived measurements would be said to be perfectly reliable, at least for the time interval over which the investigation was carried out.

On the other hand, to the degree that, within the group as a whole, the obtained measurements differ from the first measurement occasion to the second, the index will rise, casting commensurate doubt on the reliability of the measurements in question. The broad interpretation alternatives open to the investigator in this event have already been mentioned, and which alternative an investigator pursues will depend largely on the strength of his/her own conviction that the attribute being investigated really is a basic personality variable. If an investigator's convictions in this regard are weak, research efforts are likely to be redirected elsewhere; if the convictions are strong, then evidence of unreliability is likely to be framed as a technical problem, leading to a reevaluation of the fidelity of measurements from which the index of dissimilarity has been derived.

The Pearson Product-Moment Correlation Coefficient

A quantitative index of dissimilarity has three distinct and independently calculable components: elevation, scatter, and shape. Two sets of measurements will differ in *elevation* to the degree that their respective means are different; in *scatter* to the extent that their respective standard deviations are different; and in *shape* to the extent that the discrete numerical values in one array differ from their corresponding values in the other array.

The source of dissimilarity between two sets of measurements such as displayed in columns IV and V of table 2.1 must necessarily be the shape component, since each of those two sets of measurements has a mean of 0.00 and a standard deviation of 1.00 *by definition*. The investigator has therefore rendered elevation and scatter identical; shape is the only parameter that has not been predetermined.

In implicit consideration of these facts, individual differences investigators do not normally employ the Cronbach-Gleser index of dissimilarity when investigating questions of measurement reliability (or, for that matter, any of the other psychometric issues to be discussed below). Instead, the statistic most commonly employed is one known as the Pearson product-moment correlation coefficient. This statistic bears the name of its developer, Karl R. Pearson. By a widely shared convention which we will follow here, the Pearson product-moment correlation is symbolized r.

Although it is identical in meaning to Cronbach and Gleser's index of shape dissimilarity, r is somewhat easier to work with both computationally and conceptually. It is defined quite simply as *the average of the cross-products of Z-scores*:

$$r = \Sigma(Z_1 Z_2)/N \qquad\qquad (2.3)$$

Thus, the value of r for the illustrative measurements in the table is determined by (a) cross-multiplying each Z-score in column IV by its corresponding entry in column V, (b) summing these cross-products, and (c) dividing by 31. In this example, $r = .89$.

Now the range of possible values that can be assumed by r extends from -1.00 through 0.00 to 1.00. The latter value constitutes a perfect positive correlation, and will obtain if and only if every Z-score in one array of measurements is identical—both in absolute value and in sign—to its corresponding Z-score in the second array. If for each Z-score in one array its corresponding entry in the second array is identical in absolute value but opposite in sign, then a perfect negative correlation, $r = -1.00$, will obtain. To the degree that one or the other of these extremes fails to obtain, the absolute value of r will decline from unity (i.e., ± 1.00) toward zero.

If among all the positive Z-scores in one array some are paired with positive and some with negative Z-scores in the other array, then the signs of the resulting Z-score cross-products will sometimes be positive and sometimes negative. Consequently, when all the Z-score cross-products are added together, the positives and negatives will tend to cancel each other out, so that the sum of the cross-products plummets toward zero. Obviously, the average of the Z-score cross-products—which is how r is defined—will likewise diminish toward zero under these conditions.

With specific reference to temporal reliability, a correlation of zero would, of course, indicate that the measurements in question are utterly devoid of that property. Just how high a reliability coefficient must be in order to be judged "high enough" remains a matter of debate, although some ground rules in this area have been articulated. Suffice it to say that by contemporary standards, a reliability coefficient of .89 for a one-month time lag between measurements would be considered quite acceptable by most investigators.

Construct Validity

Although empirical evidence of reliability is necessary in order to establish that a given set of measurements taps some underlying personality attribute, such evidence is not sufficient. Evidence of reliability speaks only to the question of whether *something* has been measured in a consistent fashion, and not to the question of what that something is. Thus, for example, the temporal reliability coefficient of .89 obtained above would not, by itself, establish that "sociability vs. unsociability" is the underlying attribute that has been tapped. Our uncertainty in this regard exists in principle, and hence would remain even if the reliability coefficient had been found to be perfect, i.e., ±1.00.

When the personality investigator's concern shifts from the question of stability within a set of measurements over time to the question of what is being tapped by those measurements, the issue is no longer one of reliability but of *construct validity* (see Cronbach and Mechl 1955). The "multitrait-multimethod" procedure proposed over a quarter-century ago by Campbell and Fiske (1959) remains the most comprehensive framework yet articulated for addressing the issue of construct validity empirically, and so it is in terms of that framework that our discussion of this topic will proceed. (A wholly different perspective on this problem will be offered in chapter 5.)

Campbell and Fiske's point of departure was the thesis that any single personality measurement (e.g., +.41 in the case of Smith in the above example), has many possible determinants, only one of which is the level at which the attribute in question exists within the personality of the measured individual. Beyond this, individuals' scores can be influenced by other features of personality simultaneously but unintentionally tapped by the same measurements, and/or by purely methodological features of the measurement operation. The basic objective of a multitrait-multimethod analysis, therefore, is to adduce empirical evidence that putative measurements of individuals with respect to a given personality attribute are in fact determined primarily by the levels of that attribute within the personalities of the measured individuals. Individual differences variables for which such evidence can be adduced are taken as strong candidates for inclusion in the sought-after periodic table of personality elements.

As its name suggests, the minimal requirement for a multitrait-multimethod analysis is that measurements be obtained for the same individuals on each of at least two supposedly distinct attributes by each of at least two procedurally distinct methods. Thus a minimum of four measurements must be obtained for each subject, and if an investigation of temporal re-

44 Methodological Foundations

liability is to be part of the larger analysis (see below), then this minimum number increases to eight. The analysis itself is then focused on the pattern of intercorrelations among these various sets of measurements.

Suppose, for example, that in addition to measuring each of the 31 subjects with respect to the attribute "sociable vs. unsociable" (attribute A_1), measurements have likewise been generated for the same 31 subjects on the attribute "dominant vs. submissive" (attribute A_2). Suppose further that on each attribute two independent measurements have been taken for each subject: one based on the subject's self-report of his/her "typical" behaviors (method 1), and one based on ratings of the subject provided by a close friend (method 2). Finally, suppose that Pearson product-moment correlations have been computed for all pairs of the four sets of 31 measurements thus obtained, and that the results are as shown in the intercorrelation matrix given as table 2.2.

Let us first consider cell 1 of the matrix. Note that the value entered there, .88, is the correlation between measurements of attribute A_1 obtained by method 1 with a second set of measurements of attribute A_1, also obtained by method 1. In effect, therefore, the correlation in cell 1 indexes the reliability of

Table 2.2 Hypothetical Multitrait-Multimethod Correlation Matrix

| | | | Attribute | | | |
| | | | A_1 Method | | A_2 Method | |
			1	2	1	2
Attribute	A_1 Method	1	.88 (1)	—	—	—
		2	.74 (2)	.81 (3)	—	—
	A_2 Method	1	.24 (4)	.22 (5)	.90 (6)	—
		2	.16 (7)	.20 (8)	.86 (9)	.89 (10)

attribute 1–method 1 measurements as discussed previously. By the same token, the value entered in cell 3 of the matrix, .81, indexes the reliability of attribute A_1–method 2 measurements, while the values entered in cells 6 (.90) and 10 (.89) index the reliabilities of attribute 2–method 1 measurements and attribute A_2–method 2 measurements, respectively. In general, the values entered along the main diagonal of a multitrait-multimethod correlation matrix are reliability coefficients, and it is expected that each of these values will be higher than the correlations appearing off the diagonal below and/or to the left of it in the matrix.

Let us consider now cells 2 and 9 of the matrix. The value entered in cell 2, .74, is the correlation between attribute A_1–method 1 measurements and attribute A_1–method 2 measurements. The value entered in cell 9, .86, is the correlation between attribute A_2–method 1 measurements and attribute A_2–method 2 measurements. Thus each of these values constitutes what is referred to as a *monotrait-heteromethod* correlation, indexing the correspondence between two sets of measurements intended to measure the same underlying attribute, but obtained by different methods. The higher these values are, the better the evidence for *convergent* validity, i.e., the stronger the argument that two different procedures for measuring the same attribute have yielded the same results within a given group of individuals.

In contrast to the above, the values entered in cells 4 and 8 of the matrix constitute what are known as *heterotrait monomethod* correlations, indexing the correspondence between two sets of measurements intended to tap different attributes but derived by a common method. The lower these values relative to those in cells 2 and 9, the better the evidence for what is known as *discriminant* validity, i.e., the better the evidence that two distinct attributes have in fact been tapped by the respective sets of measurements. Should the correlations in cells 4 and 8 prove to be higher than those in cells 2 and 9, the evidence would suggest that the obtained measurements were determined more by the method used to obtain them than by the levels of two putatively distinct attributes within the personalities of the subjects. This pattern of findings would signal what psychometricians call *method variance*, and would contraindicate the fidelity of the measurements in question as indicators of individual differences in supposedly distinct personality characteristics.

The values entered in cells 5 and 7 of the matrix are *heterotrait-heteromethod* correlations, as they index the degree of correspondence between measurements of different attributes derived by different methods. For reasons that should be apparent at this point, these values would be expected to be among the lowest in the entire matrix.

To sum up, insofar as a personality investigator is measuring with fidelity (i.e., reliably and validly) the respective levels at which individuals are endowed with two or more theoretically distinct personality attributes, a multitrait-multimethod analysis conducted in accordance with the guidelines set forth by Campbell and Fiske (1959) should yield the following pattern of findings:

1. High correlations along the diagonal of the multitrait-multimethod matrix, indicating reliability for all attribute/measurement-method units in question.

2. High correlations in the monotrait-heteromethod cells of the matrix, indicating that procedurally different measurement operations intended to tap the same underlying attribute do in fact yield similar results within a given group of individuals.

3. Low correlations in the heterotrait cells of the matrix—especially the heterotrait-monomethod cells—indicating that measurements intended to tap some one attribute are not substantially influenced either by the method of measurement employed or by the respective levels of other attributes within the personalities of the individuals being measured.

Predictive Validity and the Quest for Empirical "Laws" of Personality Functioning

Let us suppose that, following the various procedures discussed to this point, an investigator has adduced evidence for the construct validity of two underlying attributes, A_1 and A_2, and believes that, together, those attributes might provide a viable structural model of "the" generic human personality. In the event, the investigator's next objective would be to determine empirically the way in and degree to which the identified attributes influence behavior in various situations or life domains. Under the terms of conventional "nomotheticism," the realization of this objective would be tantamount to establishing empirical laws of personality functioning; the psychometric concept of most immediate relevance to this problem is *predictive validity*. To illustrate what is involved here, it is useful to begin with the *bivariate* (two-variable) case and then extend the discussion into the more elaborate *multivariate* case.

Suppose that for each of the 31 subjects in the above example, data were available concerning the quality of their respective peer relationships. Suppose further that our hypothetical investigator theorizes that the personality attribute "sociable vs. unsociable" ought to relate lawfully—i.e., empirically—to quality of peer relations in such a way that the more sociable the individual, the better his/her peer relationships will be. Assuming that relatively high scores (i.e., positive Z-scores) on the measure of peer relations signify "good" relations while relatively low scores (negative Z-scores) signify "bad" relations, and recalling the way in which measurements of "sociability vs. unsociability" were defined, it should be apparent that in this instance our investigator would be anticipating a positive correlation between the predictor variable, sociability vs. unsociability, and the criterion variable, quality of peer relations. That is, the hypothesis asserts that positive Z-scores on A_1, indicating relative sociability, with appreciable regularity throughout the sample of 31 subjects will be paired with positive Z-scores on the criterion, indicating relatively good peer relations, while negative Z-scores on A_1 will similarly be paired with negative Z-scores on the criterion.

Let us suppose that the Pearson product-moment correlation actually obtained when measurements of A_1 are related to measurements of peer relations turn out to be $+.60$. This finding would be consistent with the hypothesis just outlined. It would also constitute preliminary evidence for the predictive validity of A_1. That is, it would constitute evidence that given normative measurements of individuals with respect to the underlying personality attribute "sociable vs. unsociable," the relative quality of peer relations is to some degree—albeit not entirely—predictable within that same group of individuals.

Of course, due caution would have to be exercised in interpreting any such finding, owing to the possibility that a second test of the same hypothesis within a new sample of subjects might yield different results. That possibility is typically addressed in what is known as a *cross-validation* study. In the context of the above example, such a study would proceed essentially as follows.

A new sample of subjects would be drawn from the same population that yielded the original sample. Then, based on (a) the measurement made of each new subject with respect to A_1 (defined in the same manner as earlier), and (b) the so-called predictive validity coefficient obtained in the first study, $+.60$, a *predicted* score for each of the new subjects with respect to the criterion variable, quality of peer relations, would be generated in the following manner:

$$\hat{Z}_{pc} = \beta_{ac}(Z_{pa}) \tag{2.4}$$

where

$\hat{Z}_{pc} =$ the anticipated or predicted measurement of person p on the criterion variable c

$Z_{pa} =$ the obtained measurement of person p on the predictor variable (in the example, A_1)

$\beta_{ac} =$ specific amount by which Z_{pa} is weighted in determining $\hat{Z}_{pc}$; in the bivariate case, β_{ac} is numerically identical to the correlation between the predictor variable, A_1, and the criterion, C, obtained in the original study (that is, to r_{ac}).

Equation (2.4) is an instance of what is generally known as a *standardized regression equation*. Such equations go hand in hand with correlational analyses, and are indeed simply alternative expressions of the same information.

In the context of the present example, therefore, generating predicted criterion scores for subjects in a cross-validation sample would be a matter of taking the measurement of each new subject with respect to A_1 (i.e., Z_{pa}) and "weighting" or multiplying it by β_{ac}. Since in the bivariate case $\beta_{ac} = r_{ac}$, β_{ac} in this case equals $+.60$. The resulting numerical value, $\hat{Z}_{pc}$, is the predicted normative measurement of person p with respect to the criterion variable "quality of peer relations."

Imagine now that, like the original sample, the cross-validation sample is composed of 31 students. If so, then it should be apparent that 31 $\hat{Z}_{pc}$ values would be generated via equation (2.4) in the fashion just described. The question is: how accurate will those predicted criterion scores prove to be? One obviously needs to obtain *actual* criterion scores for the subjects in the cross-validation sample. Once these scores have been obtained, they can in turn be correlated with the predicted criterion scores, and the resulting correlation would be viewed as an answer to the question just posed.

Since the original correlation, $+.60$, will have been artificially inflated to some degree because of "chance fluctuations" in the original data set, the correlation subsequently obtained between predicted and actual criterion values in the cross-validation sample cannot be expected to exceed, and indeed will regularly be lower than, the original r. This statistical phenomenon is known as *shrinkage*, and for obvious reasons is an obstacle in the personality investigator's quest for evidence of predictive validity.

In any event, the correlation between predicted and actually obtained criterion measurements in the cross-validation sample is the "best"—i.e., psychometrically most responsible— estimate of the actual lawful relationship between the predictor and criterion variables in question, and it is therefore in terms of this latter correlation that an investigator would couch any theoretical assertion concerning the degree to which a given personality attribute influences the behavior of individuals within some specified domain. A quantitatively precise expression of the empirically established "law" would actually be achieved by substi-

tuting the value of the cross-validated r_{ac} for the β_{ac} in equation
(2.4). Indeed, insofar as it can be argued that conventional nomothetic research yields "laws" of personality functioning at all,
such laws in their essential logical form are identical to equation
(2.4). From a substantive standpoint, of course, such laws can be
considerably more complex.

Extension to the Multivariate Case

Let us imagine that in a cross-validation study such
as just described, the correlation between actual measurements
of quality of peer relations and those predicted on the basis of
measurements of the "sociable vs. unsociable" variable turned
out to be +.50. The resultant "nomothetic law" could then be
expressed as:

$$\hat{Z}_{pc} = .50 \ (Z_{pa}) \tag{2.4a}$$

Note that had r_{ac} (and hence β_{ac}) turned out to be
+1.00 (or −1.00, for that matter), this would have meant that
the correlation between the predictor and criterion variables was
perfect. Under these conditions, never realized in practice, actual
measurements on the criterion for each and every individual in
the sample would coincide perfectly with predicted measurements based on the standardized regression equation. This would
be true *by definition*.

When *r* has an absolute value less than 1.00, actual
measurements of individuals with respect to the criterion will not
always coincide perfectly with predicted measurements. Such could
be the case for some individuals. However, for at least some and
conceivably for all, predicted values will over- or underestimate
actual ones to varying degrees. Here again, this is true *by definition*
when *r* has an absolute value less than 1.00.

Among adherents to the generic structure conception
of personality, an imperfect correlation would typically be interpreted as evidence that the behavior of individuals within the
domain represented by the criterion variable is not completely
determined by a single personality attribute, and that other fac-

tors must therefore be operating. An obvious possibility, though by no means the only one, is that additional personality attributes are influencing behavior within the domain in question. For example, the hypothetical investigator might surmise that the second component of his/her structural model of generic human personality, dominance vs. submissiveness (A_2), exerts an influence on quality of peer relations over and above the influence of sociability vs. unsociability. More specifically, s/he might hypothesize that after the influence of A_1 has been taken into account, dominant individuals experience less satisfactory peer relations than their more submissive counterparts. Reliable (i.e., cross-validated) empirical evidence to this effect would allow for—indeed would seem to mandate—a more complex expression of the "law" by which personality factors influence quality of peer relations. It is therefore worth considering briefly here how an investigator would actually go about adducing such evidence.

I noted above that when the correlation on which equation (2.4) is based has an absolute value less than 1.00, then predicted values will over- or underestimate actual ones to varying degrees. Symbolizing actual criterion values as Z_{pc} and predicted criterion values as $\hat{Z}_{pc}$, we can represent this same idea quantitatively by saying that when $|r| < 1.00$, the quantity $(Z_{pc} - \hat{Z}_{pc})$ will take on different values—at least some and perhaps all of them non-zero—from one subject to the next.

Now an array of such $(Z_{pc} - \hat{Z}_{pc})$ values, commonly referred to as *residuals*, could itself be viewed as an individual differences variable reflecting aspects of the criterion that are by definition not predictable on the basis of A_1. Any correlation between these residuals and measurements of a second personality attribute (A_2) might therefore be taken as evidence that the latter exerts some influence on the criterion over and above the effects of A_1. This is the essential logic underlying a family of statistical techniques known as multiple correlation/regression, and it is through the use of one or another of these techniques that individual differences investigators empirically accommodate the theoretical possibility of more than one factor (personality or otherwise) lawfully influencing behavior in a specified domain.

Continuing with our example, suppose that after determining the relationship between A_1 and the criterion, a set of 31 residuals (one for each subject) had been defined in the manner just discussed and in turn correlated with the A_2 measurements of those same subjects. Suppose further that the resulting (cross-validated) r turned out to be $+.40$. With this additional finding, our hypothetical investigator could now reexpress the law relating personality factors to quality of peer relations so that it reads as follows:

$$\hat{Z}_{pc} = .50 \ (Z_{p1}) + .40 \ (Z_{p2}) \tag{2.5}$$

Were we to now compute the correlation between the 31 $\hat{Z}$ values generated by equation (2.5) and the actual Z-values obtained for those same 31 subjects, we would have, in effect, the *multiple* correlation between the criterion variable and the combination of A_1 and A_2 as predictor variables. In this example, we would find that this multiple correlation is higher than either of the simple correlations between the criterion and A_1 or A_2 considered alone. Thus, by introducing additional complexity into the analysis, our hypothetical investigator could be said to have increased the overall predictive validity of his/her proposed structural model of "the" generic human personality, at least within the specific domain "quality of peer relations." Of course, investigating the predictive validity of the structural model in other domains would be a matter of repeating the basic analytic procedures just described in studies focused on other criterion variables.[3]

From what has been said to this point, it is perhaps apparent that, in principle, there is nothing to prevent an investigator from introducing still more variables into the search for the laws of personality functioning. Thus, just as equation (2.5) is a substantively more complex "law" than equation (2.4a), one can

3. The particular procedure described here is that known as stepwise multiple correlation/regression. Other procedures are possible, and the values of the β-coefficients can be influenced by the particular procedure adopted (see Kerlinger and Pedhazur 1973 for a comprehensive discussion of multiple correlation/regression). The conceptual thrust of all the variations, however, remains essentially the same.

readily imagine adding still another predictor variable and deriving another regression equation substantively more complex than equation (2.5). Note also, however, that the operative term here is "substantively," because the logic of the correlation/regression methods on the basis of which such functional "laws" are derived and expressed is the same no matter how many factors are considered.

The Problem of Identifying Relevant Attributes

To this point in the discussion we have considered, in very basic terms, the logic of the techniques by which individual differences investigators have sought reliable and valid measurements of persons' underlying personality attributes. We have also highlighted the logic of the empirical research through which putatively lawful relationships between those attributes and overt behavior would be discerned empirically and articulated quantitatively. In focusing on these matters, however, we have skirted the question of how potentially relevant attributes are identified in the first place. On what grounds, for example, might a personality investigator decide to begin by focusing on the attributes "sociable vs. unsociable" and "dominant vs. submissive," rather than some other attributes?

Historically, many approaches to this basic question have been proposed. Broadly speaking, however, the available alternatives are classifiable under two major headings: (1) theoretical/rational/intuitive, and (2) empirical (see Hase and Goldberg 1967). In the case of the former, decisions as to which attributes to investigate are rooted ultimately in educated guesses regarding which of the virtually infinite array of distinctions that might be drawn between people will prove most fruitful in subsequent research. These beliefs might themselves be grounded in a formal theory of personality [see, e.g., Phares' (1976) discussion of the development of the internal vs. external locus of control construct], or in less formally articulated but considered hunches about the nature of the generic human personality (see Murray 1938). Over against this general approach, many personality investigators have argued that the problem of identifying generic components should be handled empirically. In this context, a technique known as *factor analysis* has received extensive use.

Investigators advocating a factor analytic approach take as their point of departure the notion that within the realm of observational variables (region III in figure 2.1), entities that covary—i.e., correlate—with one another are very likely to be under the control or influence of some common underlying determinant. If so, the argument goes, then a systematic analysis of the overall pattern of intercorrelations among observational variables should yield some insight into the number and nature of the underlying determinants. In other words, the logic here is to begin not with some theory but rather with empirical knowledge con cerning the pattern of intercorrelations among variables, and then work backwards to an identification of the underlying determinants.

Factor analysis is a rather complex family of mathematico-statistical techniques, a thorough discussion of which would be far beyond the scope of the present discussion (see Nunnally 1967 for a very readable presentation, and Harman 1967 for a more in-depth explication). What follows, therefore, is a highly condensed treatment focusing on the procedure's conceptual thrust.

To this end, let us consider once again figure 2.2. Imagine that the same sort of information concerning the "typical" activity pattern of Smith has been accumulated for each of, say, 199 other individuals, and that these data have been arranged into one large matrix where each row corresponds to one of the 200 individuals and each column corresponds to one of the 18 activities. The first row of this matrix would, therefore, contain the 18 behavioral frequencies recorded for Smith. The second row of the matrix would contain the 18 behavioral frequencies recorded for subject 2, the third the 18 behavioral frequencies recorded for subject 3, and so on.

The investigator concerned to identify in these activity

patterns the underlying personality attributes relevant to an accounting of individual differences would begin by computing a Pearson product-moment correlation for every possible pair of the 18 activities. A mean and standard deviation would be computed for each column of activity frequencies, and each entry in the matrix would in turn be transformed into a Z-score based on the mean and standard deviation for the column in which it is located. The correlation between activities 1 and 2 would then be defined in the usual way, i.e., by (a) cross-multiplying each of the column 1 Z-scores by its corresponding Z-score in column 2, (b) summing these Z-score cross-products, and (c) dividing by N, which in this example is 200.

The resulting correlation, $r_{1,2}$, would index the degree to which the activities 1 and 2, "studying or reading intellectual material" and "participating in artistic or creative activities," respectively, correlate with one another within the sample of 200 subjects. In like fashion, the investigator would compute the correlation between "studying or reading intellectual materials" and each of the remaining 16 activities. The correlation between activity 2 and each of the activities 3 through 18 would in turn be computed, and so on until correlations had been computed for all possible pairs of the 18 activities.

The lower triangular matrix of intercorrelations yielded by these computations would have $[18(17)]/2 = 153$ off-diagonal entries. It is this matrix (with estimates of the reliabilities of the observational variables entered along the diagonal) that would serve as "input" to the factor analysis proper. The output of the analysis, known as a *factor loading* matrix, would have the general form depicted in table 2.3.

Note that the 18 activities, which corresponded to the columns of the original data matrix, correspond to the rows of the factor loading matrix. The columns of this latter matrix correspond to the underlying factors extracted in the course of the analysis. Unfortunately, the factor analysis itself does not tell the investigator just what the underlying factors are. Rather, their status at this point is that of "mathematical fictions" awaiting substantive psychological interpretation.

Table 2.3 Illustrative Factor Loading Matrix[a]

	Factor			
Activity	I	II	III	IV
1. Studying or reading intellectual material	.17	−.28	.42	−.18
2. Participating in artistic or creative activities	.34	.00	.03	−.14
3. Casual dating	−.03	−.06	−.39	−.03
4. Engaging in premarital sex	.14	.48	−.10	−.17
5. Participating in athletic activities	.34	.12	−.06	.47
6. Reading/viewing pornographic materials	−.20	.31	.24	−.30
7. Watching television	−.39	−.21	.08	.02
8. Listening to music	−.13	−.08	−.17	−.25
9. Working at a part-time job	.00	−.15	.47	.41
10. Playing cards	−.38	−.25	−.16	.16
11. Partying	−.22	.17	−.28	.03
12. Attending live entertainment or movies	−.12	−.07	−.13	−.23
13. Participating in outdoor activities (camping, hiking, etc.)	.32	.03	−.24	.35
14. Participating in events of a religious nature	.32	−.32	.02	−.13
15. Cutting classes	−.15	.15	.06	.32
16. Getting high on alcohol and/or marijuana	−.16	.18	−.20	−.02
17. Using drugs other than alcohol or marijuana	−.06	.34	.06	−.13
18. Attending lectures/seminars (outside of coursework)	.22	−.37	.34	−.18

[a]Intuitive interpretation of dimensions: I. Filling spare time, diversionary, or "idle" (−) vs. Physically and/or mentally involved, or "earnest" (+); II. Hedonistic, or oriented toward physical pleasure (+) vs. Nonhedonistic, or not oriented toward physical pleasure (−); III. Socially oriented (−) vs. Nonsocially oriented (+); IV. Low in motor activity (−) vs. High in motor activity (+).

SOURCE: J. T. Lamiell, The case for an idiothetic psychology of personality: A conceptual and empirical foundation, in B. A. Maher and W. B. Maher, eds., Progress in Experimental Personality Research, 11:1–64, © 1982 by Academic Press. Reprinted by permission of the publisher.

To achieve the latter, an investigator would proceed by a rational consideration of the entries in the matrix, which are known as factor loadings. Speaking again in very broad terms, variables found to correlate positively with one another in the original intercorrelation matrix will be found to have similar loadings on a given factor, while variables which originally correlated negatively with one another will be found to have opposite loadings on a given factor. Variables that were uncorrelated with one another in the original intercorrelation matrix will tend to load on different factors. For example, if two variables X and Y were uncorrelated in the original intercorrelation matrix, then X might have a substantial loading and Y a loading of zero on factor I, while Y might have a substantial loading and X a loading of zero on factor II.

In effect, each factor loading can be viewed as the correlation between a given "input variable" and a given underlying factor. Thus, the investigator's task is essentially to identify a set of underlying factors that could rationally have been expected to yield the obtained factor loadings. From a theoretical standpoint, success in this endeavor would be tantamount to identifying the covert personality attributes responsible in the first instance for the pattern of intercorrelations between observational variables with which the factor analysis began.

Consider, for example, the loadings shown under factor I in table 2.3. There we see that the activities with the highest positive values—activities 2, 5, 13, and 14, and to a lesser extent activities 1, 4, and 18, seem to reflect physical and/or mental involvement. In contrast, activities at the opposite end of this factor, most notably activities 7 and 10, and to a lesser extent activities, 6, 8, 11, 12, 15, and 16, seem to be more "diversionary" or "idle" in nature. Activities 3, 9, and 17 seem to have little to do with this factor one way or the other. On the basis of such considerations, an investigator might offer a tentative interpretation of factor I as "diversionary or idle" (−) vs. "involved or earnest" (+). Proceeding in this fashion, I have offered at the bottom of table 2.3 tentative interpretations of factors II, III, and IV as well.

Of course, the operative word is "tentative." For it is undoubtedly apparent from the above that whatever other advantages factor analysis may have over theoretical/rational/intuitive approaches to identifying attributes, neither factor analysis nor any other empirical approach can properly be seen as obviating the role of the investigator's judgment. At best, the latter is reduced to some slight degree, and it is at least arguable that all that is really accomplished is a shift of the locus of judgment from one aspect of the assessment/measurement enterprise to another.

It should also be noted here that personality attributes tentatively identified on empirical grounds are subject to the usual psychometric requirements of reliability, construct validity, and predictive validity no less than are those selected for investigation on other grounds. In the course of satisfying these requirements, an investigator would have to compute what are known as *factor scores* for individuals with respect to each underlying factor. Such scores are computed in accordance with the logic of the basic assessment model described earlier, with the loadings of the activities on a given factor (or quantitative indices derived directly from them) serving as the "weighting" component (W_{ia}) of equation (2.1). It should be clear, therefore, that there is no fundamental difference between the logic of assessment as explained earlier and the logic of factor score computation.

By the same token, however, the sense is apparent in which factor analysis is said to provide the traditional "nomotheticist" with an empirical technique for simultaneously identifying relevant attributes and specifying the W_{ia} component of equation (2.1). That is, tentative interpretations of a derived factor structure (e.g., table 2.3) are based on the alignment of factor loadings, which are themselves used, in turn, to weight the original observational variables in computing "raw" assessments (factor scores) for individuals with respect to the identified underlying attributes. This point should help to clarify my earlier allusion to the possibility of specifying the weighting component on empirical rather than intuitive/theoretical grounds.

Concluding Remarks

At the outset of this chapter I noted that, historically, the overriding objectives of conventional nomothetic inquiry have been: first, to identify the basic structural components of "the" generic human personality; second, to derive reliable and valid empirical indicators thereof; and third, to establish empirically the presumed relationships between those basic components and overt behavior. With this in mind, the focus of the present chapter has been on the basic methodo-logic of individual differences research as a vehicle for pursuing these objectives.

Throughout this discussion, I have sought to reduce complexity in the interest of clarity with respect to a few somewhat technical but fundamental matters, namely:

> (a) the grounds on which investigators select for study certain underlying dimensions of individual differences;
>
> (b) the formal nature of the procedures by which assessments of individuals with respect to those underlying dimensions are made;
>
> (c) the rationale by which interpretable measurements of individuals are derived from such assessments;
>
> (d) the basis on which those measurements are evaluated for their scientific adequacy; and
>
> (e) the nature of the empirical research through which "nomothetic laws" of personality functioning are sought and articulated.

Having considered these fundamental issues, we now have an adequate framework within which to conceptualize the major developments in personality psychology in recent years. As we take up this topic in chapter 3, we will see how the methodological tenets of individual differences research have continued to dominate the thinking of personality investigators through to the present day, even as many of those investigators (though by no means all) have abandoned the generic-structure conception of personality in the service of which those tenets were originally embraced.

3 The Legacy of Conventional "Nomotheticism" in Contemporary Personality Psychology

The Crisis of Confidence in Personality Psychology

By the mid-1960s, empirical research guided by the tenets of conventional nomotheticism had proceeded apace for more than fifty years, and in the view of some the time had arrived for a comprehensive critical evaluation of the fruits of that labor. Among the commentaries that emerged around that time (see Endler and Hunt 1966, 1968; Peterson 1968), the most influential by far was Mischel's *Personality and Assessment* (1968).

As noted previously, Mischel's major objective in that work was to discuss, in the light of empirical evidence, the "critical and controversial" issues of "consistency of particular predispositions within any individual and the utility of searching for these generalized predispositional states as the determining sources of his response to diverse situations" (p. 8). While Mischel's concern for these issues undoubtedly stemmed in part from his recognition of their implications for practical problems of behavioral prediction, he was also clearly concerned with their implications for the future directions of personality theory. In fact, if the preface to *Personality and Assessment* is any guide, it is this latter consideration—and not the former—that was uppermost in Mischel's mind:

When I started this book I intended to survey six or seven equally viable alternative theoretical approaches to personality and to examine the implications of each for personality assessment, psychotherapy, and research. In the course of this writing the field has changed and the book and my views along with it. Although a half dozen or more alternative conceptualizations each appeared to be about equally reasonable a decade ago, *the list of serious contenders now seems much shorter. This change has occurred mainly because of the voluminous and vigorous empirical researches that have become available in recent years.* The resulting evidence makes it possible to start choosing among approaches on the basis of empirical evidence rather than personal preference. (Mischel 1968:vii; emphasis added)

In the ensuing chapters Mischel would make it abundantly clear that the researches to which he had referred were studies centered around the measurement of individual differences. The "resulting evidence" on which Mischel rested his case was thus constituted of the correlation coefficients (reliabilities, validities, etc.) that, as we saw in the last chapter, such studies are specifically designed to yield.

Focusing primarily on coefficients of convergent and predictive validity, Mischel marshaled a wealth of evidence to indicate that in the realm of what he termed "non-cognitive" individual differences variables, correlations were routinely quite low—rarely exceeding $+.30$—between the personality characteristics putatively measured by those variables and other indices (e.g., alternative measures of the same characteristics, behavioral criteria, etc.) with which they should have been highly correlated if the prevailing assumptions of consistency in personality were tenable. As an illustration of the form that Mischel's argument took, consider table 3.1, which is adapted from a table that appears on p. 27 of *Personality and Assessment*.

The correlations in the table were obtained in a study conducted by Sears (1963), and Mischel was citing them as evidence pertinent to the degree of consistency with which "dependency" had been manifested by Sears' subjects (nursery school children) across five different categories of dependent behaviors. These categories were identified as: (1) negative attention seeking, e.g., attention getting by disruption or aggressive activity; (2)

Table 3.1 Intercorrelations Among Five Measures of Dependency As Reported by Sears (1963)[a]

Measure of Dependency		I	II	III	IV	V
Negative attention	I		.06	.10	.15	.37
Reassurance	II	−.24		.25	.19	.26
Positive attention	III	.23	−.11		.11	−.03
Touching and holding	IV	.04	.14	−.16		.71
Being near	V	−.03	.12	−.14	.13	

[a]Intercorrelations for Sears' girl and boy subjects are shown above and below diagonal, respectively.
SOURCE: Adapted from W. Mischel, Personality and Assessment, p. 27, © 1968 by John Wiley & Sons, Inc. Reprinted by permission of the author and the publisher.

seeking reassurance; (3) positive attention seeking, as in seeking praise; (4) nonaggressive touching or holding; and (5) being near, e.g., following a child or teacher. The correlations were reported separately for girl and boy subjects. With one notable exception, the convergent validity coefficients reported by Sears were quite low—in some cases even negative—and Mischel was pointing to this fact as evidence that the children Sears had studied were *not* consistent in their displays of dependency behaviors across the various categories investigated.

It was the steady recurrence of this pattern of findings throughout the existing literature that, in Mischel's view, contradicted a key assumption on which "the construct of personality itself rests," namely, the assumption "that individual behavioral consistencies exist widely and account for much of the variance in behavior" (p. 13). Were this assumption empirically defensible, Mischel argued, the correlations reported in the extant literature should have been substantially higher than he had found them to be. Stated otherwise, the empirical laws issuing from that literature should have revealed considerably more lawfulness than was in fact being revealed.

Comment

For our purposes here, what is of interest about Mischel's work is not the mere fact that he challenged the widely shared theoretical assumption of individual behavioral consistency—and in so doing sparked a rather serious crisis of confidence within the psychology of personality—but rather the empirical grounds on which he did so. Mischel must have believed that it was logical to evaluate the assumption of *individual* behavioral consistency in terms of the magnitudes of correlation coefficients generated in studies of individual differences. What is more, *Personality and Assessment* could not possibly have had the impact on the field that it did unless Mischel's convictions in this regard were widely shared. The vast majority of investigators within the field must have been prepared to accept the logic of Mischel's argument even if many were quite unprepared to accept his major substantive conclusions.

In confronting his contemporaries with correlations that were low when the general consensus was that they should have been high, Mischel was, in effect, challenging the field's preferred theoretical conception of personality (the generic structure view) by invoking its most fundamental epistemological tenet. Mischel thus missed the real mark. As a result, both the theoretical conception of personality that he sought to remove from the list of "serious contenders" and the epistemological tenet he invoked in the process are, to borrow Hogan's (1983) phrase, "alive and well" in contemporary personality psychology. As we will see below, generic structuralism remains, in the eyes of many, as viable a theoretical framework as it ever was, and the notion that the empirical findings generated by individual differences research incisively inform theoretical assertions about individual psychological functioning can be found at the core of every other major school of thought that *Personality and Assessment* has yet spawned.

The Rise of Interactionism

The findings that Mischel had unearthed led him to conclude that personality investigators should curtail their efforts to predict, explain, and understand behavior in terms of puta-tively stable underlying characteristics, and focus instead on what he took to be the pervasive causal influence of situational factors. Now just how sharply Mischel actually thought the traditional approach should be curtailed has itself been a matter of some debate (see Alker 1972; Bem 1972; Mischel 1973, 1977). But at the time, he was widely read to have adopted an essentially be-havioristic view that came to be referred to as "situationism."

In its extreme form, this view holds that any given instance of behavior is determined entirely by factors or forces located in the environmental settings (situations) in which that behavior occurs. Inasmuch as this view rejects explanations for behavior grounded ultimately in qualities or characteristics of persons, it obviates altogether the need for a concept of person-ality as an instrument of psychological theory. Not surprisingly, therefore, the stance that Mischel was perceived to have adopted met with considerable resistance in many quarters, and it was not long before situationism was itself being submitted to careful scrutiny.

By far the most insightful contribution in this regard was made by Bowers (1973), who criticized situationism on meta-physical and theoretical as well as empirical grounds. Unfortu-nately, the first two facets of his argument were overshadowed by the third, centered as it was around statistical evidence that be-havior was no more predictable from situational factors alone than Mischel had found it to be from personality factors (see also Ar-gyle and Little 1972; Endler and Magnusson 1976). Research find-ings showed that what were, in effect, correlations between situ-ational variables and criterion behaviors were generally as low as correlations between personality variables and criterion behav-ior.[1] If Mischel could use the latter as evidence against the as-sumptions underlying simple "trait/state" explanations of behav-

1. This is perhaps as good a place as any to point out that while in studies focusing on the influence of situational factors on behavior findings are often reported in the form of t-tests or F-tests, the latter are just special cases of correlation (see Cohen 1968; Darling-ton 1968). Hence, it is not at all inappropriate to speak of "the correlation between a situational variable and behavior."

ior, then by the same token one could use the former as evidence against the assumptions underlying "pure" situationism.

In the course of marshaling this evidence, opportunities arose to consider a number of instances in which both personality and situational factors had been deployed as predictor variables within the same study. Such studies were thought to be especially informative because they enabled direct comparisons between the two classes of variables as bases for predicting a given criterion.

In the language of correlation/regression analyses as introduced in chapter 2, research of this sort can be conceptualized according to the following general model:

$$\hat{Y}_{pt} = \beta_\mathrm{P} \, (P_{pa}) + \beta_\mathrm{S} \, (S_{pt}) \qquad\qquad (3.1)$$

where

$\hat{Y}_{pt}$	=	the predicted criterion behavior of person p at time t,
β_P and β_S	=	standardized partial regression coefficients for the personality and situational variables, respectively,
P_{pa}	=	the (presumably stable) status of person p with respect to some underlying personality attribute a,
S_{pt}	=	the prevailing situational influences on person p at time t, i.e., at the time when the criterion observation is made.

Equation (3.1) formally represents the notion that an individual's behavior at any given time t might be determined in part by some aspect(s) of his/her personality (P_{pa}) and in part by some aspect(s) of the situation in which that behavior occurs (S_{pt}).

The two β-values in equation (3.1) thus reflect the degree to which each of these two classes of variables is correlated with the criterion, Y (see discussion in chapter 2 on the relationship between β and r). It is perhaps apparent, therefore, that in some hypothetical instance where the criterion behavior is predicted perfectly by personality variable(s) and not at all by situational variable(s), r_P (and hence β_P) would assume an absolute value of 1.00 and r_S (and hence β_S) an absolute value of zero. Conversely, where the criterion behavior is predicted perfectly by situational variable(s) and not at all by personality variable(s), r_P (and hence β_P) would be zero while r_S (and β_S) would be $\pm$ 1.00. What actual studies designed in accordance with the logic of equation (3.1) revealed was that while the obtained values of r_P were typically low (as Mischel had observed), the obtained values of r_S were *also* typically low, and far too much so to justify any thoroughgoing situationism of the sort that Mischel was perceived to have advocated.

But this does not tell the whole story, because in most studies where it is possible to investigate the predictability of criterion behavior on the basis of personality and situational variables considered separately, it is also possible to determine how well the criterion can be predicted when the two classes of variables are considered conjointly. In order to represent this latter possibility formally, we must add a third term to the right-hand side of the equation, so that it now reads as follows:

$$\hat{Y}_{pt} = \beta_P(P_{pa}) + \beta_S(S_{pt}) + \beta_{P \times S}(P_{pa} \times S_{pt}) \qquad (3.1a)$$

This third term is neither redundant with nor deducible from the first two. While each of the first two terms indexes a predictor-criterion relationship obtained when one of the predictors—P or S—is considered and the other ignored, $\beta_{P \times S}$ reflects the degree to which the relationship between the criterion and one of the two predictors is itself dependent on the other predictor. A simple example will serve to clarify this point.

Suppose that in a study of the effects of different instructional techniques on the mathematics achievements of elementary school children, students have been randomly assigned to one of two different classes, one emphasizing close teacher supervision with all students proceeding through the material at the same pace, and the other designed to allow individual students to proceed at their own pace. From a research-design standpoint, these two different instructional procedures would quality as a "situational" variable.

Suppose further that individual differences in achievement motivation have been measured as a potentially relevant personality variable. Finally, suppose that the criterion variable in this study was defined by scores obtained by the students on a standardized mathematics test administered at the end of the school year, and that the results were as shown in figure 3.1.

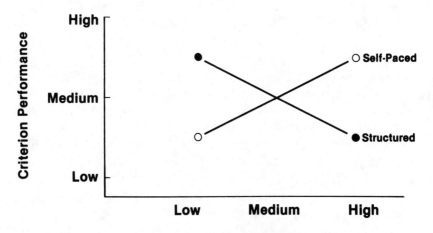

Achievement Motivation

Figure 3.1 Hypothetical Data Illustrating Person-by Situation Interaction

Note that among just those students assigned to a self-paced classroom format, the personality variable, achievement motivation, was *positively* correlated with performance on the standardized test administered at the end of the school year. Note also that among those students assigned to the highly structured instructional format, the same personality variable was *negatively* correlated with the criterion variable of test performance.

Stated in terms of equation (3.1a), a statistical analysis of these hypothetical data would render each of the first two parameters of the equation, β_P and β_S, equal to 0, and the third parameter, $\beta_{P \times S}$, equal to 1.00. The overall correlation between the criterion variable, test performance, and the personality variable, achievement motivation, is zero because the positive correlation obtained among students in the self-paced format is canceled by the negative correlation among students in the highly structured format. By itself, the situational variable, instructional format, also correlates zero with the criterion because the overall (mean) performance of the two groups of subjects did not differ. In spite of these facts, accurate predictions to the criterion would still be possible on the basis of a third predictor variable defined by considering the first two conjointly. This is what it means to say that the relationship between a criterion variable and one predictor variable is itself systematically mediated by (i.e., changed as a function of) another predictor variable.

Of course, findings as clear-cut as those in this contrived example are never really achieved. But the results of the actual studies alluded to earlier did indicate that criterion behaviors were often predicted more accurately when personality and situational variables were considered conjointly than when either of the two was considered alone (see table 1 in Bowers 1973; see also Endler and Magnusson 1976). In the face of this evidence, a great many personality investigators were persuaded to adopt a perspective on personality research that came to be known as interactionism. According to this view, the causes of an individual's behavior were likely to be discovered neither "all in the person," as the generic structuralists had allegedly assumed, nor "all in the environment," as the situationists were contending, but rather in the mutual interplay between the two. One of the chief spokespersons for this view throughout the 1970s, Norman S. Endler, stated the case as follows:

the question of whether individual differences or situations are the major source of behavioral variance, like many issues in the history of science, turns out to be a psuedo issue. . . . Asking whether behavioral variance is due to either situations or to persons, or how much variation is contributed by persons and how much by situations (an additive approach) is analogous to asking whether air or blood is more essential to life or asking to define the area of a rectangle in terms of length or width. . . . The appropriate and logical question is "How do individual differences and situations interact in evoking behavior?" (Endler 1976:63)[2]

2. Note how in this passage Endler uses the terms "individual differences" and "persons" interchangeably, as if they meant the same thing.

Comment

Viewed historically, the most striking feature of inter-actionism is that there was really nothing new in it at all. From a methodological standpoint, Cronbach had promoted the relevant research design principles in 1957. From a theoretical standpoint, Ekehammar (1974) found the literature replete with assertions to the effect that an adequate conceptualization of individual behavior/psychological functioning would have to respect the mutual interplay between personality characteristics and environmental/situational factors. Even among confirmed generic structuralists, no less prominent figures than Cattell and Eysenck had emphasized that situational factors should be expected to mediate the relationship between personal predispositions (personality traits) and behavior (see Krauskopf 1978).

In the light of these considerations, one can reasonably argue that interactionism proved so alluring to so many personality investigators at the time not because it required any fundamentally new approach to their subject matter, *but precisely because it did not*. From its inception, interactionism embraced the view that the measurement of individual differences is central to (albeit not sufficient for) the scientific study of personality, and while conceptions of interactional research faintly more sophisticated in some respects than the early version have been offered (see Golding 1975; Magnusson and Ekehammar 1975; Magnusson and Endler 1977), this basic commitment has never been compromised. As a result, interactionism has always provided a safe harbor for the belief that the knowledge generated by research incorporating individual differences variables is of direct relevance to the concerns of personality theory (see Bem 1983; Diener, Larsen and Emmons 1984). In this most fundamental respect, interactionism has remained securely tethered to the long epistemological tradition that preceded it.

A (Short-Lived) Concession to Allport

So long as the study of individual differences was to remain a central component of empirical personality research, the question of which individual differences variables to assess would continue to demand attention, interactionism notwithstanding. In one particularly noteworthy commentary on this problem, Bem and Allen (1974) conceded that Gordon Allport might have had something of importance to say on the matter after all (see the discussion of Allport in chapter 1), and suggested that headway toward a solution might require some concessions to Allport's idiographic point of view.

First, Bem and Allen argued, it might be necessary to appreciate the fact that in any given instance of personality research, some portion of the subjects being studied might not construe themselves or their behavior in terms of the underlying attribute(s) selected for study by the investigator. In effect, this would mean that the attribute(s) in question could not be applied in any psychologically meaningful way to those subjects.

But there is more, Bem and Allen noted: even among a subset of individuals within which some given attribute(s) could be meaningfully applied, psychologically important differences between those individuals could still exist with respect to the judged relevance of specific behaviors vis-à-vis those attributes. Recalling our discussion in the last chapter of the attribute "sociable vs. unsociable," for example, it could be that while there is complete consensus within a given subgroup of individuals concerning the relevance of that attribute to the activities in question (and hence to a characterization of individual differences in the engagement of those activities), there could nevertheless be substantial disagreement over what each activity signifies with respect to that attribute. Thus, while one individual might regard, say, "watching television" as a highly sociable activity, another individual might regard it as rather unsociable or aloof. In terms of assessment methodology, accommodating disagreements of this sort would require that an investigator be prepared to specify the W_{iao} component of equation (2.1) differently for different subjects.

These issues were raised by Bem and Allen within the context of a larger discussion in which they took as their point of departure the "sharp discrepancy between our intuitions [about personality], which tell us that individuals do in fact display pervasive cross-situational consistencies in their behavior, and the vast empirical literature which tells us that they do not" (1974:507–8). The literature being referred to was, of course, the low correlations with which Mischel (and others) had previously confronted the field. But faced with a choice between the conclusions seemingly mandated by those correlations and intuitive beliefs, Bem and Allen argued that it was the latter and not the former that should be trusted, and did so on the grounds that there is

a basic error in drawing inferences about cross-situational consistency from the traditional research literature in personality, an error which was identified nearly 40 years ago by Gordon Allport. The fallacy resides in the . . . nomothetic assumption that a particular trait dimension or set of trait dimensions is universally applicable to all persons and that individual differences are to be identified [solely in terms of] different locations on those dimensions. (Bem and Allen 1974:508)

The thrust of Bem and Allen's argument, then, was that the invalidity of the nomothetic assumptions under which personality investigators had been laboring was at once the source of the low correlations that investigations were so routinely turning up and the source of the discrepancy between the empirical evidence and intuitive beliefs. The evidence contradicted intuitions, Bem and Allen maintained, not because the latter were wrong, but simply because they were based "on idiographic rather than nomothetic assumptions" (p. 510). The burden of their argument was thus to show that if personality investigators would likewise abandon their nomothetic assumptions, and proceed in a fashion more compatible with idiographic intuitions, then with respect to the issue of consistency in personality, empirical findings more consonant with intuitive beliefs would be obtained.

Of course, Bem and Allen noted, adherence to these views would mean that on the basis of any one personality variable—or any one set of personality variables—an investigator could not realistically expect to do any better than predict "some of the people some of the time." This, they insisted, was simply an "idiographic fact of life." But as if to blunt the backlash that they surely expected their proposal to stir, Bem and Allen reassured the field that the rewards for conceding this fact would be paid in what had by then become "the sacred coin of the realm: bigger correlation coefficients!" (p. 512)

To demonstrate their point, Bem and Allen reported the results of a study in which their first step was to determine a priori (on the basis of what was essentially a self-report procedure) whether or not each of two personality variables, friendliness (vs. unfriendliness) and conscientiousness (vs. unconscientiousness), was applicable to a description of the personality of each of their 64 subjects. This was the "idiographic" facet of their procedure. The investigators then obtained several other independent measurements on the same subjects with respect to the same two variables. Some of the latter were based on reports concerning each subject's friendliness and conscientiousness as provided by his/her mother, father, and a peer. Other measurements were based on unobtrusive behavioral observations made by the investigators themselves.

In accordance with their basic thesis as discussed above, Bem and Allen analyzed their data so as to yield two parallel sets of intercorrelations among the various measurements obtained for each personality variable. Thus, one set of intercorrelations was computed among just those subjects for whom the personality variable in question (friendliness or conscientiousness) had been designated "applicable," and a separate set of intercorrelations was computed among just those subjects for whom the same variable had been designated "inapplicable." For illustrative purposes, the findings reported by Bem and Allen for the friendliness variable are reproduced in figure 3.2.

The correlations shown in the upper triangular portion of each cell in the figure are those obtained for the subjects

ALTERNATIVE MEASURES OF FRIENDLINESS

	I Self Report	II Mother's Report	III Father's Report	IV Peer's Report	V Group Discussion	VI Spontaneous Friendliness	VII All Variables
I							
II	.61 / .52						
III	.48 / .24	.75 / .28					
IV	.62 / .56	.71 / .40	.50 / .34				
V	.52 / .59	.34 / .41	.50 / .13	.45 / .39			
VI	.61 / -.06	.46 / -.18	.69 / -.20	.39 / .09	.73 / .30		
MEAN CORR	.57 / .39	.59 / .30	.60 / .16	.54 / .37	.52 / .37	.59 / .01	.57 / .27

Figure 3.2 Intercorrelations Among Six Measures of Friendliness Among Two Groups of Subjects

SOURCE: Adapted from D. J. Bem and A. Allen, On predicting some of the people some of the time: The search for cross-situational consistencies in behavior, Psychological Review 81:506–20, © 1974 by the American Psychological Association. Reprinted by permission of the author and the publisher.

referred to by Bem and Allen as "low variability," i.e., the subjects for whom the personality variable "friendliness" had been designated as "applicable." In contrast, the correlations shown in the lower triangular portion of each cell are those obtained for "high variability" subjects, i.e., those for whom that same personality variable had been designated as "inapplicable."

Inspecting these two parallel sets of correlations one notes that, with very few exceptions, the upper-triangular entries are substantially higher than their lower-triangular counterparts. Moreover, and although the data are not shown here, Bem and Allen reported much the same pattern of findings for the variable "conscientiousness." It was in this juxtaposition of two parallel sets of validity coefficients that Bem and Allen found empirical confirmation for their twofold thesis that (a) the low correlations obtained in previous research were born of the inappropriate nomothetic assumption of universal applicability, and that (b) by abandoning this assumption in favor of the idiographic view that any single personality variable can be meaningfully applied to some individuals but not all, research findings more consonant with the intuitive belief that individuals do display pervasive consistencies in their behavior could be obtained.

In discussing their methods and results, Bem and Allen acknowledged that while they had surrendered to each of their subjects jurisdiction over the question of whether a given personality attribute was applicable at all to a description of his/her personality, they had "stubbornly retained" jurisdiction over what they termed the "scalability" issue, i.e., the matter of determining what each of their observational variables would be taken to signify with respect to the underlying attributes in question. However, Bem and Allen noted, "when an investigator is willing to release this degree of freedom as well, his validity coefficients will reward him with an appropriate increment in magnitude" (p. 517).

Comment

Viewed from a purely conceptual/theoretical vantage point, the Allportian thrust of Bem and Allen's proposal is clear enough. Nor should it be overlooked that with respect to the rather basic problem of determining which personality variables to study (and how to define them), Bem and Allen clearly endorsed the view that the subject rather than the investigator should have the final word. Regarded more comprehensively, however, the fact that

Bem and Allen's thinking remained rooted in the epistemological tenets of the individual differences framework is also transparent.

From the grounds on which they predicated their opening allusion to the "sharp discrepancy" between intuitions and empirical evidence regarding individual behavioral consistency, through their repeated references to the notion that "bigger correlations" among individual differences variables would resolve that discrepancy, to their eventual proposals for achieving such correlations, Bem and Allen's entire argument depended for its coherence on the assumption that scientific assertions about individual behavior/psychological functioning had properly been and should continue to be informed by the findings of individual differences research. Their thesis that an investigator might first have to identify an appropriate subset of individuals before proceeding with business as usual scarcely qualified as a significant departure, and there was nothing else in their argument to suggest that any changes more radical than this would be necessary. Thus, even as Bem and Allen appeared to be striking yet another blow against generic structuralism, personality psychology's most fundamental epistemological problem was escaping detection again, disappearing once more down that shimmering hall of mirrors that are validity coefficients.

As I suggested was true of Allport's work, the most serious problem with Bem and Allen's neo-Allportian proposal was that the case against the "nomothetic" tradition was not pressed far enough. Thus, their assertion that "there is a basic error in drawing inferences about cross-situational consistency from the traditional research literature in personality" proved to be truer than they knew, inasmuch as the truly basic error—i.e., drawing *any inferences at all* about the behavior or psychological functioning of *individuals* on the basis of validity coefficients—is one that Bem and Allen themselves made.

Nor does the parallel to Allport's efforts end here. For just as Allport eventually cried uncle and retired to his corner, so has Bem come to the view that in his earlier work the case against the "nomothetic" approach had been pressed too far (see esp. Bem 1982, 1983). More recently, Bem has rejected (or at least reconstrued) what he once regarded as "the idiographic facts of life," and has embraced instead an approach that differs in no epistemologically significant respect from that version of "interactionism" discussed earlier (see Bem 1983).

Still, Bem and his colleagues had assumed the stance of idiography long enough to declare that "predicting some of the people some of the time," or maybe even "more of the people more of the time" (see Bem and Funder 1978) was the best that personality investigators could expect to do. The gauntlet had been thrown down, and nothing less than an unequivocal reaffirmation of the nomothetic commitment to the task of predicting (virtually) all the people all the time was called for (see Kenrick and Stringfield 1980). That was not long in coming.

The Emperor's "New" Clothes

In one of the most comprehensive and influential efforts yet made along these lines since the publication of Mischel's *Personality and Assessment*, Epstein (1977, 1979, 1980) argued that the "classic debate" over consistency in personality can be resolved in a way that concedes nothing either to interactionism or, in principle at least, to any idiographic facts of life. The solution, he suggests, "lies in an entirely different direction, one that is so obvious that, once pointed out, it reminds one of the fairy tale of *The Emperor's New Clothing*" (sic; 1979:197). What is needed, the argument goes, is nothing more than renewed respect for a long-standing and very basic psychometric principle.

The principle is that any single set of personality measurements (e.g., those displayed in table 2.1 in the last chapter) will inevitably be contaminated to a substantial degree by measurement error. When reliability and validity coefficients are computed on the basis of such measurements, those coefficients could very well be low not because individuals are truly inconsistent in their manifestations of the attributes in question, but because the measurement error is masking the consistency that would otherwise be discernible.

The startlingly obvious solution, Epstein teaches us, is to compute what he called "stability coefficients" (reliabilities and validities) only after measurements have been averaged over a sufficiently large number of instances. Such averaging reduces to a minimum (if it does not altogether eliminate) measurement error, and thus makes it possible for the true consistency of personality to manifest itself in the form of higher correlations. To illustrate his point, Epstein (1979) reported the results of four studies the essential nature of which is best explained in terms of the schematic data matrix shown in figure 3.3.

ASSESSMENT OCCASIONS

	1	2	3	.	.	.	o	.	.	.	t
1	$S_{1,1}$	$S_{1,2}$	$S_{1,3}$	.	.	.	$S_{1,o}$	.	.	.	$S_{1,t}$
2	$S_{2,1}$	$S_{2,2}$	$S_{2,3}$	.	.	.	$S_{2,o}$	.	.	.	$S_{2,t}$
3	$S_{3,1}$	$S_{3,2}$	$S_{3,3}$	.	.	.	$S_{3,o}$	.	.	.	$S_{3,t}$
.	.	.	.	.	.	.	.	.	.	.	.
.	.	.	.	.	.	.	.	.	.	.	.
.	.	.	.	.	.	.	.	.	.	.	.
p	$S_{p,1}$	$S_{p,2}$	$S_{p,3}$	.	.	.	$S_{p,o}$	.	.	.	$S_{p,t}$
.	.	.	.	.	.	.	.	.	.	.	.
.	.	.	.	.	.	.	.	.	.	.	.
.	.	.	.	.	.	.	.	.	.	.	.
n	$S_{n,1}$	$S_{n,2}$	$S_{n,3}$	.	.	.	$S_{n,o}$	.	.	.	$S_{n,t}$

PERSONS

Figure 3.3 Schematic Data Matrix Illustrating Basic Research Design Used by Epstein (1979)

In this figure, the rows represent different persons (1, 2, . . . p, . . . n), while the columns represent assessment occasions (1, 2, . . . o, . . . t). Each S entry within the matrix thus represents an assessment of some person p on some occasion with respect to a particular personality attribute. If the attribute in question is "sociable vs. unsociable," for example (see study 3 reported by Epstein 1979), $S_{1,1}$ would represent the assessed (un)sociability of person 1 on occasion 1; $S_{6,9}$ the assessed (un)sociability of person 6 on occasion 9, and so on. The assessments themselves would, of course, be generated in accordance with the logic of equation (2.1).

Now given data of this sort, an investigator might be inclined to index the temporal consistency of his/her subjects with respect to the attribute in question simply by correlating the assessments made of those persons on any single occasion with the assessments made on any other single occasion, e.g., by correlating the occasion 1 assessments with the occasion 2 assessments. Considering the measurement error problem just discussed, however, Epstein argued that it would be unreasonable to expect the correlation to be high for any two sets of assessments. Yet, he pointed out, most of the "stability coefficients" reported in the literature up to that time had been computed in just this way, i.e., on the basis of single assessments made on two different occasions or in two different situations.

Suppose, however, that an investigator *averaged*, say, the occasion 1 and occasion 3 assessments for each of the n subjects, and then correlated the resulting averages with similarly computed averages of the occasion 2 and occasion 4 assessments. If measurement error was in fact a major determinant of the low correlation obtained in the first instance, and if averaging assessments has the effect of reducing measurement error, then the correlation obtained in this second instance should be somewhat higher. By and large, Epstein found that this was indeed the case, and through an extension of this line of thinking, proceeded to demonstrate that the greater the number of instances over which assessments are averaged before computation of a "stability coefficient," the higher that coefficient becomes.

Illustrative of Epstein's findings in this regard are those shown in table 3.2. These correlations were obtained in a study involving 28 subjects (14 male and 14 female university students), who for a period of one month kept daily records of their most pleasant and unpleasant experiences. On each day, the subject's task was to describe his/her relevant experiences in narrative form, and then complete (a) a 90-item adjective checklist indicating felt emotions and (b) a 66-item checklist indicating the behavioral impulses s/he had and the behaviors s/he actually carried out. These data were then analyzed by Epstein in accordance with the general scheme described above.

The results displayed in table 3.2 summarize the "stability coefficients" Epstein obtained from assessments of positive emotions. For each of those emotions, it can be seen that, when based on assessments made either on the first two or last two days of the month, the obtained stability coefficients were rather low, and indeed not terribly different in magnitude from those that Mischel had found in his review of the extant literature. However, when assessments were averaged over all odd days of the month and then correlated with assessments averaged over all even days of the month, the resulting "stability coefficients" were substantially higher, and hovered around an r of .88.

Table 3.2 Some "Stability Coefficients" for Positive Emotions

	"Stability Coefficients"		
Emotion	Day 1 vs. Day 2	Last Day vs. Next-to-Last Day	All Odd Days vs. All Even Days
Happy	−.03	.22	.92
Kindly	.40	.29	.89
Calm	.43	.34	.88
Adequate	.37	.44	.87
Unified	.46	.44	.87
Energetic	.49	.34	.86
MEAN r:	.36	.36	.88

SOURCE: Adapted from S. Epstein, The stability of behavior: I. On predicting most of the people much of the time, Journal of Personality and Social Psychology 37:1097–1126, © 1979 by the American Psychological Association. Reprinted by permission of the author and the publisher.

After determining empirically that this pattern of findings would hold both for other categories of individual differences variables—not just positive emotions—and for other kinds of data—peer ratings and direct observations of behavior as well as self-reports—Epstein concluded that

> The classic debate on stability in personality can be resolved by noting that the problem lay in a failure to take into account error of measurement as it relates to temporal reliability. Single items of behavior, no matter how carefully measured, like single items in a test, normally have too high a component of error of measurement to permit demonstration of high degrees of stability. Once this is recognized, the solution to two related problems becomes apparent. First, the contradictory findings between a few studies that have reported stability in personality using data derived from ratings and a much larger number of studies that failed to find evidence of stability using data derived from the direct measurement of behavior can be accounted for by the observation that the former studies examined adequate samples of behavior, whereas the latter examined single events. Second, the failure to relate self-ratings, ratings by others, and personality inventories to objective behavioral criteria can be accounted for by the unreliability of the behavioral criteria, which almost always consisted of single items of behavior, usually measured in a laboratory setting. . . . [In short], error of measurement appears to be the crucial consideration in demonstrating stability in personality and in relating self-ratings and ratings by others to objective data. (Epstein 1979:1121)

Comment

As part of the same study in which the findings shown in table 3.2 were obtained, Epstein (1979) also inspected "within-subject reliability coefficients" (p. 1110), i.e., correlations between variables within a given category (positive emotions, negative emotions, impulses, etc.) computed for single subjects. Now when he analyzed his data this way—on a subject-by-subject basis—Epstein found that even when the "stability coefficients" were based on assessments that had been averaged over the maximum number of odd and even days, their magnitudes varied substantially across individuals, ranging all the way from $r= -.17$ to $r= +1.00$ (see Epstein 1979:1111, table 3). He concluded from these findings—quite properly—that his 28 subjects had not been equally consistent in their respective manifestations of the various sets of attributes he had chosen to assess.

Since these findings were quite literally staring him in the face, Epstein might at least have conceded Bem and Allen's (1974) point that given any single set of investigator-specified personality variables, one cannot realistically expect to find evidence of "behavioral stability" in more than some of the individuals one has studied. Better still, Epstein might have achieved some insight into the fact that the variations in his within-subject correlations flatly negated the relevance of his "high" between-subjects correlations to the question at hand: If within a given matrix of assessments some individuals can be found to be inconsistent even when conventional between-subjects correlations *based on the same matrix of assessments* are high, then the latter cannot possibly be indexing "consistent behavioral tendencies *in individuals*" (Epstein, 1979:1104; emphasis added), and *this* was the issue over which the "classic debate" Epstein claimed to be resolving had arisen in the first place.

But Epstein did not see matters this way, and so concluded his 1979 presentation with a startling non sequitur:

> According to our findings, it is not necessary to select particular [sub]classes of people to demonstrate stability unless one has failed to obtain a sufficient sample of behavior to begin with, in which case one needs individuals with unusually high stability to compensate for a high degree of error of measurement. As demonstrated in the present article, given an adequate sample of behavior to begin with, it should be possible "to predict most of the people much of the time." (Epstein 1979:1124)

Thus has it been revealed to personality investigators how they might, to paraphrase Epstein, both warm the Emperor and advance the cause of science (1979:1122). Merely by cloaking the former in a classically nomothetic principle concerning measurement error, he demonstrated to the satisfaction of many that high "stability coefficients" can be achieved in properly tailored individual differences research, and that the trait conception of personality must therefore be "alive and well" after all (Epstein 1977).

Through empirical evidence of the sort produced by Epstein (see also Block 1977), many contemporary investigators have found license to pursue with renewed vigor the mission of generic structuralism as it was defined some sixty years ago by the discipline's founding fathers. The Emperor's old clothes are now being paraded most exuberantly (though by no means exclusively) in the programmatic efforts of Buss and Craik to advance what they are calling an "act frequency" approach to personality (see, e.g., Buss and Craik, 1980, 1981, 1983a, 1983b, 1983c, 1984a, 1984b, 1986). Whatever new wrinkles there might be, there is no mistaking this approach's grounding in the time-honored conviction that the study of individual differences is the *sine qua non* of a science of personality.

Cognitive Personality Psychology

Some, of course, suspect that further progress in the psychology of personality will require a good deal more than renewed sensitivity to the problem of measurement error. As mentioned in chapter 1, more than a few contemporary investigators are persuaded that for the foreseeable future the most important theoretical advances in the field will be made through systematic inquiry at what Mischel has termed "the interface of cognition and personality" (1979:740). Because I concur with the basic thrust of "cognitive personality psychology," I will have more to say about it in later chapters. Still, a brief commentary on the current direction of this movement is warranted here.

As one might expect, this "new" development is not without its historical precedent. As early as 1955, George Kelly had offered a formal theory of personality which was nothing if not a commitment to the thesis that an understanding of what an individual *does* requires an understanding of how that individual *thinks*. In the Kellian view, "a person's processes are psychologically channelized by the ways in which he [sic] anticipates events" (1955:46), and events are themselves anticipated in terms of one's *personal constructs*. As one means of assessing personal constructs at the level of the individual, Kelly devised a technique known as the role construct repertory (REP) test.

Recognizing the continuity between Kelly's seminal efforts and more recent developments, Rorer and Widiger (1983:456) have recently remarked that "With the growing interest in cognitive theories generally, George Kelly's personal construct theory, with its idiographic emphasis and its rejection of much of the logical empiricist position, has come to be accepted by many as a classic that was ahead of its time."

But precisely for this reason, we do well to consider what has become of Kelly's views during the thirty-odd years that they have been extant. The following commentary by Sechrest—who studied under Kelly as a graduate student at Ohio State in the 1950s—is as revealing as it is sobering:

> In the late 1950s and early 1960s some really exciting developments growing out of Kelly's theorizing were expected. Jerome Bruner . . . referred to Kelly's work as the greatest single contribution to the theory of personality functioning of the decade ending in 1955, and Kelly had produced a group of active and dedicated students. Yet nothing much has happened in the decades since 1965, and *the major developments have to do with the utility of the Role Construct Repertory Test rather than with the theory itself.* The literature about Kelly's theory in any given year is sparse, and, in the opinion of this writer, not inspiring. It is not clear why. (Sechrest 1983:235–36; emphasis added)

The reason, I would suggest, is that very little of the empirical research carried out in Kelly's name has preserved either his idiographic emphasis or his anti-empiricist views. On the contrary, with respect to its implications for personality research, Kelly's theory has been used by many investigators as little more than a convenient excuse for tracking the correlates of *individual differences* in personal constructs. By grossly misreading Kelly and then co-opting his REP technique for their own purposes, ersatz "Kellians" have hitherto focused most of their attention on the patterns of intercorrelation between measures of individual differences in personal construct systems on the one hand, and measures of individual differences in such other attributes as cognitive complexity (Crockett 1965) and cognitive differentiation/integration (Landfield 1976) on the other.

The problem with this stems from the fact that Kelly's theory was not and is not about individual differences in cognitive complexity, integration/differentiation, or even, for that matter, personal construct systems. Although such differences are readily *accommodated* by Kelly's theory, the theory itself is about *the construing process* as it transpires *at the level of the individual*, and about the relationship between an individual's constructions of events and his/her actions. For reasons to be explained more fully in chapter 4, there is nothing in knowledge about the differences between individuals' construct systems (or the correlates thereof) that can illuminate these matters. The empirical research alluded to by Sechrest thus informs us about the utility of an assessment technique devised by Kelly but not about Kelly's theory because that is all such research can do.

Nowadays one finds a good deal less talk about personal constructs per se (but see Mancuso and Adams-Webber 1982), and commensurately greater attention being given over to "scripts," "schemas," and "prototypes." All these and similar concepts refer, in one way or another, to cognitive structures in terms of which individuals acquire and organize their knowledge about objects, persons, events, etc. The theoretical interest in these hypothetical structures is rooted in the notion that the subjective knowledge they "contain" has everything to do with the task of understanding what an individual does vis-à-vis any given set of circumstances. Beneath the modern parlance, however, one finds clear evidence of a continuing commitment to the view that a cognitive psychology of personality must still be an individual differences psychology of personality.

At first blush, this assertion might seem belied by the

fact that much of the recent research has been of a highly experimental—as opposed to correlational—nature. Precisely for this
reason, however, Higgins, Kuiper, and Olson (1981) have argued
that the role of personality factors in cognition is being systematically obscured rather than illuminated. Accordingly, those authors have emphasized "the need to get personal" in this research domain, and to this end have called for programmatic
studies of individual differences in scripts, schemas, prototypes,
etc. (see Broughton 1984).

Consistent with this view and reminiscent of Bem and
Allen's efforts, Markus (1977, 1983) has sought to document empirically the usefulness of assessing individual differences in the
content of self-schemas as a way of achieving (among other things,
perhaps) higher predictive validity coefficients in the search for
consistency in behavior. Similarly, Mischel is now of the view that
the future of personality assessment lies in the study of "person
variables" that reflect individual differences in such cognitive activities as "selective attention and encoding, rehearsal and stor-
age processes, cognitive transformations, and the active construction of cognitions and actions" (1977:251). In one of his most
recent contributions to the literature (Mischel 1984), he offers
empirical evidence—in the form of high validity coefficients, naturally—as testimony to the utility of this approach.

In seeking to focus attention on how persons think,
rather than on "traits" and "types" that somehow "impel" them
to act in certain ways, cognitive personality psychologists are
clearly—and in my view appropriately—trying to break free of the
more traditional conceptions of the discipline's subject matter.
At the same time, however, this entire movement gives every indication of being no less constrained than its ancestors by the
view that knowledge about the personality of cognition is properly acquired through empirical research involving individual differences variables of one sort or another. The names being attached to the variables may well be changing, but the underlying
epistemology remains the same. Barring a radical departure from
this view, I would suggest that some years hence, analysts of "the
cognitive movement" in personality psychology will puzzle, much

as did Sechrest in the passage cited above, as to just what went wrong.

Concluding Comments

The past two decades have not been tranquil ones within the psychology of personality. Confronted with the empirical evidence marshaled by Mischel (1968), the major task within the discipline seemed to be one of repairing or reconstructing its very foundation. As Mischel himself put it, the challenge was to somehow reconcile the

shared perception of continuity with the equally impressive evidence that on virtually all of our dispositional measures of personality substantial changes occur in the characteristics of the individual longitudinally over time and, even more dramatically, across seemingly similar settings cross-sectionally. (Mischel 1969:1012)

For most of the past twenty years, the literature of personality psychology has been singularly devoted to meeting this challenge. Accordingly, we have considered here several of the most prominent viewpoints that have been articulated to date, including "situationism," "interactionism," "quasi-idiography," "refined generic structuralism," and "cognitivism."

Unquestionably, serious differences persist between proponents of these various schools of thought over a variety of matters. As I have emphasized throughout, however, there is at least one fundamental legacy of conventional "nomotheticism" that survives intact, namely, the notion that the scientific study of personality and individual differences research are essentially isomorphic endeavors. So thoroughly embedded in contemporary thought is this notion that it has outlived extended and often acrimonious debates among personality psychologists that in all likelihood could not have arisen but for that notion.

Many individual differences investigators have opted

to "sit out" these disputes, secure in their belief that the correlation coefficients and regression equations yielded by their research advance the cause of behavioral prediction quite apart from
any impact they might be said to have on the future directions of
theory. In a text revealingly entitled *Personality and Prediction: Principles of Personality Assessment*, Wiggins spoke directly to this point:

> The field of applied personality assessment has not been
> deeply concerned with the problem of which of two correlated person-
> ality measurements "causes" the other. Prediction, the main goal of as-
> sessment, can be accomplished in total ignorance of such theoretical
> niceties. As a matter of fact, that strategy of personality assessment
> which has come to be known as the "empirical approach" is openly
> intolerant of such attempts to bring theoretical enlightenment into the
> realm of prediction studies. The basic paradigm of personality assess-
> ment calls for the prediction of a "criterion" from tests or other proce-
> dures which yield quantifiable information about individuals. . . . The
> criterion is that which we (or those who bear the financial burden of
> our enterprises) wish to predict. Predictors are, literally, anything we can
> employ to increase the accuracy of forecasts. (J. S. Wiggins 1973:12)

Now insofar as the goal of individual differences research is defined as generating predictions about the status of individuals
with respect to certain criterion variables in such a way that errors of prediction are minimized on the average, i.e., across individuals, and inasmuch as this purely technical objective is (meth-
odo)logically accessible without "causal" analyses and all other
theoretical niceties, there are good reasons for investigators to
reject attempts to bring "theoretical enlightenment" into the realm
of prediction studies.

But as it happens, there are also very good reasons to
reject attempts by individual differences investigators to bring their
particular brand of empirical "enlightenment" into the realm of
personality theory. The sword wielded by Wiggins in the above-
quoted passage cuts both ways. Unfortunately, the vast majority
of investigators within what Fiske (1978b) has so aptly termed a
"chronically ill specialty" have never seen matters this way. It is
here, I will now try to show, where the source of the illness lies.

4 Fundamental Errors of Reasoning in the Psychology of Impersonality

That individuals can be said to differ from one another in some extraordinarily large number of ways is evident to anyone who has ever pondered the matter. Moreover, the existence of viable techniques for representing certain of these differences quantitatively, and for tracking them over time and across behavioral domains, has long been a fait accompli. For these reasons alone, it seems safe to say that those who are committed above all else to the measurement and study of individual differences will always have (a) something to do, and (b) ways of doing it. But the question before us here is not whether individuals differ (they do), or whether certain of the ways in which they differ can be studied empirically (they can). The question is whether individual differences research, in any of its various guises, speaks decisively to the concerns of personality theory. Conventional wisdom has long been that it does. I will argue in the present chapter that it does not.

I noted in chapter 1 that any theory of personality is first, last, and always a conception of *individual* behavior/psychological functioning, and in launching the present discussion I would reiterate that this thesis has never been seriously disputed. Undoubtedly, the reason is that one is hard-pressed to imagine what the subject matter of a personality theory would otherwise be. In any case, we must bear in mind here that the notion that "the study of personality is essentially the study of individual differences" rose to the status of dogma among investigators within the field not out of any opposition to the theoretical concern for individual functioning, but rather out of the conviction that such research is uniquely suited to the task of reconciling that very concern with two other facets of any legitimately scientific enterprise: methodological rigor and the search for general principles. We saw in chapter 2 that it was in the service of this conviction that personality investigators embraced the measurement and statistical analysis techniques of individual differences research in the first place, and in chapter 3 that this same conviction has emerged unscathed from a tumultuous crisis of confidence within the discipline that has left few other stones unturned.

In order to understand why individual differences research cannot advance personality theory, therefore, it is necessary to confront the epistemological problems to which this fundamental conviction gives rise. These problems are embedded within three broad areas of traditional concern to classical nomotheticists: (a) the problem of identifying those basic human tendencies that define the "elements" of personality; (b) the issue of temporal and transsituational (in)consistency in personality; and (c) behavioral prediction and the establishment of empirical laws of personality.

The Psychologist's Fallacy

As I mentioned in chapter 1, the case against individual differences research as a medium for the advancement of personality theory is logically quite straightforward: the empirical findings generated by individual differences research cannot be interpreted at the level of the individual, and consequently cannot possibly inform in an incisive manner a theory of *individual* behavior/psychological functioning. Moreover, and for this very reason, individual differences research cannot possibly be suited to the task of establishing general laws or nomothetic principles concerning individual behavior/psychological functioning. That is, the empirical findings generated by such research cannot logically establish that something is the case for *each of many* individuals.

In short, the kind of knowledge that individual differences research can legitimately be said to yield is neither "idiographic" nor "nomothetic" vis-à-vis the concerns of personality theory. Nor can the methodological rigor of such research ever compensate adequately for these deficiencies. As important as methodological rigor is in some respects, it is simply not enough.

The task before us, then, is to make salient the errors of reasoning by which the empirical findings are made to *seem* interpretable at the level of the individual. As we shall see, these errors are really just different versions of a single error, identified long ago by William James as *the psychologist's fallacy*. According to James, this fallacy occurs whenever the empirical properties of *data* are uncritically assumed to reflect psychological properties of the *persons* observations on whom generated the analysis of those data. A simple example may help to clarify the nature of the pitfalls inherent in this fallacy.

Before a political election, it is common for pollsters to survey representative samples of the voting population in an attempt to forecast the outcome of the election. Let us say for the sake of discussion that in one such poll, it has been found that 51 percent of the sampled voters favor candidate A, while 49 percent favor candidate B. Thus, the findings indicate that within the sample as a whole, there is a slight preference for candidate A, and if the poll was conducted with sufficient care, these findings might well enable the pollster to accurately forecast the outcome of the election. On the other hand, no one would seriously interpret such findings as evidence that within each voting person there is a "mild preference" for candidate A over candidate B. Indeed, if this were the case, an accurate poll would have revealed that candidate A was favored by 100 percent of the voters, and candidate B by no one. A 51–49 percent outcome might reflect any one of a very large number of underlying dynamics, one of which is that 51 percent of the sampled voters adamantly prefer candidate A while 49 percent just as adamantly prefer candidate B. And if everyone's preference is "adamant," then no one's is "mild," the narrow overall results notwithstanding.

By the same token, while a 99–1 percent outcome could be pointed to as evidence that there is an "overwhelming" preference for candidate A within the sample as a whole, such data would not constitute evidence that any voting person has an overwhelming preference one way or the other. This could be true, but (among other possibilities) it might just as well be true that each voter in the 99 percent has but a mild preference for A, and each voter in the 1 percent but a mild preference for B. In this instance, no one in the sample could properly be said to have an "overwhelming" preference.

The point, of course, is that whatever trends might be revealed by the results of an election poll. they are properly regarded as trends *in the data*, i.e., in the overall pattern revealed by the votes. Whether or not there are any voting *persons* who "have" psychological inclinations corresponding to the identified trends is a matter on which the available data are altogether mute.

Now if one's objective is simply to forecast the outcome of an election, the distinction just drawn is irrelevant. If, on the other hand, one's objective is to gain knowledge about persons who cast votes, then the distinction is crucial, and when it is permitted to go unrecognized—or worse, simply ignored—the fallacy of which James spoke is at play. Unfortunately, this is precisely what has happened within mainstream personality psychology. The theories within this discipline are unarguably theories of *persons*, and so empirical research that would inform those theories must yield knowledge about persons. Ultimately, individual differences research fails to truly inform us about persons for the same basic reasons that election polls fail to truly inform us about voters, and as we shall presently see, matters are only made to seem otherwise by "virtue" of superficially different versions of the psychologist's fallacy.

A pollster can afford the luxury of ignoring whatever epistemological problems attend this fallacy because what is central is not really knowledge about the persons who produce the data, i.e., the voters, but knowledge about the pattern of the data produced, i.e., the votes. The personality researcher cannot afford a comparable "luxury" because in his/her role as one who would advance our understanding of persons, s/he must make empirical inquiries that yield knowledge about persons. The question, then, boils down to whether it is this kind of knowledge that the study of individual differences variables does yield. Let us consider the matter.

The Quest for Knowledge
Concerning Basic Human Tendencies

As explained in chapter 2, the methodological tenets of classical "nomotheticism" were originally adopted in concert with generic structuralism, a theoretical perspective according to which any one individual's personality is regarded as a variation on some underlying structure presumed to be common to all persons. For obvious reasons, the primary task of investigators committed to advancing this conception of personality has been to identify empirically the component elements of the presumed generic structure. Discussions of current research programs devoted to this objective can be found sprinkled throughout the current literature (see, e.g., Bem 1983; Buss and Craik, 1983a, 1983c, 1984; Golding 1978; Mehrabian and O'Reilly 1980; Royce 1978; Wiggins 1979), and although the efforts diverge from one another in some respects, they have all been undertaken in the service of a common and by now familiar conviction that

personality is that branch of psychology which is concerned with providing a systematic account of the ways in which *individuals differ from one another.* . . . [Thus] the principal goal of personality study is to provide a systematic account of *individual differences in human tendencies* (proclivities, propensities, dispositions, inclinations) to act or not to act in certain ways on certain occasions. (Wiggins 1979: 395; emphasis in the original)

For our purposes here, it is the term "human tendencies" that requires careful scrutiny. Its centrality to the thinking
of most personality investigators is amply reflected in the fact
that the empirical literature of the field is replete with—indeed,
virtually defined by—claims to bits of knowledge concerning the
differential "tendencies" that people have as a result of (or at
least as a function of) differences between them with respect to
certain underlying personality characteristics. But just what do
such assertions mean? As claims to knowledge concerning human tendencies, what is the nature of the empirical evidence on
which those claims rest, and what does that evidence really tell
us about human tendencies? It is when we begin to look closely
at these matters that things begin to unravel.

Let us consider the simple example shown in figure
4.1, which displays in scatterplot form a correlational relationship
between assessments taken on 27 individuals for each of two hypothetical individual differences variables, X and Y. These variables could be anything one liked, but for the sake of discussion,
let us say that assessments on variable X represent individual
differences in some underlying personality characteristic, while
assessments on variable Y represent individual differences on some
criterion variable hypothesized to be related to X. I am using these
data to illustrate the most rudimentary kind of empirical evidence
on which individual differences investigators stake their claims to
knowledge about basic human tendencies. As indicated in the
figure, the actual Pearson product-moment correlation for these
data is .76, and although the point is not critical to the argument,
it can be noted in passing that as the validity coefficients typically go in the field, this is a generous correlation.

Now upon inspecting these data, one might reasona-
bly assert: "There is a tendency for high Xs to be paired with high
Ys, and for low Xs to be paired with low Ys." Worded just so,
there is nothing at all wrong with this statement from an epistemological standpoint. That is, the statement says what the data
actually show. Note, however, that from the standpoint of a theory of persons, there is really nothing informative about the
statement either. For if one asks *where* the asserted tendency is,

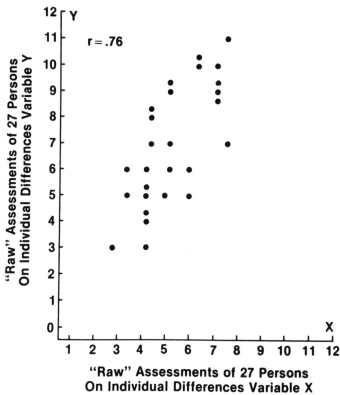

Figure 4.1 Scatterplot of Hypothetical Data Depicting Relationship Between Two Individual Differences Variables, X and Y

the answer can only be that it is in the collection of data points to which the assertion is tied. That is, the tendency being referred to is *there in the data array*, and since that data array is not defined for persons-as-persons, but only for persons-as-group, the tendency revealed by that data array cannot constitute knowledge about the tendencies of the persons-as-persons represented therein.

To be sure, matters can be and usually are made to seem otherwise, but this is accomplished only by a bit of semantic legerdemain according to which empirical findings of the sort depicted in figure 4.1 would be claimed as evidence that "people"—i.e., those persons—to whom an investigator has assigned "high" scores on variable X *have* a tendency to be high on variable Y, while "people" assigned low scores on X have a tendency to be low on Y. Worded thusly, this claim sounds relevant to the concerns of personality theory precisely because it does assert that some bit of knowledge about the tendencies of persons-as-persons has been acquired. But if the validity of claims rested in their mere assertion, we would never have need for empirical evidence.

If the term "tendency" can be logically grounded at all to data of the sort displayed in figure 4.1, it can be so only by virtue of its reference to the strength or magnitude of the relationship between the variables in question. In the present example, therefore, one might sensibly say that while X and Y (whatever they may be) are not perfectly related, they "tend" to be related, and the strength of the tendency is indexed quantitatively by the r-value of .76. Again, all is logically in order to this point, so long as it is kept firmly in mind that in the phrase "they tend to be related," the term "they" can only refer to the *variables* X and Y, the term "tend" can only refer to the r-value .76, and that while each of these entities is defined for persons-as-group, none is defined for persons-as-persons.

But it is precisely in the failure to keep these points in mind that the problem typically arises. In the second interpretation of the data in the figure, the entities to which the tendencies are being attributed are persons-as-persons. In the usual course of such interpretations, the magnitude of the psychological tendencies that the persons-as-persons putatively "have" is seen to be indexed by or at least proportional to the observed empirical tendency that is merely there in the data for persons-as-group. Thus, if one is presented in the results section of a research report with a high correlation between X and Y (whatever X and Y may be in any given instance), one will be invited to conclude in the discussion section of the report that persons high on X "have a 'strong' " tendency to be high on Y, while persons low on X "have a 'strong' " tendency to be low on Y. If the correlation between X and Y is low (as it usually is), the adjectives before "tendency" will be modified accordingly.

The conviction that the empirical findings generated by individual differences research speak to the concerns of personality theory is undoubtedly nourished greatly by interpretations of this sort. But permitting them to go unchallenged requires us to look past, among other things, the fact that within such arrays of data, the knowledge that can be claimed concerning *any* person, in each case and hence for *all* the persons-as-persons, is contained entirely within a single data point located at the intersection of the two assessments it "joins." The "joining" is literally achieved in the derivation of *r* by the operation of computing the cross-products of the Z-score transformations of the two assessments made of each person [see equation (2.3)].

The first thing to be recognized is the obvious but by no means conceptually trivial fact that, as such, single data points reveal no "tendencies" of any kind. In the context of figure 4.1, the empirical content of the term "tendency" *is* the magnitude of the correlation between X and Y as variables. It follows that that term has no content in reference to *any* person. As it is brought to bear on such data, then, the concept of "tendency" is empirically empty apart from the correlation that defines it, and there is no logical way to translate *that* meaning of the term "tendency" at the level of the discrete data points. Since it is only at the level of discrete data points that persons-as-persons are represented in the data, it also follows that there is no logically coherent way to "discover" in the tendency revealed by a correlation computed for such data any tendency—psychological, behavioral, or other—in any of the persons studied.

Obviously, empirical findings that do not disclose the tendencies of *any* person cannot sensibly be said to provide knowledge about the tendencies of persons in general (each of many). That is, such findings cannot be said to yield knowledge that is nomothetic in the only sense of the word to which a theory of persons would be compelled to bow: it tells us nothing of individual behavior/psychological functioning.

Nothing that has been said to this point argues that the central theoretical assertion of generic structuralism is invalid. As it happens, I will argue later and on rather different grounds that there are good reasons to suspect that it is. But here the point is that if the central assertion of generic structuralism *is* valid, the empirical findings generated by individual differences research cannot establish that fact.

Having said this much, I should comment here on several ancillary matters. First, the argument developed above does not hinge on any peculiarities in the hypothetical data displayed in figure 4.1. It applies no matter what kind of individual differences variables X and Y might be said to represent (i.e., traits, types, features of personal construct systems, scripts, schemas, prototypes, self-concepts, or what have you), no matter what kind of correlation the resulting r-value is said to be (reliability or validity, predictive or construct, etc.), and no matter how large or small that correlation is. Further, the argument holds no matter how many correlations are produced, and without regard to nuances in the research designs from which they are culled (e.g., the argument applies fully to the empirical findings of research that is "interactional" in the sense discussed in chapter 3). So long as the empirical findings in question are constituted of relationships involving individual differences variables (and if they are not, the research is not individual differences research to begin with) the argument stands.

I should also state explicitly here that neither is the argument compromised by individual differences research that yields multiple rather than simple correlations. In deriving a multiple R, a single individual differences variable which we may symbolize as Y' is, in effect, manufactured as some combination of two or more X variables. Thus the multiple correlation between the criterion (or some other variable), Y, and these two or more Xs is the simple correlation between Y and Y', because the latter variable, Y', *is* the two or more Xs. In short, a multiple R is really just a special kind of simple r, and it is this fact that renders the above argument applicable.

Finally, and with reference to the assertion that in data

of the sort depicted in figure 4.1 the knowledge that can legitimately be claimed concerning persons is for each person contained in a single data point, the epistemological emphasis belongs on the term "single" and not on the term "data point." Personality psychology's epistemological problems are rooted neither in measurement nor in the quantitative analysis of data per se. They are rooted in the fact that as a result of the *kind* of measurement and the kinds of quantitative analyses endemic to individual differences research, the knowledge actually yielded merely begs the questions supposedly being investigated. Convictions to the contrary can be preserved only by indulging reasoning that is patently fallacious in just the sense identified by William James.

If we have found this to be so as regards the continuing quest for knowledge concerning "basic human tendencies," it is no less so as we take up once again that long-running controversy over temporal and transsituational (in)consistency in personality.

The Consistency vs. Inconsistency Controversy in Epistemological Perspective

We saw in the last chapter that the allegedly crucial theoretical debate over the degree to which individuals are "behaviorally consistent" over time and across situations has been waged almost exclusively in terms of the magnitudes of reliability and validity coefficients generated in studies involving individual differences variables. Such was the ammunition with which Mischel (1968) began the debate, and such has been the ammunition with which others have sought, in various ways, to resolve it.

From an epistemological standpoint, the "given" in the debate has always been that the magnitude of a "stability coefficient" computed for an individual differences variable constitutes adequate empirical grounds for a generalization concern-

ing the degree of consistency with which individuals have manifested an underlying attribute. In this view, a "high" correlation
is taken to mean that in general the individuals studied have
been consistent in their respective behavioral displays of the attribute in question, and a "low" correlation to mean that in general the individuals studied have been inconsistent. With this
doctrine in mind, let us consider the data plotted in Figure 4.2.

These data were obtained in an actual study not unlike that described in chapter 2 (see Lamiell 1982; Lamiell, Trierweiler, and Foss 1983a). More specifically, each of 11 male and 8
female college students was asked to indicate, on three different
occasions separated by two-day intervals, the frequency with which
s/he had engaged, during the preceding two days, in each of the
18 activities listed in figure 2.2. Using the values shown for factor
III in table 2.3 to define the W component of equation (2.1), the
latter was applied in the usual way to these self-reported activity
protocols so as to generate three assessments of each subject
with respect to the underlying attribute "sociable vs. unsociable."

Following the standard procedures discussed in chapter 2, each of these assessments was transformed into a normative measurement (Z-score), and it is the latter that are plotted
in figure 4.2 for each of the 19 subjects. Thus, each line in the
figure represents a single individual, and the slope of a line reflects the degree to which an individual's normatively measured
status with respect to the attribute in question (i.e., his/her Z-
score) differed from the first measurement occasion to the second (left panel), and from the second measurement occasion to
the third (right panel). In other words, the slope of any given line
reflects the (in)consistency of the individual represented by that
line over the two-day interval in question; the steeper the slope,
the less the consistency. As indicated at the top of the figure, the
Pearson product-moment correlation coefficient is +.60 for the
occasion 1–occasion 2 measurements and −.01 for the occasion
2–occasion 3 measurements.

The first thing to be noted about figure 4.2 is that the
ordinate (Y-axis) is defined in terms of Z-scores. The appropriateness of this derives from the dual fact that (a) personality mea-

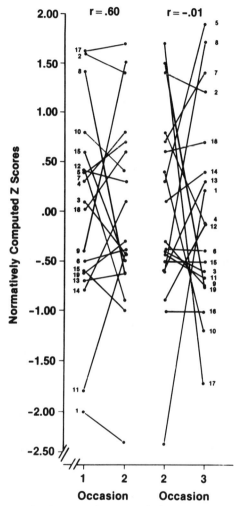

Figure 4.2 A "Microscopic Picture" of Data Underlying Two Reliability-Coefficients

SOURCE: J. T. Lamiell, The case for an idiothetic psychology of personality: A conceptual and empirical foundation, in B. A. Maher and W. B. Maher, eds., *Progress in Experimental Personality Research*, 11:1–64, © 1982 by Academic Press. Reprinted by permission of the publisher.

surements within the individual differences paradigm are defined in terms of normatively computed Z-scores, and (b) a conventional "stability coefficient" expresses the average of the cross-products of Z-scores.

When disputants in the consistency-vs.-inconsistency controversy speak of debating (in)consistency in *behavior*, a conceptual gap is immediately created between the issue being debated and the empirical grounds of the debate. Under the very best of conditions (never realized at that; see below), the coefficients generated merely constitute evidence of consistency in *the positioning of individuals relative to their group mean*, because that is the meaning of the normatively defined measurements on which correlations are based.

But consistency in positioning relative to a group mean and consistency in the behavior of individuals are two rather different matters. It is entirely possible for the behavior of individuals to change dramatically without altering their positions relative to a group mean, and it is also possible for individuals' positions within a distribution to change despite perfect consistency in behavior.

So putting aside the assertions (and, apparently, the genuine beliefs) of those who have claimed to be debating temporal and transsituational (in)consistency in the "behavior of individuals," we find when we look closely that the kind of evidence being debated does not, in fact, speak directly to the question of *behavioral* (in)consistency at all. And as if this were not problem enough, we also find when we look closely that the evidence does not speak directly to the question of *individual* (in)consistency either—"behavioral" or otherwise.

Consider the data plotted in the left-hand panel of figure 4.2, for which the "stability coefficient" equals + .60. The "logic" of disputants in the controversy is that a "stability coefficient" of this magnitude is evidence that "in general" the 19 individuals investigated were highly consistent from the first measurement occasion to the second in their relative manifestations of the measured attribute. The magnitude of a "stability coefficient" computed for a given variable supposedly indexes or is directly proportional to the degree of consistency with which the underlying attribute has been manifested by the individuals one has studied. And yet one need only glance at the left panel of the figure to see that the reasoning is simply wrong. Even relative to each other, the 19 individuals in the sample were not equally (in)consistent. While it is true that the measurements obtained on occasions 1 and 2 were indeed quite similar for some of the individuals (especially persons 2, 5, 6, 13, and 17), it is also true that the pairs of measurements were dissimilar for other individuals (especially persons 8, 9, 12, 14, and 15). The conclusion is inescapable that these latter five individuals were, as individuals, quite *inconsistent* in their relative manifestations of the measured attribute.

The "high stability coefficient" of +.60, therefore, does *not* constitute evidence that *in general* the 19 individuals were "highly" consistent from the first measurement occasion to the second. One need only look at the data to see that *no* single assertion concerning the degree of consistency manifested by the individuals in the sample could legitimately be said to hold in general.

Shifting our attention to the right-hand panel of the figure, we find exactly the same problem despite the fact that for those data the "stability coefficient" is − .01. Conventional wisdom has it that a correlation of this magnitude (essentially zero) constitutes evidence that "in general" the 19 individuals investigated were utterly inconsistent from the second measurement occasion to the third in their relative manifestations of the measured attribute. Here again, however, the most striking feature of the data is that the 19 individuals were not equally (in)consistent. When we inspect the data aggregated into the statistic $r = -.01$ on a case-by-case basis, we find that the obtained measurements for some individuals were indeed quite disparate from the second measurement occasion to the third (persons 1, 5, 8, 9, 10, and 17); but we also find that for other individuals (persons 2, 3, 6, 14, 15, 16, and 18) the two obtained measurements were very similar, and in some cases virtually identical. These individuals, then, were *as individuals* quite consistent in their relative manifestations of the attribute in question, the "low stability coefficient" notwithstanding. The latter value, therefore, cannot possibly constitute evidence that "in general" the 19 individuals investigated were inconsistent.

Contrary to the epistemological "given" on which the entire controversy has been based, there is but one circumstance under which a conventional "stability coefficient" constitutes legitimate grounds for a generalization concerning the temporal or transsituational consistency of individuals. That circumstance obtains when the "stability coefficient" in question is unity, i.e., when $r = 1.00$, for only then can it legitimately be said that what holds for persons *in the aggregate*, i.e., as a group, also holds for *persons in general*, i.e., for each of however many individuals there are in the group. This hypothetical state of affairs has been depicted with fictitious data in figure 4.3, using an N of 19 so as to facilitate comparisons with the actual data shown in figure 4.2.

In contrast to the actual data shown in figure 4.2, we see in figure 4.3 that the slopes of the lines are the same for all 19 subjects. This is necessarily the case when $r = 1.00$; r can equal 1.00 only when the two Z-scores cross-multiplied in the course of computing r are identical for each individual in the sample, and if this condition is met, then it is by definition true that every individual has been found to be perfectly consistent in the sense captured by normative measurement. Thus, a "stability coefficient" of 1.00 does constitute unambiguous grounds for an inference concerning consistency at the level of the individual precisely because that is the one condition under which it can be said that what holds for persons-as-group also holds in general for persons-as-persons.

The error of reasoning that typically arises in this context results from a failure to account for the fact that when the "stability coefficients" generated by individual differences research are less than 1.00 (and they always are), their interpretability as measures of (in)consistency in individuals is not merely changed in proportion to their deviations from unity but *altogether negated*. Thus, by a seemingly straightforward but in fact fallacious

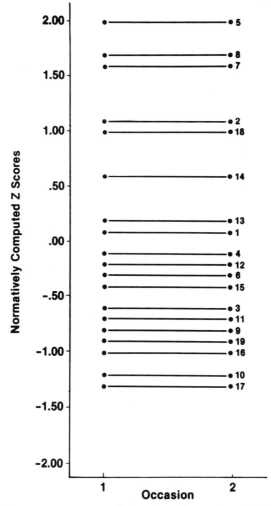

Figure 4.3 A "Microscopic Picture" of Hypothetical Data for Which the "Consistency Coefficient," r, Equals 1.00

extension of reasoning that applies only when the coefficients are unity, "high" (but not perfect) correlations constitute evidence that individuals are "highly" consistent and "low" correlations evidence that individuals are inconsistent. As figure 4.2 clearly illustrates, a "high" but not perfect "stability coefficient" does not mean that in general individuals were highly consistent, nor does a "low" stability coefficient mean that in general individuals were inconsistent. Neither coefficient means anything other than that the individuals within the group for which it was computed were not equally (in)consistent, which is another way of saying that with respect to the question of (in)consistency in personality, "high" and "low" coefficients mean the same thing.

Note that the argument here is not that individuals must be shown to manifest certain attributes with perfect consistency over time and across situations in order to validate the theoretical assumption of consistency in personality. Indeed, I know of no spokesperson for the consistency thesis who has ever asserted such an extreme view. The argument is that in order to defend the claim that one is studying empirically the degree of consistency with which particular attributes are manifested by individuals, one must at the very least be dealing with empirical findings that are both (a) relevant to the question of (in)consistency and (b) interpretable at the level of the individual. It just so happens that the "stability coefficients" generated by individual differences research fail to qualify in the latter regard unless they are perfect, and they cannot be perfect unless each of the individuals under investigation *is* perfectly consistent in the sense captured by normative measurement.

Note also that one cannot properly extract from the above argument any conclusion to the effect that such coefficients "at least" provide empirical grounds for statements on the degree of consistency manifested by "some" individuals. For as improbable as it may seem at first blush, not even this is true. It is true that given a conventional "stability coefficient" that is less than unity, an investigator can know—indeed must know—that any statement s/he might make concerning degree of consistency manifested will be applicable at most to some of the individuals within the group for which that coefficient has been derived. But there is no guarantee that the statement will hold for *any* individual, nor is there any way to find out whether the statement holds without investigating the matter at the level of the individual.

At its core, then, the epistemological problem here is not merely that given a conventional "stability coefficient" that is less than unity one is unable to frame a single answer to the question "How consistent?" that can legitimately be said to hold for all individuals within the group. The problem is actually more serious than that, and is embedded in the fact that given only such a coefficient it is impossible to provide an answer to the question "How consistent?" for any individual. To illustrate this point, let us conduct a little exercise.

Returning momentarily to figure 4.2, cover the data points plotted therein so that only the "stability coefficients" shown at the top of the figure are visible. Using as a guide either one of those two coefficients—it does not matter which one—pose to yourself the question: how consistent was subject 1 over the time interval in question? So long as you do not actually inspect the data for subject 1, you will find that your answer to this question can only be some variant of the phrase: "Cannot say." If you repeat the process for each of the 19 subjects, you will find at the end that you have been forced to respond "Cannot say" nineteen times, and I would reiterate that it does not matter which of the two panels in figure 4.2 you use to conduct the exercise. Nor would it matter if the "stability coefficients" in question were of magnitudes other than those cited in this particular example, provided that none was unity. Thus, we find that empirical evidence of the sort that classical "nomotheticists" have always regarded as uniquely suited to the task of determining what holds "for everyone" (i.e., people in general) provides us with an answer to the simple question How consistent? *for no one.*

Now one might observe here that since conventional "stability coefficients" are, after all, constituted of information about individuals (i.e., the normative measurements represented by Z-scores), an investigator might at any time "unpack" or "disaggregate" those coefficients and thereby access the data needed to determine the (in)consistency of any given individual (as I have done in constructing figure 4.2). However, when one appreciates that an investigator would necessarily have had access to the required data prior to and wholly apart from the computation of a "stability coefficient," it becomes obvious that vis-à-vis questions concerning individual (in)consistencies any such computation would be, at best, superfluous.

What Does the Available Empirical Evidence
Concerning (In)consistency in Personality Really Mean?
        As misguided as the "classic" consistency debate has been in most respects, the mass of empirical findings that investigators have brought to bear on that debate does, paradoxically, say something of considerable consequence for the age-old nomothetic vs. idiographic controversy, at least as the latter has traditionally been conceived.
        As I have tried to explain above, all the available evidence when properly interpreted means that individuals have yet to be found equally (in)consistent in their respective manifestations of any one of the hundreds of individual differences variables that have to date been investigated. Now when this fact is juxtaposed with the traditional "nomothetic" tenet that it is just those attributes manifested with some appreciable degree of consistency by individuals in general that define the basic structure of "the" human personality, one is forced to conclude that after some six decades of rigorous research, compelling empirical evidence has yet to be adduced for so much as a single basic component of the presumed generic structure. Stated otherwise, if (a) any given individual's personality is to be regarded as but a quantitative variation on some underlying generic personality the structural elements of which are common to all, and if (b) the existence of these presumed structural elements is to be inferred from empirical evidence that they are manifested overtly with some degree of consistency over time and across situations (the exact degree of consistency required has never been specified) then (c)

the search for structural elements common to all is logically tied to the search for evidence that those elements are manifested overtly with a degree of consistency common to all.

But we have seen that the available empirical evidence means that every underlying attribute studied to date *has not* been manifested with a degree of consistency common to all. Hence, we have yet to identify an attribute that on the basis of the available evidence can be said to *be* common to all, and so the long-coveted but still mythical periodic table of nomothetic personality elements remains empty.

Of course, no amount of failure in the search for such "elements" will ever conclusively prove that success can never be achieved. It is nevertheless both ironic and deserving of our serious reflection that in their fervent (and continuing) search for these "elements," the "nomotheticists" who to date have so thoroughly dominated empirical personality psychology have managed to produce overwhelming evidence that (a) the theoretical assumptions that have historically driven their quest (i.e., the assumptions of generic structuralism) are almost certainly false, and that (b) the "antiscientist" of personality psychology banished to his corner some twenty years ago as punishment for admonishing his colleagues on just this point was—if not certainly, then certainly beyond reasonable doubt—correct all along.

We saw in chapter 3 that for a time during the mid to late 1970s, Daryl Bem and his colleagues made some attempt to rekindle Allport's insights. Unfortunately, neither Allport's nor Bem's thinking ever fully circumvented the "nomothetic" monolith, and so both eventually capitulated—Allport with manifest reluctance, Bem more in the fashion of a Prodigal Son. In the light of what has been said to this point, however, perhaps there is hope that on purely logical grounds contemporary "nomotheticists" can eventually be persuaded that the empirical findings they themselves have trained on the (in)consistency controversy actually build a stronger case for the assumptions of the traditional idiographic position than traditional idiographists ever managed to build for themselves.

Behavioral Prediction and the Quest
for "Nomothetic Laws"

Yet a third key tenet of classical nomotheticism is that the findings of research incorporating individual differences variables can contribute to the practical objective of predicting behavior, and simultaneously serve the more theoretical objective of demonstrating that behavior is at least systematically related to—and perhaps actually caused by—qualities or attributes with which the personalities of individuals are endowed in varying amounts. Further, insofar as the construct validity of variables intended to represent those qualities is established, the empirical findings generated can, if properly cross-validated, serve as grounds for articulating the "nomothetic laws" of personality functioning.

We discussed earlier the logic by which the prediction of behavior on the basis of personality variables proceeds. To recapitulate briefly, the level of prediction achieved within a given behavioral domain is indexed by the magnitudes of the correlations between some specified criterion variables(s) and personality variables. As predictor variables, the latter may be considered either singly, multiply, or in combination with other predictors such as situational variables. The actual mechanics of prediction are accomplished by means of regression equations that describe correlational relationships mathematically. While the exact form assumed by a given prediction equation will depend upon the specific features of the research design, the underlying logic is always the same (see equations (2.4), (2.5), (3.1), and (3.1a). With all this in mind, then, let us see what individual differences research actually offers in the way of behavioral prediction and "nomothetic laws."

To begin with, when a personality investigator speaks of "predicting a person's behavior" on the basis of findings generated by individual differences research, all that can really be meant is that the investigator can *formulate* a prediction about that person's behavior. The accuracy of a prediction necessarily remains open to question when the basis for the prediction is a less-than-perfect correlation, and since for all intents and purposes predictions of this sort are always based on less-than-perfect correlations, claims to be "predicting a person's behavior" should really not be made. With this much established, the fallacious reasoning embedded in traditional conceptions of the personality-and-prediction enterprise begins to surface.

Consider the fact that one can formulate a prediction about an individual's behavior without benefit of the knowledge yielded by any kind of research. One can simply decide to formulate a prediction "out of the blue" and do so. This being the case, systematic empirical research can scarcely be regarded as enabling one to do something that one could not otherwise do. What, then, is special about research-based predictions?

If one puts this question to advocates of conventional "nomotheticism," the answer is routinely and inevitably of a form that can be paraphrased as follows: Well, yes, one can formulate predictions about an individual's behavior without the knowledge yielded by systematic empirical research. But one who formulates a prediction "out of the blue" is in no position to say anything about the accuracy of that prediction. On the other hand, one whose prediction is informed by empirical research can address the question of accuracy, and in comparison to out-of-the-blue predictions, this is what is special about predictions based on the findings of individual differences research.

The most serious problem with this view is that when a prediction about a person's behavior is "informed" by the findings of individual differences research, one *cannot*, in fact, specify ahead of time the accuracy of that prediction. What the empirical findings entitle one to speak about is the *average* of the (squared) errors of prediction *in the long run*, i.e., across individuals. See figure 4.4 in this regard.

The hypothetical three-variable regression equation shown in the figure can be thought of as having been derived from empirical research in which three "personality" variables, X_1, X_2, and X_3 were related via multiple correlation/regression procedures (see chapter 2) to some criterion variable Y. The *b*-coeffi-

Hypothetical three-variable regression equation:
$$\hat{Y} = a + b_1(X_1) + b_2(X_2) + b_3(X_3)$$

Person	A Posteriori Error of Prediction	A Priori Value
1	$(Y - \hat{Y})$	Unspecifiable
2	$(Y - \hat{Y})$	Unspecifiable
3	$(Y - \hat{Y})$	Unspecifiable
4	$(Y - \hat{Y})$	Unspecifiable
5	$(Y - \hat{Y})$	Unspecifiable
6	$(Y - \hat{Y})$	Unspecifiable
7	$(Y - \hat{Y})$	Unspecifiable
8	$(Y - \hat{Y})$	Unspecifiable
9	$(Y - \hat{Y})$	Unspecifiable
10	$(Y - \hat{Y})$	Unspecifiable
GROUP	Average of squared $(Y - \hat{Y})$ values	Average of squared $(Y - \hat{Y})$ values (on cross-validation)

Figure 4.4 Schematic of the Epistemology of Prediction Errors in Individual Differences Research

Note: $\hat{Y}$ represents the predicted criterion value for a given person based on the regression equation, while Y represents the actually obtained criterion value for that person.

cient shown adjacent to each X-variable specifies the value by which an individual's "raw" assessment on that variable must be "weighted" (cross-multiplied) in generating the value of $\hat{Y}$ for that individual. For our purposes here, it is permissible to think of each b-coefficient as the correlation between its corresponding X-variable and actually obtained values of the criterion variable, Y, although strictly speaking matters are not quite this simple (for a highly readable discussion of how b-coefficients are related to and derived from correlation coefficients, see Kerlinger and Pedhazur 1974).

Now if $\hat{Y}$ represents a given individual's predicted status and Y his/her actual status on the criterion variable, then the degree of error in (or accuracy of) the prediction made for any one person is given by the quantity $(Y - \hat{Y})$ as determined for that person. With this in mind, my previous assertion about the knowledge actually yielded by individual differences research as regards accuracy-of-prediction is formally represented at the bottom of the middle column in Figure 8. That is, competently executed research of this sort yields knowledge about the *mean* value of $[(Y - \hat{Y})^2]$ for the *sample* of subjects, i.e., for persons-as-group.

Thus, an investigator whose predictions about individuals are based on the findings of individual differences research cannot specify ahead of time degree-of-accuracy for any one of those predictions, i.e., for any person-as-person. Indeed, if it were possible to specify ahead of time the accuracy of or degree of error in one's prediction for an individual, i.e., if it were possible to specify the value of $(Y - \hat{Y})$ on a case-by-case basis, then there would no longer *be* any "error of prediction." One would by definition be in a position to account for "error" ahead of time, and hence to ensure that all subsequent predictions were perfectly accurate!

This last point helps to illuminate the only condition under which the knowledge yielded by individual differences research does in fact enable an investigator to specify ahead of time the accuracy of a prediction about a given individual. That condition is met when the correlation (simple or multiple) on which the prediction equation is based is perfect (i.e., ± 1.00). In that and only that instance, the error of prediction for any given individual can be known ahead of time precisely because it is *by definition zero for each and every individual.* When the correlation is less than unity, however, error of prediction is *by definition indeterminate at the level of the individual* and hence *unspecifiable for each and every individual.* In fact, for any given individual, the error of prediction can take on any value permitted by the scale on which the criterion variable is defined. No greater precision than this can legitimately be claimed, and this much "precision" can be claimed without benefit of any research knowledge. And so we are right back where we started.

Of course, none of this should be taken to mean that the knowledge yielded by individual differences research is of no use whatsoever. On the contrary, such knowledge does have uses, and there is even a sense in which it can be said that such knowledge serves the objective of behavioral prediction. All actuarial prediction schemes are rooted in the notion that maximizing predictive accuracy means minimizing errors of prediction in the long run, i.e., on the average. In individual differences research this average is computed across persons—"the long run" literally runs over persons—and predictive accuracy is thus knowledge about persons-as-a-group but not knowledge about persons-as-persons. Within the individual differences framework there are only two ways around this conclusion. One is strict reliance on perfect correlations as the bases for prediction. The other is the psychologist's fallacy. The former option is practically inaccessible, and the latter is scientifically unacceptable.

Beyond the implications for behavioral prediction per se, it should be clear that nothing is left of the notion that individual differences research can yield "nomothetic laws" of relevance to personality theory. We have already seen that within the traditional paradigm, the very concept of "lawfulness" in behavior is tied directly to evidence that behavior is to some degree predictable. But since the knowledge yielded by individual differences research concerning behavioral predictability is actually knowledge about no one, it cannot possibly constitute knowledge about everyone. Since the nomothetic concerns of personality theory are properly understood as concerns for laws that hold for persons in general and not merely persons in the aggregate, such "laws" as individual differences research might be said to yield are, from the perspective of personality theory, simply irrelevant.

Summary and Conclusion

In this chapter, we have considered from an epistemological standpoint three issues that, historically, have been of central significance to classical "nomotheticists." My overriding objective here has been to explain why the empirical findings generated by individual differences research can be made to seem interpretable at the level of the individual only by the dubious grace of variations on what William James called the psychologist's fallacy. Thus, in discussing (a) the search for basic human tendencies, (b) the "classic" debate over (in)consistency in personality, and (c) the issue of behavioral prediction as it pertains to the search for "nomothetic laws" of personality functioning, we have seen that in each case knowledge of a sort that for purely logical reasons cannot even be articulated apart from its reference to persons-as-group is nevertheless being interpreted, discussed, and archivally recorded as if it constituted knowledge of persons-as-persons.

Perhaps the belief that individual differences research yields knowledge about the behavior or psychological functioning of individuals is rooted ultimately in the fact that the "raw material" for such research is, after all, constituted of observations, assessments, and measurements of individuals. That is, the input for such research is information that is interpretable at the level of the individual. The problem lies at the other end, so to speak, in the fact that the empirical "output" is not interpretable for individuals—the nature of the input notwithstanding—and that it is the output on which interpretations that sound relevant to the concerns of personality theory are being imposed.

Since logically, the knowledge yielded by individual differences research cannot be divorced from its aggregate statistical moorings, it is not at all inappropriate to view such research as providing us with what amounts to a psychology of impersonality. The knowledge there is really knowledge about individual differences variables, not knowledge about individuals. It is in this sense that the knowledge is impersonal and, in the final analysis, it is for this reason that one is entitled to reject attempts by individual differences investigators to bring their particular brand of enlightenment into the realm of personality theory. If one seeks knowledge about individuals, then one must study individuals. Moreover, if one wishes to establish that something holds·for individuals in general—i.e., nomothetically—then one must show that it holds for each of many individuals and not merely for aggregates of individuals.

In concluding this chapter, I should perhaps emphasize once more the fact that the problem here does not lie with individual differences research per se. That is, I am not arguing that individual differences research is of no conceivable use. The argument is aimed directly and specifically at individual differences research as a framework for the advancement of personality theory.

For this purpose, the inadequacies of the traditional paradigm are epistemological. Hence they remain no matter what kinds of individual differences variables are taken up for investigation (traits, types, cognitions, etc.), and whether or not those variables are studied in conjunction with other kinds of variables (e.g., within the context of interactional research designs). In short, the inadequacies of the traditional paradigm vis-à-vis the concerns of personality theory are built into that paradigm and cannot be remedied under any version of it (see Lamiell 1985; Lamiell and Trierweiler 1986a, 1986b; Paunonen and Jackson 1986). Hence, as long as the view prevails that "the study of personality is essentially the study of individual differences," there will be no genuine theoretical advances within this field.

5 On the Epistemology of "Objective" Personality Measurement

Though for the decidedly critical thrust of the last chapter my outlook on the field of personality psychology might seem nihilistic, I hope to establish in the remainder of this book that such is not at all the case. On the contrary, I would contend that a viable psychology of personality could exist even if another study of individual differences was never to be carried out. The task at this point, therefore, is to somehow fashion an alternative conception of basic personality research that both accommodates the arguments of the previous chapter and at the same time respects the overriding theoretical objectives and scientific concerns of the discipline.

In taking up this mission, however, we do well not to ignore the lessons of the past. We saw in chapter 1, for example, that Gordon Allport's abiding misgivings about the adequacy of the dominant "nomothetic" framework led him to insist that inquiry in the psychology of personality must proceed in a more "idiographic" fashion. Unfortunately, neither Allport nor anyone in his intellectual patrimony has ever been seen by mainstream investigators to have offered a great deal in the way of methodological guidelines for such inquiry. Indeed, most of what little empirical research Allport himself directed was actually of the conventional "nomothetic" variety (cf. Hall & Lindzey, 1978), and that which was not (e.g., Allport, 1967) has long been viewed by most personality researchers as far too biographical or impressionistic to qualify as properly scientific (cf. White, 1972, 1975; Runyan, 1983). Thus, in expressing a view that undoubtedly remains widespread among contemporary personality investigators (see, e.g., Pervin, 1985), Daryl Bem has remarked that

The problem with [recommending] an idiographic approach has always been that one is never quite sure what to do next. To the extent that one accepts psychology's goal as the construction of general nomothetic principles, the idiographic approach appears to be biography rather than science, a capitulation to the view that a science of psychology is impossible because "everybody is different from everybody else." It is this pessimism that seems largely responsible for the fact that the field's respect and admiration for Gordon Allport has never been translated into research programs based on his conception of personality. (Bem 1982: 23–24)

If the relevant past speaks to us at all, it seems to say that the kind of thinking that has dominated empirical personality psychology throughout this century cannot successfully be countered on terms other than its own. Since those terms are the terms of quantification, it is now our burden to dig beneath the limits of our earlier discourse, past the correlational analyses and resultant aggregate statistics that are really but the visible superstructure of individual differences research, and down into the nature of the assessment and measurement operations that are its very core. For as paradoxical as it may seem, it is in the epistemology of formal measurement that, I believe, the roots of a viable alternative can begin to take hold.

The Technology of Person Characterization Revisited

In the conclusion to chapter 4, I noted that while the aggregate statistical "output" of individual differences research is for all intents and purposes never interpretable for any individual, the measurements aggregated into those statistics are of individuals, and are thus, by definition, interpretable for individuals.

Hence, were the statistical analyses endemic to individual differences research to be undone or circumvented altogether, one could, on the basis of the underlying measurements, construct for a given individual "Smith" a profile having the essential form of that displayed in figure 5.1. Note that in the figure the abcissa demarcates three different attributes with respect to which Smith has been measured, while the ordinate represents the scale in terms of which the measurements have been expressed. In this example, the scale has been arbitrarily defined so as to range from 0.00 at one extreme to 1.00 at the other.

It should be mentioned in passing that while profiles of the sort shown in the figure almost never appear in journal or textbook presentations of the findings of empirical personality

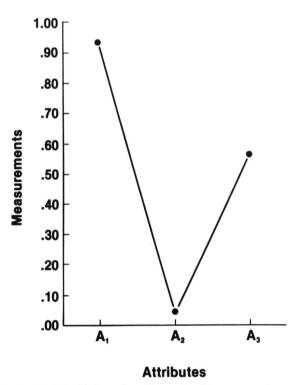

Figure 5.1 "Portrait" of Smith Based on Normative Measurements

research—one is much more likely to see tables of correlations—the construction and use of such profiles in clinical settings is rather routine (compare figure 5.1, for example, with the illustrative MMPI profile that can be found in virtually any introductory psychology textbook). But our main purpose here is to draw attention to the fact that the task of constructing even so simple a profile as this on the basis of assessments that have been made of Smith would quite literally be impossible in the absence of some coherent rationale for deciding precisely what the Y-axis coordinate of each assessment should be. That is, while drawing data points and connecting them with lines is no particular problem in itself, the task of determining in the first instance just where the data points should be located with respect to the Y-axis requires a rationale. The question before us, then, is: Just what is the usual rationale?

Review of Basic Assessment and Measurement Operations
          We know from chapter 2 that the rationale required here is usually supplied by the logic of normative measurement operations. However, it is now necessary to probe the entire matter much more closely.
          Let us first recall equation (2.1), which represents the essential features of formal personality assessment:

$$S_{pao} = \Sigma_{i=1}^{m}(OV_{pio})(W_{iao}) \tag{5.1}$$

where

S_{pao} = the "raw" assessment made of person p with respect to attribute a on occasion o,

OV_{pio} = an item of information obtained on occasion o concerning the behavior of person p, expressed as a value of observational variable i,

W_{iao} = the weight or importance attached to observatonal variable i as a reflection or instantiation of underlying attribute a on occasion o, and

$\Sigma_{i=1}^{m}$ = the additive combination rule under which the

$[(OV_{pio})(W_{iao})]$ units, of which there are m, are combined into the "raw" assessment, S_{pao}.

Continuing along the lines of the example in chapter 2, let us suppose that as part of an attempt to assess Smith's personality on the basis of behavioral self-reports, information such as that shown in figure 5.2 has been obtained. Thus, via the protocol shown there Smith is telling us that he typically devotes "very much" time or effort to studying or reading intellectual material, "little" time/effort to artistic or creative activities, "very little or no" time/effort to casual dating, and so on.

To illustrate the use of the equation, let us say that

Activity	Very little or no time/effort 0	1	Little time/effort 2	3	Moderate time/effort 4	5	Substantial time/effort 6	7	Very much time/effort 8	9
1. Studying or reading intellectual material.									X	
2. Engaging in artistic or creative activities.			X							
3. Casual dating.	X									
4. Engaging in athletic/physical fitness activities.					X					
5. Working at a part time job.					X					
6. Engaging in discussions/debates about science, philosophy, religion, politics, sports, etc.			X							
7. Partying.				X						
8. Getting high on marijuana or alcohol.				X						
9. Nurturing a close familial relationship or personal friendship.									X	
10. Engaging in activities of a religious nature.	X									
11. Attending lectures, seminars, etc. outside of coursework.	X									
12. Cutting classes for casual reasons.			X							
13. Nurturing an intimate relationship with a spouse/mate/lover.	X									
14. Watching television.			X							
15. Reflecting/thinking in quiet solitude.							X			
16. Engaging in political activities.	X									

Figure 5.2 "Smith's" Self-Reported Activity Pattern

SOURCE: J. T. Lamiell and S. J. Trierweiler, Personality measurement and intuitive personality judgments from an idiothetic point of view, Clinical Psychology Review 6:471–91, © 1986 by Pergamon Press, Ltd. Reprinted by permission of the publisher.

Smith's activity protocol is to be numerically coded by means of an arbitrary 0–9 scale according to the scheme depicted across the top of the figure. Following this scheme, Smith's protocol would thus be scored as follows:

8,2,0,4,4,2,3,3,8,0,0,2,0,2,6,0

These values define the OV component of the equation.

Finally, let us suppose that the particular attributes with respect to which Smith is to be assessed in this instance are (1) "warm/impassioned vs. cool/dispassionate," (2) "withdrawn/introverted vs. outgoing/extraverted," and (3) "pleasure/fun-oriented vs. work/achievement-oriented," and that the weights or "relevance values" to be used in generating the desired assessments, as determined in one or another of the ways discussed in chapter 2, are as shown in table 5.1. Note that for purposes of the assessment operation, the numerical values shown in a given column of table 5.1 define the W component of equation (5.1). Note also that each set of weights is defined (arbitrarily) on a scale ranging from -1.00 to $+1.00$, and that the "legend" in table 5.1 indicates the direction in which the activities have been scaled with respect to each attribute. For attributes 1, 2, and 3, therefore, activities with negative weights are being regarded as more "warm/impassioned," "withdrawn/introverted," and "pleasure/fun-oriented," respectively, while activities with positive weights are being regarded as more "cool/dispassionate," "outgoing/extraverted," and "work/achievement-oriented," respectively.

Now, by simply cross-multiplying each of the activity frequency values displayed row-wise above by its corresponding weight for a given attribute as displayed column-wise in table 5.1, and by then summing the cross-products thus obtained, the reader can verify that as "raw" assessments of Smith with respect to attribute 1, 2, and 3, equation (5.1) yields in these instances the values -4.43, -3.77, and -3.02, respectively. The question now, as always, is what do these "raw" assessments mean? To what coordinate on the Y-axis of figure 5.1, for example, shall we say that the "raw" assessment of Smith with respect to attribute 1, -4.43, corresponds?

Table 5.1 Weights or "Relevance Values" of 16 Activities for Three Attributes

	Attribute		
Activity	1	2	3
1. Studying or reading intellectual material	+.30	−.26	+.19
2. Engaging in artistic or creative activities	−.12	+.20	−.08
3. Casual dating	−.20	+.15	−.19
4. Engaging in athletic/physical fitness activities	+.03	+.08	.00
5. Working at a part time job	−.21	+.20	+.08
6. Discussing/debating science, religion, philosophy, etc.	−.32	+.08	+.09
7. Attending parties	−.07	+.14	−.32
8. Getting high on marijuana/alcohol	+.12	+.11	−.50
9. Nurturing a familial or personal friendship	−.50	−.13	−.10
10. Engaging in activities of a religious nature	−.21	−.21	+.06
11. Attending lectures/seminars outside of coursework	−.07	.00	+.14
12. Cutting classes for casual reasons	+.06	−.18	−.40
13. Nurturing an intimate relationship with spouse/lover	−.39	+.14	+.16
14. Watching television	+.06	−.16	−.41
15. Reflecting/thinking in quiet solitude	−.27	−.40	.00
16. Engaging in political activities	+.18	+.14	−.11

Attribute 1: Warm or impassioned (−) vs. cool or dispassionate (+)
Attribute 2: Withdrawn or introverted (−) vs. outgoing or extraverted (+)
Attribute 3: Pleasure or fun-oriented (−) vs. work or achievement-oriented (+)

SOURCE: J. T. Lamiell and S. J. Trierweiller, Personality measurement and intuitive personality judgments from an idiothetic point of view, *Clinical Psychology Review* 6:471–91, © 1986 by Pergamon Press, Ltd. Reprinted by permission of the publisher.

We must recall at this point our earlier discussion of the fact that, lacking some larger context within which to embed the "raw" assessment −4.43, its meaning as a statement about the level at which Smith's activity protocol reflects some underlying attribute remains inchoate, and that it is precisely for this reason that in any formal, quantitative approach to the characterization of an individual, a clear distinction must be maintained between an assessment and a measurement. The latter is the result of an operation whereby the former is *contextualized*, and it is via this contextualization process that an intelligible answer to the question is achieved.

As we know only too well by now, the view that has dominated empirical personality psychology throughout the present century is that "all meaning for a given score of a person derives from comparing his [her] score with those of other persons" (Kleinmuntz 1967:45). This notion is the essence of normative measurement, which is in turn the technical centerpiece of the "nomothetic" approach. To embrace normative measurement, therefore, is to commit oneself to the view that *scientific knowledge about what kind of a person any given individual "is" is properly acquired and conveyed through comparisons of that individual with others.*

Having detailed previously the mathematical operations by which normative measurements of an individual are derived, we will simply note that, in an actual study from which the example here has been taken, the group means for attributes 1, 2, and 3 obtained when Smith was assessed along with 39 of his (representatively sampled) peers were found to be -7.53, -0.97, and -3.45, respectively. The corresponding standard deviations were 2.14, 1.56, and 2.65, respectively. At this point we invoke equation (2.2):

$$Z_{pao} = (S_{pao} - \bar{S}._{ao})/\text{SD}._{ao} \tag{5.2}$$

and determine by means of this equation that the Z-transforms of the obtained assessments of Smith for attributes 1, 2, and 3 are $+1.45$, -1.79, and $+.16$, respectively. These latter values, then, constitute normative measurements of Smith with respect to the three attributes in question.

If we now wished to proceed with various correlational analyses, we would repeat for each of Smith's 39 peers the transformation operation specified by this equation and then continue along the course outlined in chapter 2. However, our focus here is really on a matter that lies beyond such analyses; namely, the matter of how a profile of Smith might actually be constructed *after* the attribute measures in question had been "properly validated" and hence "scientifically legitimized." For this purpose, it turns out, the three normative measurements of Smith derived above are not altogether sufficient.

The problem that arises stems from the fact that while Z-transforms of "raw" assessments are defined on a scale that is in theory infinite, a profile such as that displayed in figure 5.1

cannot be constructed without resorting to reference axes that are in practice finite. Let us consider how this problem has typically been resolved within the "nomothetic" framework.

Framing a Normative "Portrait" of Smith

One of the most important yet most frequently overlooked assumptions underlying "nomothetic" inquiry is that each of the basic attributes comprising "the" generic human personality is distributed more or less normally within the population. In figure 5.3, I have sought to depict the relevance of this assumption to our present concerns by aligning the infamous bell-shaped curve adjacent to the Y-axis, and by demarcating the points

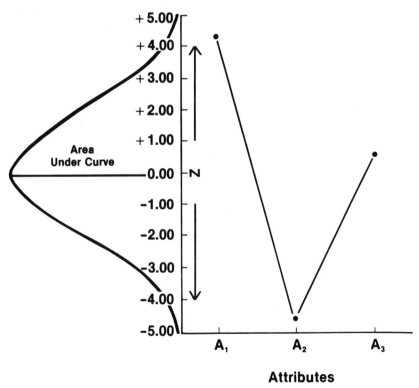

Figure 5.3 The Normal Curve as a Rationale for the Definition of "Levels"

along the latter in terms of the former. Thus, the midpoint of the Y-axis is zero in accordance with the fact that the normal curve is centered about that point where $Z = 0$. Similarly, the remaining numerical values shown along the Y-axis increase positively as the axis is ascended and negatively as it is descended, in accordance with the fact that Z-scores—the measurements whose meanings are at issue here—deviate in both a positive and negative direction from zero. In short, the *meanings* that a personality investigator seeks to convey via his/her assertions concerning the levels at which various personality attributes are manifested by an individual are based ultimately in a concept of *levels* that is itself rooted in that theoretical construction known as the normal curve.

Now for reasons alluded to previously, it is no accident that figure 5.3 has been drawn in such a way that the "tails" of the normal curve never actually touch the Y-axis. On the contrary, that feature reflects the subtle but conceptually crucial fact that, as a theoretical construction, the normal curve extends to infinity in either direction from its midpoint. In theory, therefore, there is neither a "top" nor a "bottom" to the normal curve. Over against this abstraction, however, lies the concrete and stubborn reality that in order to manufacture a tangible profile of Smith, the Y-axis with reference to which the measurements of Smith are to be plotted must necessarily have a top and a bottom. Were it otherwise, the desired profile would never be completed, because we would be busy drawing and demarcating the Y-axis forever (or, more precisely, until we reached the limits imposed by our own finitude as mortal beings).

Thus, the very concept of levels—and let us not lose sight of the centrality of this concept to the whole idea of person characterization—brings with it and requires for its concrete, practical sensibility reference to the notions "full" and "empty." That is, the concept requires some sort of boundedness in order for the meanings it subsumes to be coherently defined.

Now inasmuch as the term "define" itself has Latin roots meaning to put "limits about" (*fines* + *de*), we should not be surprised to discover that it is just by putting limits about the normal curve and thus rendering it finite that "nomotheticism" achieves its solution to the problem. This solution can be paraphrased as follows: "We hereby embrace the view that beyond certain points along the theoretically infinite scale of normative measurements (Z-scores) *there is for all practical purposes no more normal curve.*" In effect, personality investigators agree among themselves to wink at the fact that the normal curve is infinite, and to embrace instead the mathematically treasonous but realistically necessary view that it is finite. By means of this convention, the tails of the bell-shaped curve can, as it were, be "pinched against" the Y-axis at some point, and the seemingly simple problem of constructing a tangible profile of Smith is made soluble.

To illustrate, let us suppose that the Z-values $+3.70$ and -3.70 have been specified as the points along the theoretically infinite scale of Z-values at which the normal curve will be truncated. Of course, since any decision in this matter is ultimately arbitrary, other Z-values might be selected instead. It happens, however, that 3.70 represents an absolute value of Z beyond which the area under the curve is zero to two decimal places (.00). Thus, the area under the normal curve encompassed by the distance from $Z=0$ to $Z=|3.70|$ is, to two decimal places, $|.50|$, or half of the total area under the curve. Equivalently, the area under the normal curve encompassed by the distance from $Z=-3.70$ to $Z=+3.70$ is, again to two decimal places, $|1.00|$ or 100 percent of the total area under the curve.

By consulting a table of normal curve equivalents of Z-scores set up in accordance with these conventions (see, e.g., table 3 in Edwards 1964), one can determine that the value $Z=+1.45$ corresponds to a location on the scale of Z-values for which the area under the normal curve between that location and the arbitrarily determined bottom of the scale, $Z=-3.70$, is 93 percent of the total area under the curve. On a numerical scale ranging from .00 at one extreme to 1.00 at the other, therefore, the meaning of $Z=+1.45$ as an finite normative measurement of the level at which Smith has displayed attribute 1 on occasion 1 would be expressed as .93. We thus determine by these conventions that for purposes of constructing a tangible profile of Smith,

.93 is the proper Y-axis coordinate of the original assessment of Smith with respect to attribute 1.

Continuing in this fashion, we can determine by consulting a table of normal curve equivalents that $Z = -1.79$, the obtained normative measurement of Smith for attribute 2, corresponds to a location on the scale of Z-values below which lies 4 percent of the total area under the normal curve. Similarly, $Z = +.16$, the obtained normative measurement of Smith for attribute 3, corresponds to a location on the scale of Z-values below which lies 56 percent of the total area under the curve. Following the reasoning just explained, therefore, we determine that for purposes of constructing a tangible profile of Smith, the values .04 and .56 are the proper Y-axis coordinates of the original assessments of Smith with respect to attributes 2 and 3.

At long last, we have come full circle to figure 5.1. In effect, the profile shown there is the "portrait" of Smith that emerges when assessments made of him are operated on—framed, as it were—in the conventional normative fashion. It bears reemphasis at this juncture that for the logic of the operations by which it has been constructed, if not for its stark simplicity, figure 5.1 differs in no fundamentally significant respect from, say, a standard MMPI profile (see Harris 1980).

There are, of course, good reasons to wonder just how much figure 5.1 (or, for that matter, an MMPI profile) could actually tell us about Smith. It is important to keep in mind, however, that our concern is not with the portrait per se but with the logic by which it was constructed. For it is in the thinking by which such portraits are generated and not in the portraits generated by such thinking where the significant epistemological issues lie.

The task of teasing out these issues is best begun by posing the question, *on what grounds* might Smith have been measured *normatively* with respect to attributes 1, 2, and 3 in the first place? As we know from our earlier discussions, the traditional "nomothetic" answer to this question would be couched in terms of the reliability and validity coefficients gleaned from individual differences research. More specifically, such coefficients would be pointed to as scientific proof that normative measurements of Smith and his peers with respect to attributes 1, 2, and 3 tap, with adequate if not unremitting fidelity, the levels at which the respective personalities of individuals are endowed with those attributes.

But we also know from our earlier discussions that to "answer" the question just raised by pointing to reliability and validity coefficients is to not answer the question at all, because that question inquires about the grounds for measuring *an individual* and the coefficients would not be interpretable for individuals—Smith or anyone else. Hence, there would be no good reason to accept such coefficients as any justification, least of all a scientific one, for portraying Smith in the fashion of figure 5.1. Moreover, the question On what grounds? demands an answer, at least if the measurements we derive of individuals are to be regarded as significant of anything beyond the technical/mathematical operations by which we derive them.

Rather than invoking irrelevant aggregate statistics, one might instead adopt a Kleinmuntzian stance and simply assert as a basic reality of psychological measurement that "all meaning for a given score of a person derives from comparing his [her] score with those of other persons." The argument on this view would be that measurements of Smith's personality are properly derived normatively simply because that is the only way in which scientifically legitimate measurements of individuals' personalities can be derived. As we shall see presently, this argument is not defensible either. It happens, however, that a closer analysis of this view does move us further toward the heart of matters. With the Kleinmuntzian thesis in mind, therefore, let us inspect as a kind of "test case" the value .93, derived as a finite normative measurement of Smith with respect to attribute 1.

Clearly, this measurement signifies that, in comparison with his peers, Smith has been found to be relatively high with respect to *something*. But what? What is the characteristic "of Smith" that in this instance is being signified by the normative measurement .93, and how are we to know? In itself, the normative measurement .93 will never yield an answer, and without an answer to this question, the measurement would be of scant interest to one seriously disposed to learning something of *psychological* import about the person Smith. Of course, if one is not so disposed, then none of this really matters. In this event, however, we are reduced to discussing not psychological measurement but mere psychotechnology, a purely mechanical exercise *seeming* to qualify as psychological measurement only by the dubious grace of (a) the language in terms of which numerical quantities are labeled and discussed, and (b) the errors of reasoning discussed in chapter 4.

So how do we know what .93 is supposed to mean? The answer, it turns out, is in *the assessment operation itself*. We know that in this instance a measurement of .93 signifies that Smith has been found by an investigator to be relatively "cool/dispassionate" as opposed to "warm/impassioned" because we know how the observational variables on which the original assessment was based have been scaled by the investigator with respect to that underlying attribute. Put more precisely, because we know (a) that numerically low Ws (negative weights) have been assigned to activities that are being viewed as more or less "warm/impassioned," (b) that numerically high Ws (positive weights) have been assigned to activities that are being viewed as more or less "cool/dispassionate," and (c) how the available information about Smith has been combined into an overall assessment, we are able to know (d) that, in this instance, the numerically high measurement .93 signifies relative dispassionateness, and (e) that in this same instance a numerically low measurement *would* have signified relative warmth. Thus, we find that even after a "raw" assessment has been normatized, an epistemologically crucial facet of the measurement's meaning remains embedded in an understanding of the procedure by which that "raw" assessment was originally generated.

While these considerations are all quite simple enough on their surface, they do serve to clarify a point that for quite some time has escaped the attention and/or concern of mainstream "nomotheticists," specifically, that any given normative measurement of a person ultimately depends for its psychological—as opposed to merely mathematical—interpretation on a frame of reference defined not by group norms at all, but by the *alternative possibilities* built into the procedure used to generate the assessment from which that normative measurement was derived. Moreover, since some such procedure must necessarily exist in the mind and in the methods of a sentient investigator before any group norms can ever materialize, the conclusion is inescapable that normative measurement is itself rooted ultimately in—indeed impossible wholly outside of—a frame of reference that is fundamentally *nonnormative*.

Thus, contrary to the long-dominant Kleinmuntzian view, it is *never* true that *all* meaning for a given assessment of a person derives from comparing that assessment with assessments of other persons. From here it is but a short step to the realization that meaningful psychological measurements of persons could be derived even if normative comparisons were dispensed with altogether.

Interactive Measurement as an Alternative Rationale for the Characterization of Persons

In the view of most if not all contemporary psychometricians, there is but one viable alternative to measuring persons normatively, and that is to measure them *ipsatively*. Drawing its name from the Latin term for "himself" (*ipse*), ipsative measurement refers to a procedure whereby the meaning of any one assessment of an individual is defined not with reference to assessments of other individuals, but instead with reference to other assessments of that individual. Put more formally, rather than interpreting an assessment made of person p for attribute a on occasion o with reference to assessments made of other persons for the same attribute on the same occasion. [See the $\bar{S}._{ao}$ and $SD._{ao}$ terms of equation (5.2)], one might interpret an assessment of person p for attribute a on occasion o with reference to assessments of person p for other attributes on the same occasion (quantities definable as $\bar{S}_{p\cdot o}$ and $SD_{p\cdot o}$), or with reference to assessments of person p for the same attribute on other occasions (quantities definable as $\bar{S}_{pa\cdot}$ and $SD_{pa\cdot}$).

While the possibility of measuring individuals in these particular nonnormative ways has long been recognized (see Lamiell 1982), ipsative measurement operations have been exercised programmatically only by a relative few, and hence have never played a very prominent role in empirical personality research (Tyler 1978). Nor at this point in our discussion should that observation come as any great surprise. So long as the tenets of conventional "nomotheticism" were to rule the thinking of personality investigators, normative measurement would naturally remain the method of choice, and the options afforded by ipsative measurement would, just as naturally, be viewed as poor cousins; technically possible, to be sure, but neither particularly appropriate conceptually nor especially worthwhile empirically (see esp. in this regard Block 1957; Eysenck 1954; Heilbrun 1963).

It is conceivable that, at some point in the future, ipsative measurement will assume a much more prominent role in empirical personality research. But be this as it may, the objectives of our inquiry are better served at this point by shifting the focus away from ipsative measurement and onto the fact that, prevailing wisdom aside, there is still another alternative. Indeed, in a 1944 *Psychological Review* article, no less a paragon of conventional psychometry than Raymond B. Cattell identified *three* basic models for psychological measurement: normative, ipsative, and *interactive*.

As Cattell thought of it, interactive measurement is

measurement in terms of the actual physical and biological effects of behavior, usually, in test situations, *within a restricted framework defined by the test*. It recognizes the oneness of the organism-environment and pays tribute to the oft-forgotten fact that a trait is never resident only in the organism but is a relation between the organism and the environment. (Cattell 1944:293; emphasis added)

In stating that interactive measurement concerns "the actual physical and biological effects of behavior, usually," Cattell seems to have been guarding, with just a tinge of hesitancy, a belief linked to a distinction he drew later in the same article between the kinds of data on which psychological measurements are based. Cattell distinguished "behavioral" data from "introspective" data, arguing that the former derive from and are hence properly expressed in terms of "dimensions of the external world," while the latter derive from and hence can only be expressed in terms of "dimensions of consciousness" [see Fiske's (1979) more recent distinction between "the two worlds of psychological phenomena"]. Cattell went on to argue that while scientifically legitimate interactive measurements could be derived within the realm of "behavioral" data, such measurements could not legitimately be derived in the realm of "introspective" data. Indeed, Cattell labeled measurements of the latter sort "false interactive or false absolute," and declared further that valid interactive measurement based on introspective data—i.e., observations rooted in dimensions of consciousness—would be "impossible in the absence of E.S.P." (p. 294).

Now even if we were to grant for the moment Cattell's highly dubious assumption that there is somewhere a domain in which scientific observations can be made wholly apart from "dimensions of consciousness" (reason-free, as it were) few, we hope, would be prepared to defend the view—and to his credit Cattell certainly did not—that the "raw" assessments underlying personality measurements lie in that domain. On the contrary, even Cattell recognized that the "raw" assessments with which personality investigators work contain elements of human judgment (reflected most obviously though by no means exclusively in the weighting), and he argued that for so long as this was the case, investigators would have to continue to rely on normative and/or ipsative measurement operations.

Still, Cattell left no doubt at all about his high regard for the essential nature of interactive measurement. Indeed, he averred that "interactive quantification is the queen of measurement," (p. 299), and did so on just these grounds:

In the first place, true ipsative measurements and true normative measurements are bound to be founded on interactive measurement. In the second place, the interactive measurement is not only more fundamental but also more permanent, surviving the dissolution of populations or the vagaries of cultural change. . . . Finally—and this is the most important feature of interactive measurement—attention to interactive units forces the psychologist to analyze more profoundly the psychological functions he is measuring. If individuals can be given a score simply from putting them in rank order—and people can be put in rank order for anything under the sun—there is very little incentive to find the exact nature of the thing with respect to which they are being put in rank order. (Cattell 1944:299–300).

In the light of these remarks, it seems clear that there was but one thing standing between Cattell and an unqualified endorsement of interactive measurement as a technical foundation for empirical personality research. The impasse was constituted of his own doubt that, *sans* ESP, such measurement was possible with data that had been "sullied" by human judgment, and hence rooted not in "the literal logical dimensions of the external world," but instead, to one degree or another, in mere "dimensions of consciousness." Had Cattell only appreciated what by then had been widely accepted by scientists in other disciplines, i.e., that *all* scientific measurement is ultimately "sullied" by human judgment (consider, e.g., the well-known Heisenberg principle), it seems likely that he would have viewed matters quite differently, and most unlikely that his highly insightful views on interactive measurement would have disappeared so completely from the psychometric scene.

In any event, it must surely be clear by now that the sharp bifurcation drawn by Cattell between "literal dimensions of the external world" and (mere) "dimensions of consciousness" is indefensible. Perhaps less obvious, but no less true, is that as we loose ourselves from this false bifurcation, we simultaneously free ourselves to beckon back the queen that Cattell scorned.

Framing an Interactive "Portrait" of Smith
Consistent with Cattell's insight that interactive measurement is measurement in terms of a restricted framework de-

fined by the test, a formal model for deriving interactive measurements of an individual with respect to any given personality attribute might be defined as follows:

$$I_{pao} = \frac{S_{pao} - S'_{pao\ min}}{S'_{pao\ max} - S'_{pao\ min}} \tag{5.3}$$

where

I_{pao}	=	the interactively derived measurement of person p with respect to attribute a on occasion o,
S_{pao}	=	is defined, as previously, by equation (5.1), and
$S'_{pao\ max}$ and $S'_{pao\ min}$	=	respectively, the maximum and minimum assessments obtainable in a particular instance given the OV_{pio}'s, W_{iao}'s, and integration function Σ of equation (5.1).

With this equation before us, let us recall for illustrative purposes that in our earlier example the derived "raw" assessment of Smith for attribute 1 was −4.43. In order to transform this "raw" assessment into an interactive measurement of Smith with respect to attribute 1, the first step would be to determine the values of S'_{min} and S'_{max} in equation (5.3). By reflecting briefly on the procedure by which the S-value −4.43 was itself derived, it can readily be seen that S'_{min} would have been obtained if Smith's activity protocol (figure 5.2) had indicated that each activity weighted negatively with respect to attribute 1 (table 5.1) was engaged in with a maximum frequency value of 9, while each activity weighted positively with respect to that attribute was engaged in with a minimum frequency of 0. That is, if contrary to the pattern of activity frequency values displayed earlier Smith's activity protocol had instead assumed the pattern

0,9,9,0,9,9,9,0,9,9,9,0,9,0,9,0

then the same assessment operation that yielded the value −4.43 would instead have yielded the value −21.24. By exercising equation (5.1) with the data just displayed row-wise as the OV component, and the values shown for attribute 1 in table 5.1 as the W component, the reader can easily verify this calculation.

By the same token, it can be seen that the obtained assessment of Smith would have equaled S'_{max} if his activity protocol had indicated that each activity weighted positively with respect to attribute 1 was engaged in a with maximum frequency value of 9, while each activity weighted negatively with respect to that attribute was engaged in with a minimum frequency value of 0. Thus, had Smith's activity protocol assumed the pattern

9,0,0,9,0,0,0,9,0,0,0,9,0,9,0,9

then the same assessment operation that yielded the value -4.43 would instead have yielded the value $+6.75$. In this instance, therefore, the S'_{max} parameter of equation (5.3) equals $+6.75$.

If we now substitute the values -4.43, -21.24, and $+6.75$ for S, S'_{min}, and S'_{max} in equation (5.3), simple arithmetic verifies that in this instance $I_{pao} = .60$. It is this value, expressed on a scale ranging from 0.00 to 1.00, that would be said to constitute an interactive measurement of the degree to which the activity protocol actually obtained from Smith reflects the attribute "warm/impassioned vs. cool/dispassionate."

By the same token, for the second of the three attribute dimensions designated in table 5.1 (for which the obtained "raw" assessment of Smith was -3.77), the values of S'_{min} and S'_{max} are -12.06 and $+11.16$, respectively. The values of S'_{min} and S'_{max} for the last of the three attributes (for which the obtained "raw" assessment of Smith was -3.02) are -18.99 and $+6.48$, respectively. By equation (5.3), therefore, the derived interactive measurements of Smith for attributes 2 and 3 turn out to be .36 and .63, respectively.

In figure 5.4, the interactive "portrait" of Smith yielded by the three measurements just derived is juxtaposed with the normative "portrait" of Smith displayed previously in figure 5.1.

Unlike the normative profile, the interactive profile of Smith was constructed without any reference at all to assessments of other persons. Technically, the reason for this is that in

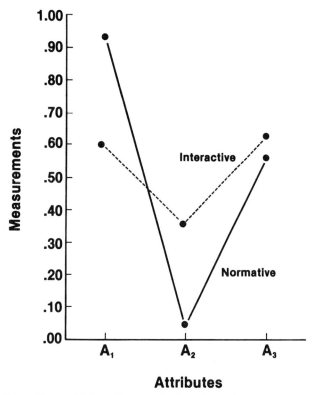

Figure 5.4 Normative and Interactive "Portraits" of Smith

interactive measurement, the reference points for contextualizing any one assessment of a given individual are defined not by assessments of other individuals (nor by other assessments of the same individual, as is true in ipsative measurement), but by the highest and lowest assessments that *might possibly* have been made of that same individual under the constraints inevitably imposed by the assessment procedure itself. This is what Cattell meant when he spoke of interactive measurement as "measurement within a restricted framework defined by the test."

One implication of the foregoing is that the interactive profile shown in figure 5.4 could have been constructed just as it was, and would look just as it does, even had we somehow known ahead of time that Smith was the only person to whom attributes 1, 2, and 3 could be meaningfully applied, and that, as a consequence, there would not *be* any assessments of other persons with respect to those attributes. Under those circumstances, the normative profile of Smith could not even have been constructed, and there would be no juxtaposition to consider.

But as we conclude this chapter, let us place the technicalities to one side in deference to the fact that, in the long run, there is a great deal more at stake here than the suggestion that personality investigators substitute one computational algorithm for another. One does not simply appropriate a model for psychological measurement without adopting the epistemological stance that goes with it, and we saw earlier that what "goes with" normative measurement is the view that knowledge about who Smith "is" is properly grounded in the consideration of who others are.

In the case of interactive measurement, the outlook is altogether different, and is defined by the thesis that *knowledge about who Smith is is properly grounded in the consideration of who Smith is not but might otherwise be.* On this latter view, it is held (among other things) that whether or not there are any "Joneses" to whom we might point as visible exemplars of who Smith is not is ultimately irrelevant.

Without doubt, this essentially dialectical view of person characterization will be rejected by many who believe that "it is meaningless to interpret the behavior of an individual without a frame of reference of others' behavior" (Epstein 1983:381). But we have seen that the psychological interpretation of any measurement of an individual's behavior—as opposed to the mere computation of a number based on observations about behavior—*always* requires a frame of reference that is other than and prior to the group norms to which Epstein has alluded, and hence that one must eventually revert to this frame of reference *even when the measurement in question is normative.* Now since the nonnormative frame of reference to which one reverts consists of the alternative possibilities built into the assessment procedure itself, and since this is merely the frame of reference to which interactive measurement adheres throughout, it follows that Epstein is simply wrong, and that, in this respect at least, Cattell was quite correct: "true ipsative measurements and true normative measurements are bound to be founded on interactive measurements," (Cattell 1944:299).

As a model for interactive measurement, therefore, I would contend that equation (5.3) is really nothing more—or less—than a particular representation of the dialectical reasoning process from which all psychological measurement emerges, and without some vestige of which neither normative nor ipsative measurements would be interpretable as anything except numbers. And before interactively derived "portraits" such as that shown in figure 5.4 are in their own turn dismissed either as in principle invalid for lack of ESP or as the products of a purely mathematical exercise devoid of genuine theoretical import, let us reserve judgment long enough to consult the personalities that, in the last analysis, matter the most. Let us consult, as it were, "the Smiths" themselves.

6 On the Epistemology of Subjective Personality Judgments

The suggestion that person characterization can be explored not only from the point of view of an investigator (as has been our approach up to now) but also from the point of view of the subjects is not, of course, a novel one. On the contrary, even before the well-known research on impression formation conducted by Solomon Asch (1946), the study of what Bruner and Tagiuri (1954) would later term "naive, implicit personality theories" (p. 649) had come to be viewed by many investigators both in the United States and abroad as an important topic of inquiry in its own right (see Allport 1937a; Schneider 1973; Wegner and Vallacher, 1977).

However, it is significant if not surprising that empirical research in this domain has to date been thoroughly dominated by the view that subjective personality judgments—including not only those made by laypersons but also those made by trained clinical psychologists in therapeutic settings—are themselves grounded in considerations of a normative, individual differences nature.[1] That is, just as it has long been assumed that

1. See, e.g., D'Andrade (1965); Dawes (1986); Ebbesen (1979, 1981); Funder (1980); Gara and Rosenberg (1981); Goldberg (1968); Harris (1980); Jackson (1969); Jackson and Messick (1963); Jones and Young (1972); Kim and Rosenberg (1980); Lay and Jackson (1969); Mulaik (1964); Norman (1967); Norman and Goldberg (1966); Ostrom and Davis (1979); Passini and Norman (1966); Rosenberg, Nelson, and Vivekananthan (1969); Shweder (1975, 1977a, 1977b, 1980, 1982); Shweder and D'Andrade (1979, 1980); J. Wiggins (1979, 1980); N. Wiggins (1973).

in order to derive objectively meaningful measurements of Smith an investigator must explicitly compare Smith with others, so has it also been widely—and uncritically—assumed that in order for Smith to frame subjectively meaningful judgments about Jones (or, for that matter, about himself), Smith must implicitly compare Jones (or himself) with others.

My major concern in the present chapter is to submit this assumption to close critical scrutiny. As the discussion unfolds, I will argue and present empirical evidence to the effect that, from the subjective point of view, the process of characterizing a person—oneself or another—is fundamentally a matter of distinguishing that person from the person s/he is not but might otherwise be, and only secondarily, incidentally, and never necessarily a matter of differentiatng that person from others. I will argue, in other words, that subjective assertions concerning the personality characteristics of self and others are grounded in a reasoning process that is essentially dialectical in nature, and thus represented more faithfully by the logic of interactive measurement than by the logic of normative measurement.

Conceptualizing the Study of Subjective Personality Judgments

Suppose that in a study of Smith's subjective personality impressions he is presented with a series of, say, 40 activity protocols like that depicted by figure 5.2, and told that each protocol describes the typical behavior pattern of one of his peers. Smith is asked to consider for a few moments the activity frequency information available in each protocol, and then to rate that protocol according to his own judgment of the degree to which it reflects each of the three underlying attributes discussed for illustrative purposes in chapter 5. It is explained to Smith that in each instance he should express his subjective judgment of the "target" by encircling a number on a 21-point scale, where 0 corresponds to one pole of the attribute being judged (warm/ impassionate, withdrawn/introverted, or pleasure/fun-oriented, as the case may be) and 20 corresponds to the other pole of that same attribute (cool/dispassionate, outgoing/extraverted, or work/achievement-oriented, as the case may be).

After Smith has provided us with the 120 requested ratings (40 targets 3 ratings each), the problem is to account for the reasoning process through which he did so. How, that is, did Smith determine in any given instance that a particular number on the rating scale would, better than any other number on that scale, express his subjective judgment of a particular target with respect to a particular attribute? In short, what do the ratings *mean to Smith*, the person who made them?

Rudiments of the Traditional Actuarial Approach

In order to appreciate the manner in which we will approach these questions later, it is helpful to have some basic familiarity with the analytic techniques that, in one form or another, have dominated the study of subjective and clinical personality judgments to date. With this in mind, let us consider table 6.1, in which are displayed data taken from an actual study patterned after the example just described (Lamiell and Trierweiler 1986a).

Note that each row in table 6.1 save the last represents one of the 40 targets rated by Smith. Each column in the larger (40×16) matrix on the right corresponds to one of the 16 activities in terms of which information about the targets was presented to Smith. Each entry in this matrix thus represents the frequency value of activity i for target t, numerically coded for purposes of quantitative analysis according to the same 0–9 scoring scheme adopted for illustrative purposes in chapter 5. Each column in the smaller (40×3) matrix on the left represents one of the three attribute dimensions in terms of which Smith rated the targets. Each entry in this matrix thus represents the numerical rating that Smith assigned to target t for attribute a.

Once the data have been organized in this fashion,

Table 6.1 Data Matrices For Correlation/Regression Analyses of Smith's Subjective Ratings

Target	A₁	A₂	A₃	X₁	X₂	X₃	X₄	X₅	X₆	X₇	X₈	X₉	X₁₀	X₁₁	X₁₂	X₁₃	X₁₄	X₁₅	X₁₆
	Attribute Ratings			Informational Cues															
1	10	8	13	8	2	0	4	4	2	3	3	8	0	0	2	0	2	6	0
2	5	15	4	2	0	7	8	0	8	8	9	7	0	0	2	6	2	2	2
3	4	9	8	2	4	2	2	4	2	4	4	4	0	0	2	6	2	2	0
4	8	8	12	7	2	0	0	0	4	0	0	9	1	0	0	8	0	2	0
5	8	12	11	7	1	3	2	5	8	5	0	9	0	2	0	9	4	9	3
6	9	14	8	8	3	1	5	0	3	5	3	5	2	1	2	2	2	4	2
7	14	8	8	4	1	3	3	1	6	5	4	7	2	2	3	0	2	3	1
8	7	13	7	4	2	6	8	8	2	9	8	4	7	2	0	7	1	3	2
9	7	8	7	8	5	2	4	6	5	6	3	6	4	2	2	5	1	2	2
10	5	5	8	7	3	5	9	9	3	5	1	6	3	3	1	7	3	9	1
11	7	8	8	4	1	4	8	0	4	4	1	2	0	2	2	7	2	5	0
12	8	8	7	7	5	7	7	0	4	5	4	8	6	1	1	2	0	8	0
13	8	13	8	7	3	2	9	4	1	6	2	7	4	1	1	7	1	7	0
14	7	10	8	8	4	3	3	8	2	6	6	8	2	0	1	4	2	8	1
15	7	10	12	7	2	5	5	7	2	6	4	7	1	1	2	5	4	4	0
16	6	13	4	4	3	7	8	0	5	7	7	8	0	5	5	8	3	8	1
17	6	14	8	5	3	7	7	5	9	9	5	9	1	3	3	3	1	5	1
18	8	8	14	6	1	0	2	6	6	2	0	9	2	2	0	9	0	4	1
19	9	14	9	9	3	6	6	8	5	7	4	7	2	3	0	5	1	0	0
20	7	9	11	5	2	4	6	5	2	6	5	4	1	1	3	3	1	5	4
21	12	7	9	7	4	0	4	0	3	3	2	6	3	2	0	7	2	4	1
22	12	8	11	6	4	1	7	5	2	4	4	6	1	1	0	6	2	7	2
23	8	12	12	5	2	0	6	0	6	6	4	8	0	2	4	8	2	5	2
24	10	7	12	7	1	2	2	1	2	2	2	8	2	0	0	2	0	4	0
25	10	12	14	8	2	2	4	6	4	4	4	8	0	0	2	0	0	4	0
26	8	12	10	5	7	7	7	6	6	6	1	3	3	4	7	4	4	5	0
27	8	12	7	4	2	4	6	0	4	7	5	7	3	4	1	5	3	6	2
28	7	13	4	4	1	0	9	0	6	7	7	5	0	1	4	7	2	4	0
29	6	13	6	6	4	4	7	0	6	8	7	7	2	3	7	8	4	2	2
30	13	13	7	8	1	3	9	6	4	7	3	5	5	0	3	2	4	2	0
31	11	7	5	6	5	3	4	0	3	6	4	4	2	1	0	0	2	5	3
32	8	7	8	9	4	3	7	1	5	6	1	6	6	3	1	1	1	5	1
33	8	13	12	6	3	5	6	4	3	4	4	6	2	1	1	3	3	3	1
34	7	8	12	7	4	3	5	4	2	6	4	8	5	0	1	4	2	5	0
35	10	8	11	7	4	4	9	4	4	4	0	9	0	2	0	4	4	4	3
36	8	8	11	5	4	5	8	2	4	4	3	5	0	5	4	7	0	5	2
37	7	14	11	4	2	0	4	6	4	4	0	6	2	2	0	8	4	6	0
38	9	11	15	7	4	4	5	4	2	4	1	4	0	2	1	2	2	4	0
39	7	12	18	9	0	0	8	0	7	1	0	9	6	0	0	9	1	3	0
40	7	12	9	7	2	0	7	4	8	3	2	8	3	2	3	9	7	5	4
Means	8.2	10.4	9.5	6.2	2.8	3.1	5.8	3.3	4.2	5.1	3.3	6.6	2.1	1.6	1.8	5.0	2.1	4.6	1.1

the usual procedure would be to conduct a series of multiple correlation/regression analyses. In each such analysis, the vectors in the right-hand matrix of table 6.1 would serve as the predictor variables, and one of the vectors in the left-hand matrix would serve as the criterion variable. In this example, therefore, three separate analyses would be conducted, and the result of each analysis would be a regression equation having the following general form:

$$\hat{R}_{ta} = c + b_{1,a}(X_{t,1}) + b_{2,a}(X_{t,2}) + \ldots + b_{16,a}(X_{t,16}) \qquad (6.1)$$

In this equation, $\hat{R}_{ta}$ represents the "best" (least squares) *estimate* of R_{ta}, Smith's actual rating of target t with respect to underlying attribute a. The equation thus indicates that a postdiction ("prediction" after the fact) of the rating Smith actually made of any one of the 40 targets could be derived by (a) cross-multiplying the coded frequency value of each informational cue (i) describing that target, X_{ti} (e.g., $X_{t,1}$, $X_{t,2}$) by its corresponding partial regression coefficient b_{ia}, (b) summing these cross-products, and then (c) adding to this sum the value of the regression constant, c.

For reasons alluded to in chapter 4, the simple correlation between Smith's actual ratings of the 40 targets and the estimates thereof derived via equation (6.1) would equal the multiple correlation between Smith's actual ratings and the cue variables $X_1, X_2, \ldots, X_{16}$. Provided that this correlation is of a sufficiently high magnitude, its associated regression equation would be offered as a formal representation of the reasoning process through which Smith framed his impressions of the targets with respect to the attribute in question. More specifically, each b_{ia} coefficient would be interpreted to reflect the relative weight or importance that Smith placed on informational cue i in rating each target with respect to a, and the summation operation would serve to represent the manner in which Smith combined subjectively weighted bits of information, the $[b_{ia}(X_{ti})]$ values, into his overall impression of each target. To lend some concreteness to these notions, the results of the three multiple correlation/regression analyses conducted on the data displayed in table 6.1 are shown in table 6.2.

Table 6.2 Regression Equations Providing Best Least-Squares Estimates of Smith's Ratings of the Targets ($\hat{R}_{ta}$) With Respect to Each of the Three Attributes

Attribute	Regression Equation	
1	$\hat{R}_{ta} = 11.6 + .11(X_1) - .18(X_2) - .35(X_3) + .09(X_4)$	
	$- .03(X_5) - .06(X_6) - .16(X_7) + .04(X_8)$	
R = .71	$+ .01(X_9) + .02(X_{10}) + .57(X_{11}) - .22(X_{12})$	
	$- .51(X_{13}) + .20(X_{14}) - .10(X_{15}) + .04(X_{16})$	(a)
2	$\hat{R}_{ta} = 5.4 + .18(X_1) - .28(X_2) - .02(X_3) + .07(X_4)$	
	$+ .01(X_5) + .31(X_6) + .58(X_7) + .19(X_8)$	
R = .72	$- .01(X_9) - .17(X_{10}) - .12(X_{11}) - .04(X_{12})$	
	$+ .17(X_{13}) + .40(X_{14}) - .20(X_{15}) - .52(X_{16})$	(b)
3	$\hat{R}_{ta} = 13.1 + .08(X_1) - .32(X_2) + .07(X_3) + .08(X_4)$	
	$+ .32(X_5) - .26(X_6) - .74(X_7) - .45(X_8)$	
R = .81	$+ .40(X_9) - .07(X_{10}) - .07(X_{11}) + .36(X_{12})$	
	$- .06(X_{13}) - .34(X_{14}) - .18(X_{15}) + .14(X_{16})$	(c)

The "Mystery" of the Additive Constant

To this point in the discussion nothing has been said concerning the additive constant term c in equation (6.1) beyond the fact that it exists. Nor is this unusual when viewed within the context of the relevant literature, for in the eyes of most contributors to that literature an additive constant is of no interpretive consequence whatsoever. Indeed, if mention is made of the additive constant at all, which is rare, this is usually only by way of a passing (and rather uninformative) allusion to the fact that its value depends on "how the subject used the rating scale" to express his/her judgments of the targets. While this is indeed what the additive constant represents, the question of *why* a subject might have "used the rating scale" in a particular way is far from inconsequential, especially if one's objective is to achieve a *theoretically based understanding of the judgments* and not merely an actuarial accounting of the variance in the ratings. Unfortunately, the extant empirical literature in this domain scarcely recognizes distinction between these two vastly different objectives (see Lamiell, Trierweiler, and Foss 1983b), and therein lies the problem.

From a purely mechanical standpoint, the need for an additive constant in equation (6.1) stems from the fact that if $\hat{R}_{ta}$

values, i.e., estimates of a subject's actual ratings, were computed simply as the sum of the $[b_{ia} (X_{ti})]$ cross-products, the numerical values thus obtained could for some—or, conceivably, even all—targets fall outside the range of the response scale in terms of which the subject was constrained to make the ratings. In the present example, this means that the values of $\hat{R}_{ta}$ could for cer-tain targets be less than 0 or greater than 20, and as estimates of the ratings that Smith actually made of the targets on a scale ranging from 0 to 20, such values clearly would not do. The technical problem, therefore, is to somehow "adjust" or "correct" the regression-based estimates of Smith's ratings so that they always fall within the permissible numerical range of his actual ratings.

The solution to this problem begins by determining the mean value of each of the informational cues (X-variables) across the 40 targets. Each of these mean values is then cross-multiplied by its corresponding b-coefficient, and the cross-products are then summed. The resulting value, which we may symbolize $\hat{R}_{avg \cdot a}$, estimates the rating that Smith *would* presumably have assigned to the hypothetical "average target" with respect to attribute a. This value is then compared with $\overline{R}_{\cdot a}$, the *average* of the ratings that Smith *did* assign to the *actually presented* targets with respect to that attribute. The amount by which $\hat{R}_{avg \cdot a}$ must be adjusted in order to equate it with $\overline{R}_a$ defines c, and it is by c that the sum of the $[b_{ia} (X_{ti})]$ cross-products must be "corrected" so as to ensure that the resulting values of $\hat{R}_{ta}$ consistently fall within the permissible limits of R_{ta}.

By exercising these procedures on the means displayed in the bottom row of table 6.1, the reader could verify that the values of the additive constants in equations (a), (b), and (c) in table 6.2 are as shown. From a conceptual standpoint, however, further clarity concerning the role played by c can be achieved by considering equation (6.2), which is simply equation (6.1) reexpressed in standardized form.

$$\hat{Z}_{ta} = \beta_{1,a} (Z_{t,1}) + \beta_{2,a} (Z_{t,2}) + \ldots + \beta_{16,a} (Z_{t,16}) \qquad (6.2)$$

Note that in this equation there is no additive constant. Thus, the problem of accounting for how Smith "used the response scale" seems to have been eliminated. Note also, however, that in equation (6.2) neither the predictor nor the criterion variables are expressed in their original form. Instead, each variable has been *reexpressed normatively*, i.e., in terms of Z-scores based on its mean and standard deviation computed across the targets.

Now because each variable on the right-hand side of equation (6.2) is expressed normatively, *the mean of each is zero by definition*, as we saw in chapter 2. Following the procedure just described for determining additive constants, therefore, it should be apparent that if one were to actually set each of the predictor variables in equation (6.2) equal to its mean, cross-multiply each mean by its corresponding β-coefficient (standardized b-coefficient), and then sum the cross-products, the resulting value, $\hat{Z}_{avg \cdot a}$, would always be zero no matter what values the β-coefficients assumed. Moreover, because the mean of the Z-transforms of Smith's actual ratings, i.e., $\bar{Z}_{\cdot a}$, would likewise be zero by definition, the amount by which $\hat{Z}_{avg \cdot a}$ would have to be adjusted in order to equate it with $\bar{Z}_{\cdot a}$ would necessarily equal zero, and hence would be computationally trivial in equation (6.2). Thus, the equation "lacks" an additive constant not because the constant's business in equation (6.1)—to account for how Smith "used the response scale"—has somehow been circumvented, but because that business has been conducted by the alternative and wholly equivalent procedure of expressing all the variables in standardized form.

The point of this discussion is to draw attention to the fact that when Smith's ratings of the targets with respect to a given attribute are submitted to a conventional correlation/regression analysis, the logic of the analysis demands that the rating Smith actually made of each target be transformed normatively and hence *interpreted by the investigator relative to Smith's ratings of the other targets*. While this demand is "hidden away" in the additive constant of equation (6.1), it is betrayed more clearly by the manner in which the predictor and criterion variables are defined in equation (6.2), and it is established finally by the fact that from a conceptual as opposed to merely mechanical standpoint, there is really no difference between equations (6.1) and (6.2).

Now if Smith himself was "using the response scale" normatively as he produced his ratings, then the demand might be of no particular consequence. That is, if the *meanings* that Smith intended to convey as he rated the targets were grounded in considerations of individual differences, then it is at least arguable that the normative transformation operation built into the analytic procedure by which equations (a), (b), and (c) in table 6.2 were derived preserved those meanings, and in this sense faithfully captured Smith's own reasoning process. However, if Smith was not "using the response scale" normatively to begin with, the nature of the reasoning process underlying his ratings will not only have been missed by the regression analyses but will actually have been distorted. Since it is conceivable that Smith was reasoning in other than a normative fashion when he made his ratings, and since, as we have now seen, the logic of a conventional correlation/regression analysis will simply not admit of this possibility, it follows that if our objective is to understand what Smith meant by his ratings, an alternative approach is required.

Rudiments of a Nonactuarial Approach

As a point of departure here, let us make explicit the analogy that can be drawn between the manner in which a personality investigator formally *assesses* persons with respect to underlying attributes and the manner in which Smith subjectively *judges* persons with respect to underlying attributes. That is, just as the former process can be represented in terms of the by now familiar expression

$$S_{pao} = \Sigma_{i=1}^{m} \ (OV_{pio}) \ (W_{iao})$$

so can the latter process be represented in terms of the expression

$$J_{tao} = \Sigma_{i=1}^{m}(X_{tio})(R_{iao}) \qquad\qquad (6.3)$$

where

J_{tao} = the covert subjective judgment that Smith makes of target t with respect to attribute a on occasion o,

X_{tio} = one of m items of information on which Smith is to base his judgment of target t with respect to attribute a on occasion o,

R_{iao} = Smith's view of the relevance of informational item i to a judgment of any given target with respect to attribute a on occasion o, and

$\Sigma_{i=1}^{m}$ = the manner in which Smith combines subjectively weighted items of information about a given target into an overall impression or subjective judgment.

As a formal representation of the manner in which Smith judges any given target, equation (6.3) does bear a resemblance to equations (6.1) and (6.2). However, on the right-hand side of equation (6.3) there is no additive constant, nor have the component variables been expressed in standardized form. As a direct result, the term on the left-hand side of the equation represents not an actuarial postdiction of Smith's overt rating of target t, but rather a quantitative estimate of Smith's *covert judgment* of target t.

The centrality of this latter distinction to our present concerns can scarcely be exaggerated. For if the analogy being drawn here between formal personality assessments and subjective personality judgments is a useful one, then it follows that just as an investigator must explicitly contextualize his/her "raw" *assessment* of a person in order to translate that assessment into an objectively meaningful *measurement*, so also must Smith implicitly contextualize his covert *judgment* of a person in order to translate that judgment into a subjectively meaningful response scale *rating*. The question, then, concerns the nature of the subjective contextualization process, and, obviously, this question cannot be addressed within a research framework where no clear distinction is drawn to begin with between a covert judgment—the entity contextualized—and an overt rating—the result of the contextualization.

Conversely, once this distinction is made, and its formal similarity to the assessment-measurement distinction recognized, the possibility is readily seen of representing alternative *theories* of the subjective contextualization process by means of the different measurement operations discussed in chapter 5. That is, if Smith's covert judgments of others are framed in accordance with a normative reasoning process, and if J_{tao} values generated in accordance with equation (6.3) can be used to represent those covert judgments, then an application of normative measurement operations to those J_{tao} values should yield reasonably accurate predictions of the overt ratings that Smith actually assigns to individual targets in a task of the sort described previously. By the same token, if the reasoning process by which Smith subjectively contextualizes his covert judgments of others conforms more closely to the operations of interactive measurement, then an application of those operations to J_{tao} values derived via equation (6.3) should yield more accurate predictions of the ratings that Smith actually assigns to the targets.

To investigate these alternatives empirically, it is first necessary to define the R_{iao} component of equation (6.3), i.e., Smith's view of the relevance of each informational item i to each of the underlying attributes in terms of which he has been asked to rate the targets. The issue here, then, is nothing other than what Bem and Allen (1974) identified as the "scalability" issue (see chapter 3), and under the terms of conventional correlation/regression analyses, this issue is addressed in terms of the b-coefficients of equation (6.1) or the β-coefficients of equation (6.2). An alternative procedure is to simply request Smith to rate each activity in accordance with his view of its relevance to each underlying attribute. As it happens, the numerical values shown previously in table 5.1 are those that, in a rating exercise of just this sort, were actually obtained from the particular "Smith" whose data are being discussed here. Thus, just as those values served previously to define the W_{iao} component of equation (5.1), so will we now employ them to define the R_{iao} component of equation (6.3).

In accordance with this equivalence and with the analogy drawn above, the same numerical values derived previously via equation (5.1) to illustrate an investigator's "raw" assessments of the target protocols with respect to the three underlying attributes will serve us here, in the form of the J_{tao} values of equation (6.3), as quantitative estimates of Smith's covert judgments of the same target protocols with respect to the same attributes. It follows that if Smith was reasoning normatively as he translated his covert judgments into overt ratings, then we would expect his ratings of the particular target represented by figure 5.2 to assume the pattern of the normative measurements displayed in figure 5.4. Conversely, if Smith's reasoning was better represented by the logic of interactive measurement, then we would expect his ratings to correspond more closely to the pattern of the interactive measurements in figure 5.4. Together with those two sets of measurements, the three attribute ratings, 10, 8, and 13, that Smith actually made of the target in question are plotted in figure 6.1.

Note that in this figure there are two Y-axes. The reason for this is that while the normative and interactive profiles were originally articulated in the "language" of a .00-to-1.00 scale, Smith was asked to rate the target by speaking in the "language" of a 0-to-20 scale. To compare the three profiles, it is necessary to express them all in the same "language." With this in mind, it can be seen that the three normative measurements derived in chapter 5 and shown in figure 5.1, .93, .04, and .56, interpolate linearly onto a 0-to-20 scale as the values 18.60, .80, and 11.20. By the same token, the three interactive measurements derived in chapter 5, .60, .36, and .63, interpolate linearly onto a 0-to-20 scale as the values 12.0, 7.2, and 12.6, respectively. The question is: precisely how (dis)similar are each of these two sets of values to the ratings Smith actually made, 10, 8, and 13?

In terms of the Cronback-Gleser procedure for indexing dissimilarity, discussed in chapter 2, the maximum possible

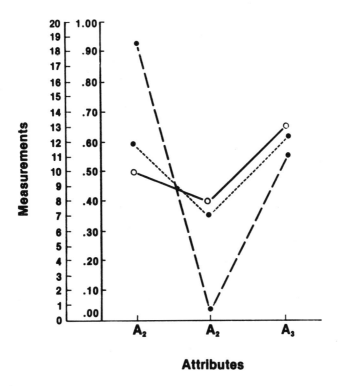

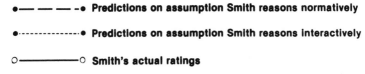

●— — — —● **Predictions on assumption Smith reasons normatively**

●·············● **Predictions on assumption Smith reasons interactively**

○————————○ **Smith's actual ratings**

Figure 6.1 Comparison of Smith's Actual Ratings with Predictions Based on Alternative Theoretical Conceptions of the Reasoning Process

dissimilarity of any set of predicted ratings to Smith's actual ratings is given by the expression $[(10-0)^2+(8-20)^2+(13-0)^2]^{1/2}$, which equals 20.32. Expressed as a ratio of this value (see Budescu 1980), the dissimilarity between Smith's actual ratings and those predicted under a normative theoretical conception of his reasoning process would be given by the expression $\{[(10-18.60)^2+(8-.80)^2+(13-11.20)^2]^{1/2}/20.32\}$, which equals .57. In contrast, the dissimilarity between Smith's actual ratings and those predicted under an interactive theoretical conception of his reasoning process would be given by the expression $\{[(10-12.00)^2+(8-7.20)^2+(13-12.60)^2]^{1/2}/20.32\}$, which equals .11. In comparison, the two values .57 vs. .11 merely reflect quantitatively what a casual glance at figure 6.1 reveals visually: the interactively based predictions correspond much more closely to the ratings Smith actually made than do the normatively derived predictions.

It would thus appear that when, for example, Smith rated the target "10" with respect to the first of the three attributes, he did not mean that he judged the target to be "neither particularly warm/impassionate nor particularly cool/dispassionate" relative to others, but that he judged the target to be "neither particularly warm/impassionate nor cool/dispassionate" *relative to how he would have judged the target had the presented activity pattern been other than it was.* It is as if Smith subjectively "anchored" the end points of the response scale, 0 and 20, by formulating covert judgments bearing a close resemblance to the S'_{min} and S'_{max} values of the interactive measurement model [see discussion of equation (5.3)], and that he *selected* his rating of the target so that the *physical* pattern defined by the relationship between his rating and the end points of the response scale would preserve the *psychological* pattern defined by the relationship between his judgment of the target's activity protocol and his judgments of its polar negations. It appears, in other words, that the *meanings to Smith* of the response scale ratings that he actually made of the target were grounded in considerations of an essentially dialectical nature, and hence that he was not "using the response scale normatively" at all.

Further Evidence for the Dialectical Nature of Subjective Personality Judgments

Although the material just presented was drawn from an actual study, it nevertheless merely represents the results obtained by investigating one particular subject's ratings of one particular target with respect to three particular attribute dimensions. But in an ongoing program of research patterned after the nonactuarial methods just described, where many different subjects have rated many different targets with respect to many different attribute dimensions, the results have consistently—indeed, overwhelmingly—pointed to the superiority of interactive measurement over normative measurement as a formal representation of the subjective contextualization process. Since this line of inquiry is instructive not only for its theoretical implications but also by virtue of its formal, paradigmatic structure, it will repay us to consider some of the relevant research in greater detail.

Subjects and Procedure

The subjects for this investigation were 40 undergraduate students at a large midwestern university, and data were gathered during three separate sessions of up to one hour each, scheduled at one-week intervals. In the first session, each subject was presented with a list of 64 personality trait adjectives (taken from Rosenberg, Nelson, and Vivekanathan 1968), and asked to select the three adjectives that best represented his/her own personality. The subject was then asked to think of three adjectives opposite in meaning to those that had been selected. Using the adjective pairs thus obtained to define the opposite poles of three 11-point rating scales, each subject was asked, in the latter part of the first session, to rate each of the 18 activities listed in table 6.3 below. That is, the subject was asked to indicate the degree to which each activity reflected each of the three attribute dimensions s/he had designated. These ratings were in turn used to define the subjective "relevance values" (R_{iao} component) of equation (6.3) as discussed above, and were numerically coded for purposes of subsequent analysis along an integer scale ranging from −5 through 0 to +5.

For purposes of obtaining these ratings, the location on the rating scale coded −5 was labeled "Extremely ——," with the blank space being filled by the adjective in a given pair said by the subject to characterize him/herself. The location on the scale coded +5 was labeled "Extremely ——," with the blank space taken by the opposite adjective in the pair. The midpoint of the rating scale (coded 0) was labeled "Neither extremely —— nor extremely ——," and was to be used by the subject to assert that a given activity indicated nothing one way or the other with respect to the attribute dimension in question. Each subject rated all 18 activities on his/her first-designated dimension, then on the second dimension, and then on the third. In this way, each subject provided a total of 54 activity ratings: 18 activities, the same for all subjects, on each of three attribute dimensions, specified individually by each subject. Table 6.3 displays the ratings actually obtained in this phase of the study from one of the 40 subjects, who will be referred to as "Rex."

In the second data collection session, each subject was provided with a blank activity protocol identical in its basic format to figure 6.2. The subject was asked to fill in the blank protocol, indicating the frequency with which s/he "typically" engaged in each of the 18 activities. The activity frequencies shown in the figure are those indicated by Rex to describe his own typical behavior pattern.

In the last data collection session, each subject was presented with the self-descriptive activity protocol s/he had completed during session 2, along with 30 additional activity protocols said to represent the self-reported activity patterns of 30 of his/her peers. These latter protocols were in fact obtained by having representatively sampled undergraduate students indicate their "typical" activity patterns. As in our earlier example, the subject's task here was to consider each activity protocol and then rate that protocol with respect to each of the three attribute dimensions s/he had previously designated. Each subject rated his/her own self-reported activity protocol first, and then rated

Table 6.3 Ratings By the Subject "Rex" of 18 Activities With Respect to Each of Three Self-Designated Attribute Dimensions

	Attribute Dimension		
	1	2	3
	Intelligent (−)	Critical (−)	Sociable (−)
	vs.	vs.	vs.
Activity	Unintelligent (+)	Receptive (+)	Unsociable (+)
1. Studying or reading intellectual materials	−5	−1	0
2. Participating in artistic or creative activities	−2	0	−1
3. Casual dating	0	1	−3
4. Engaging in premarital sex	3	0	0
5. Participating in athletic activities	0	0	−4
6. Reading/viewing pornographic materials	1	0	3
7. Watching television	2	3	−1
8. Listening to music	0	−1	2
9. Working at a part time job	−1	0	−1
10. Playing cards	0	−1	−3
11. Partying	1	3	−4
12. Attending live entertainment or movies	0	−2	−3
13. Participating in outdoor activities (camping, hiking, etc.)	−1	0	−2
14. Participating in events of a religious nature	−2	0	−2
15. Cutting classes	4	0	0
16. Getting high on alcohol and/or marijuana	1	2	0
17. Using drugs other than alcohol or marijuana	4	3	1
18. Attending lectures/seminars outside of coursework	−5	3	−1

SOURCE: J. T. Lamiell, M. A. Foss, R. J. Larsen, and A. Hempel, Studies in intuitive personology from an idiothetic point of view: Implications for personality theory, *Journal of Personality* 51:438–67, © 1983 by Duke University Press. Reprinted by permission of the publisher.

the remaining 30 protocols in terms of the same attribute dimension. Following this, the subject again rated all 31 protocols with respect to his/her second-designated attribute dimension. Finally, the subject rated all 31 protocols again with respect to his/her third-designated attribute dimension. All 93 of these ratings (31

M x   F___

Self-reported Frequency

Activity	Never or almost never	Seldom	Occasionally	Frequently	As often as possible
1. Studying or reading intellectual material				X	
2. Participating in artistic or creative activities		X			
3. Casual dating			X		
4. Engaging in pre-marital sex	X				
5. Participating in athletic activities				X	
6. Reading/viewing pornographic materials		X			
7. Watching television				X	
8. Listening to music				X	
9. Working at a part time job				X	
10. Playing cards			X		
11. Partying			X		
12. Attending live entertainment or movies				X	
13. Participating in outdoor activities (camping, hiking, etc.)				X	
14. Participating in events of a religious nature			X		
15. Cutting classes		X			
16. Getting high on alcohol and/or marijuana			X		
17. Using drugs other than alcohol or marijuana	X				
18. Lectures/seminars (outside of coursework)			X		

Figure 6.2 Rex's Self-Reported Activity Protocol
SOURCE: J. T. Lamiell, M. A. Foss, R. J. Larsen, and A. Hempel. Studies in intuitive personology from an idiothetic point of view: Implications for personality theory. *Journal of Personality* 51:438–87. © 1983 by Duke University Press. Reprinted by permission of the publisher.

targets, 3 attribute dimensions each) were made on 11-point integer scales, where the numerically low extreme of the scale (0) was labeled with that adjective of a given pair said by the subject to characterize him/herself, and the numerically high extreme of the scale (10) labeled with that adjective of a given pair said by the subject to characterize the opposite of him/herself.

Data Analysis and Results

Consistent with a central theme of this text, the data were analyzed separately for each of the 40 subjects. In the interest of both clarity and consciseness, however, detailed results will be presented only for the subject Rex. This will be followed by a summary of the results obtained across the entire sample of 40 individuals.

Proceeding as described in our foregoing discussion of Smith, data analysis began by generating the J_{tao} values of equation (6.3). Using the 31 (targets) $\times$ 18 (activities) matrix of activity frequency values to define the X_{tio} component of that equation (coded according to the same 0–9 scheme we have been using throughout), and the 18 (activities) $\times$ 3 (attributes) matrix of subjective "relevance values" to define its (R_{iao}) component, a postmultiplication of the former matrix by the latter yielded the 31 (targets) $\times$ 3 (attributes) matrix of J_{tao} values shown in Table 6.4. In accordance with the rationale explained previously, therefore, the nonparenthesized entries in the table are to be viewed here as quantitative estimates of Rex's covert subjective judgments of each of the 31 targets (himself and 30 others) with respect to each of three attribute dimensions designated by Rex himself.

Shown at the bottom of each column in the table are the mean and standard deviation of the J_{tao} values in that column. Based on these values, the Z-transform of each J_{tao} value was then computed in the usual fashion [see equation 2.2]. Each parenthesized entry in the table thus represents the Z-transform of its corresponding J_{tao} value.

Also shown at the bottom of table 6.4 are the values

Table 6.4 Quantitative Estimates of Rex's Covert Judgments of Self and 30 Others with Respect to Three Self-Designated Attribute Dimensions[a]

| | Attribute Dimension | | |
| | 1
Intelligent (−)
vs.
Unintelligent (+) | 2
Critical (−)
vs.
Receptive (+) | 3
Sociable (−)
vs.
Unsociable (+) |
Target			
1 (Self)	−43(−.43)	44(+1.76)	−129(−2.83)
2	−16(+.82)	17(−.14)	−55(+.08)
3	12(+2.12)	62(+3.03)	−52(+.20)
4	−16(+.82)	17(−.14)	−43(+.55)
5	−26(+.36)	−1(−1.40)	−32(+.98)
6	−12(+1.01)	30(+.78)	−73(−.63)
7	−16(+.82)	19(.00)	−66(−.35)
8	−24(+.45)	9(−.70)	−63(−.23)
9	−79(−2.10)	10(−.63)	−37(+.79)
10	−69(−1.64)	−8(−1.90)	−19(+1.50)
11	−74(−1.87)	10(−.63)	−74(−.67)
12	−61(−1.26)	19(.00)	−67(−.39)
13	−50(−.75)	18(−.07)	−96(−1.53)
14	−69(−1.64)	22(+.21)	−97(−1.57)
15	−21(+.59)	20(+.07)	−34(+.91)
16	−37(−.15)	−6(−1.76)	−19(+1.50)
17	−27(+.31)	23(+.28)	−43(+.55)
18	−4(+1.38)	21(+.14)	−33(+.94)
19	−28(+.27)	22(+.21)	−38(+.75)
20	−16(+.82)	4(−1.05)	−43(+.55)
21	−25(+.41)	16(−.21)	−77(−.78)
22	−17(+.78)	25(+.42)	−30(+1.06)
23	−46(−.57)	28(+.64)	−98(−1.61)
24	−32(+.08)	26(+.49)	−57(.00)
25	−19(+.68)	30(+.78)	−47(+.39)
26	−48(−.66)	5(−.98)	−52(+.20)
27	−53(−.89)	27(+.56)	−51(+.24)
28	−31(+.13)	36(+1.20)	−48(+.36)
29	−32(+.08)	26(+.49)	−87(−1.18)
30	−45(−.52)	3(−1.12)	−67(−.39)
31	−23(+.50)	14(−.35)	−41(+.63)
mean	−33.77	18.97	−57.03
standard deviation	21.54	14.21	25.41
$J_{tao\ min}$	−144	−45	−255
$J_{tao\ max}$	+144	+135	+54

[a] For each J_{tao} value shown in this table, its corresponding Z-score is shown in parentheses. See text for details.

SOURCE: J. T. Lamiell, M. A. Foss, R. J. Larsen, and A. Hempel, Studies in intuitive personology from an idiothetic point of view: Implications for personality theory, Journal of Personality 51:438–67, © 1983 by Duke University Press. Reprinted by permission of the publisher.

of J'_{min} and J'_{max}, which the reader may recognize as the subjective analogues of the S'_{min} and S'_{max} parameters of the interactive measurement model defined by equation (5.3). By reviewing our discussion of that equation, the reader will be able to verify that, for the person Rex, the J'_{min} and J'_{max} values associated with each attribute dimension are as indicated.

Continuing as we did with Smith, the normal curve equivalent of each Z-score in table 6.4 was determined and then reexpressed (via linear interpolation) in the "language" of the 0–10 scale used by Rex to rate the targets. The resulting values are displayed in panel 1 of table 6.5, and they constitute *predictions* of Rex's actual ratings of the targets *under the theoretical assumption* that his reasoning process could be understood in terms of the logic of tradition *normative* measurement. In parallel fashion, each J_{tao} value in table 6.4 was, in conjunction with its corresponding J'_{min} and J'_{max} values as shown at the foot of the table, reexpressed under the logic of equation (5.3) and then translated (once again via linear interpolation) into the 0–10 response "language" used by Rex. The resulting values are shown in panel 2 of table 6.5, and they constitute *predictions* of the ratings that Rex would actually assign to the targets *under the theoretical assumption* that his reasoning process could be understood in terms of the logic of *interactive* measurement. Panel 3 in table 6.5 displays Rex's actual ratings of each of the 31 targets with respect to each of the three attributes he had designated.

With all this in mind, let us consider the first row of data in table 6.5. The first three entries there indicate that if Rex rated his own activity protocol on the basis of normative considerations, then his "self-portrait" with respect to the three attribute dimensions in question should have been well approximated by the values 3.34, 9.61, and 0.02. If on the other hand, the reasoning process underlying Rex's self-characterization was interactive in nature, then his ratings should have been better approximated by the values 3.51, 4.94, and 3.44.

As the ratings Rex actually assigned to his own activity protocol were 3, 5, and 2, the maximum possible dissimilarity to this "self-portrait" is given by the expression

Table 6.5 Predicted Ratings, Actual Ratings, and Proportional Profile Dissimilarity Values Computed For the Subject Rex for Each of 31 Targets

	1 Predicted Ratings Based on Normal- Curve Model (PR-N)			2 Predicted Ratings Based on Interactive Model (PR-I)			3 Actual Ratings (AR)			4 Proportional Profile Dissimilarity Values	
	Attribute			Attribute			Attribute			AR vs.	AR vs.
Targets	1	2	3	1	2	3	1	2	3	PR-N	PR-I
1 (Self)	3.34	9.61	0.02	3.51	4.94	3.44	3	5	2	.43	.13
2	7.95	4.45	5.32	4.44	3.44	6.09	6	5	5	.22	.26
3	9.83	9.99	5.78	5.42	5.94	6.20	9	9	6	.09	.34
4	7.95	4.45	7.10	4.44	3.44	6.62	3	5	6	.49	.21
5	6.41	0.80	8.38	4.10	2.44	6.92	5	6	6	.60	.38
6	8.44	7.81	2.65	4.58	4.17	5.45	4	6	4	.48	.23
7	7.95	5.01	3.62	4.44	3.56	5.70	3	7	4	.46	.35
8	6.75	2.42	4.07	4.17	3.00	5.81	4	4	6	.36	.10
9	0.18	2.64	7.85	2.26	3.06	6.74	2	3	7	.16	.03
10	0.51	0.29	9.33	2.60	2.06	7.38	2	4	9	.30	.19
11	0.31	2.64	2.52	2.43	3.06	5.41	1	5	4	.24	.23
12	1.03	5.01	3.47	2.88	3.56	5.66	0	5	5	.15	.29
13	2.26	4.73	0.63	3.26	3.50	4.62	5	7	2	.32	.40
14	0.51	5.84	0.58	2.60	3.72	4.59	3	6	2	.24	.28
15	7.23	5.29	8.18	4.27	3.61	6.85	5	5	7	.26	.16
16	4.40	0.39	9.33	3.72	2.17	7.38	4	5	8	.43	.26
17	6.23	6.12	7.10	4.06	3.78	6.52	4	4	5	.38	.16
18	9.17	5.57	8.28	4.86	3.67	6.88	7	8	6	.33	.40
19	6.06	5.84	7.73	4.03	3.72	6.70	4	6	5	.35	.28
20	7.95	1.46	7.10	4.44	2.72	6.52	8	6	5	.45	.43
21	6.58	4.17	2.16	4.13	3.89	6.99	5	6	3	.24	.34
22	7.82	6.64	8.56	4.41	3.89	6.99	9	7	9	.09	.41
23	2.85	7.37	0.53	3.40	4.06	4.55	3	4	3	.36	.14
24	5.73	6.90	5.01	3.89	3.94	6.02	4	4	5	.32	.10
25	7.54	7.81	6.54	4.34	4.17	6.38	4	6	6	.39	.18
26	2.54	1.63	5.78	3.33	2.78	6.20	4	4	5	.29	.19
27	1.86	7.14	5.94	3.16	4.00	6.24	2	3	5	.36	.17
28	5.51	8.85	6.39	3.92	4.50	6.34	3	7	4	.34	.31
29	5.33	6.90	1.19	3.89	3.94	4.95	6	6	3	.19	.32
30	3.01	1.31	3.47	3.44	2.67	5.66	2	5	5	.39	.06
31	6.92	3.63	7.36	4.20	3.28	6.59	5	7	9	.34	.36
Mean										.32	.26
Standard deviation										.12	.11

SOURCE: J. T. Lamiell, M. A. Foss, R. J. Larsen, and A. Hempel, Studies in intuitive personology from an idiothetic point of view: Implications for personality theory, *Journal of Personality* 51:438–67, © 1983 by Duke University Press. Reprinted by permission of the publisher.

$[(3-10)^2 + (5-0)^2 + (2-10)^2]^{1/2}$, which equals 11.75. Expressed as a ratio of this value, the dissimilarity of the normatively based predictions to Rex's actual self-ratings is defined as $\{[(3.34-3)^2 + (9.61-5)^2 + (0.02-2)^2]^{1/2}/11.75\} = .43$, and this is the value entered in the first row of panel 4 in table 6.5, under the heading AR (actual ratings) vs. PR-N (predicted ratings based on normative model). In contrast, the dissimilarity of the interactively based predictions to Rex's actual self-ratings is defined as $|[(3.51-3)^2 + (4.94-5)^2 + (3.44-2)^2]^{1/2}/11.75| = .13$, and so this is the value entered in the first row of panel 4 of the table, under the heading AR vs. PR-I (actual ratings vs. predicted ratings based on interactive model). As we found to be the case with Smith, therefore, it appears that, in this instance too, the logic of interactive measurement represented more faithfully the subjective contextualization process than did the logic of normative measurement.

Nor does this finding appear to be limited to the case in which Rex rated himself. On the contrary, a target-by-target comparison of the profile dissimilarity values shown in panel 4 of table 6.5, all of which were determined in accordance with the procedures just described, indicates that for 21 of the 31 targets Rex rated (including himself), the predictions derived from the interactive model of the subjective contextualization process better approximated his actual ratings than did the predictions derived from the normative model. Consistent with this picture, a comparison of the mean dissimilarity values shown at the bottom of table 6.5 (.32 vs. .26) revealed a statistically significant difference in favor of the interactive model.

The data for each of the other 39 individuals who served as subjects in this study were analyzed in a fashion identical to that just described. Since space limitations preclude a complete presentation here of the results for each subject, the findings have instead been summarized in table 6.6. The table displays, for the normative and interactive models, respectively, the mean proportional profile dissimilarity values obtained for each of the 40 subjects across the 31 rated targets. Obviously, the normative model did not fare well in this sample of the individuals as a formal

Table 6.6 Mean Proportional Profile Dissimilarity Values Computed for Each of 40
Subjects Based On 31 Rated Targets

	Mean Proportional Profile Dissimilarity Values		
Subject	AR vs. PR-N	AR vs. PR-I	Correlation of AR vs. PR-N Values With Target Order
("Rex") 1	.32	.26*	(−.10)
2	.34	.18*	(+.13)
3	.46	.41	(+.12)
4	.42	.19*	(−.08)
5	.44	.30*	(−.10)
6	.36	.15*	(−.43)#
7	.34	.28*	(−.20)
8	.47	.45	(+.25)
9	.38	.18*	(+.16)
10	.30	.21*	(+.10)
11	.40	.38	(−.13)
12	.31	.28	(+.18)
13	.42	.20*	(−.52)#
14	.43	.36*	(−.18)
15	.37	.31*	(−.02)
16	.30	.21*	(+.23)
17	.43	.27*	(−.06)
18	.41	.32*	(−.40)#
19	.38	.29*	(+.07)
20	.34	.17*	(+.35)##
21	.31	.18*	(+.44)##
22	.42	.27*	(.00)
23	.39	.31*	(+.18)
24	.39	.27*	(+.31)##
25	.40	.28*	(−.29)
26	.31	.21*	(+.18)
27	.37	.27*	(−.16)
28	.40	.28*	(+.03)
29	.38	.30*	(−.57)#
30	.48	.37*	(−.04)
31	.39	.41	(+.08)
32	.41	.34*	(+.14)
33	.31*	.38	(−.27)
34	.41	.21*	(−.21)
35	.39	.24*	(−.09)
36	.39	.36	(+.02)
37	.43	.36*	(+.03)

Subject	Mean Proportional Profile Dissimilarity Values		Correlation of AR vs. PR-N Values With Target Order
	AR vs. PR-N	AR vs. PR-I	
38	.44	.20*	(−.20)
39	.46	.30*	(+.22)
40	.42	.25*	(−.06)

Note: * indicates that the indicated profile dissimilarity value was significantly lower (p < .05) than its comparison value. # indicates a statistically significant trend for predictions based on normative model to increase in accuracy over the sequence of 31 rated targets; ## indicates a statistically significant trend in the opposite direction.
SOURCE: J. T. Lamiell, M. A. Foss, R. J. Larsen, and A. Hempel, Studies in intuitive personology from an idiothetic point of view: Implications for personality theory, Journal of Personality 51:438–67, © 1983 by Duke University Press. Reprinted by permission of the publisher.

representation of the subjective contextualization process. On the contrary, there was only one individual (subject 33) for whom that model significantly outperformed the interactive model. For 6 subjects, the statistical analyses failed to reveal any clear advantage of one model over the other, and for 33 of the 40 subjects, the interactive model was manifestly superior.

Probing the data further for more substantial evidence of a normative reasoning process on the part of the subjects, some additional analyses were undertaken. The rationale for these analyses was that if subjective personality judgments are routinely mediated by considerations of a normative nature, then in research of this sort one ought to find, at the very least, some indication that the dissimilarity between actual ratings and those predicted on the basis of the normative model decreases in magnitude (reflecting an increase in the accuracy of the normatively based predictions) as the subject "works through" the sequence of targets, i.e., as s/he (presumably) becomes more familiar with the immediately prevailing sample norms. Consistent with this rationale, Pearson product-moment correlations were computed for each subject between the temporal order of the rated targets (1–31) and the profile dissimilarity values computed for the normative model (i.e., values of the sort displayed in table 6.5 under the heading AR vs. PR = N).

The correlations thus obtained are shown as the par-enthesized entries in table 6.6. For subjects 6, 13, 18, and 29, there was indeed some indication that normative measurement operations yielded increasingly accurate predictions of actual rat-ings as those subjects progressed through the targets. For the remaining 36 subjects, no such evidence was found. Indeed, for subjects 20, 21, and 24, these analyses revealed a significant trend for the predictions derived on the basis of the normative model to *decrease* in accuracy over the sequence of targets. On balance, there is no evidence here to support any generalization that nor-mative considerations will become increasingly relevant to the deliberations of the intuitive personologist as s/he gains increas-ing familiarity with prevailing sample norms.

Interpretive Comment

Given the complexities of the foregoing, it is desirable at this point to reiterate the thesis for which I would offer in supportive evidence the findings just presented: *Subjective charac-terizations of self and others are not—as the ersatz "nomotheticists" of scien-tific personality psychology would have it—routinely mediated by considera-tions of individual differences.* Instead, person characterization from the subjective point of view seems to engage much more regu-larly a reasoning process that is essentially *dialectical*, i.e., a pro-cess whereby the psychological context for each judgment is gen-erated "on the spot," as it were, through a mental *negation* of the information on which the judgment is to be based.

This implies that from the subjective point of view each person is being judged not with reference to others but *with reference to the person(s) s/he is not but might otherwise be*, and that whether or not these latter "persons" do or did ever really exist in some sample or population of persons is irrelevant. Put more concretely, I am suggesting here that when Smith is presented with information concerning the behavior of Jones and asked to judge, say, how "introverted vs. extraverted" Jones is, Smith is naturally inclined to consider how introverted and how extraverted Jones might *possibly* be judged to be, given (a) the information on which the judgment is to be based [formally represented above by the X_{tio} component of equation (6.3)], and (b) how he, Smith, construes that information with respect to the attribute introverted vs. extraverted [formally represented above by the R_{iao} component of equation (6.3)]. I am suggesting that on the basis of these considerations, Smith intuitively *generates* "images" of what Jones's behavior pattern would have had to look like in order to warrant a judgment of extreme introversion on the one hand, and a judgment of extreme extraversion on the other hand, and that covert judgments corresponding to these "images"—judgments that we may symbolize, after equation (5.3), as J'_{min} and J'_{max}—serve Smith as the psychological context within which he frames the *meaning* of his judgment of the information about Jones that was actually presented. As noted earlier, I am suggesting finally that if Smith is asked to express his subjective judgment in the "language" of a rating scale anchored by the numerical values 0 and 10 Smith will *select* an actual rating AR such that the resulting physical pattern [0—AR—10] mirrors the precedent psychological pattern $[J'_{min} - J_{tao} - J'_{max}]$.

Concluding Remarks

In chapter 5, reference was made to Epstein's recent assertion that "it is *meaningless* to interpret the behavior of an individual without a frame of reference of others' behavior" (1983:381; emphasis added). In the light of the results obtained with the subjects of the research just discussed it would appear that I am not the only one who believes quite otherwise, and I will argue in chapter 7 that this is of no small consequence for the future of theoretically guided personality research. As we conclude the present chapter, however, there are some formal aspects of the above research that should not go unremarked.

First, and by way of a contrast to analytic methods that have traditionally dominated the study of person characterization from the subjective point of view, it should be reiterated that the research we have been discussing is nonactuarial in nature. It was designed and carried out not merely to account for the variance in Smith's (rating) behavior, but to evaluate alternative theoretical conceptions of the psychological processes underlying the *production* of that behavior. In this context the normative and interactive models for psychological measurement served to formally represent the alternative theoretical conceptions in question. Divergent predictions concerning *how Smith would behave* (rate the targets) were based on contrasting hypotheses concerning *how Smith was thinking*, and not on information concerning how Smith had behaved (rated other targets) in the past. Prediction was not the end in itself, but rather a means to the larger theoretical end of *understanding what Smith was saying.*

Second, it must be remembered that each of the 40 individuals who served as subjects for the research was studied *as an individual*, and that the substantive attribute dimensions in terms of which the targets were rated were specified by and for each subject individually. At no point were questions taken up concerning the differences between those individuals. Each subject was a self-contained study unto him/herself, and the results were both generated and reported in such a way as to be interpretable at the level of the individual.

Third, nothing in the procedure logically undermined the search for a general principle of individual psychological functioning. As noted several times previously, a general principle of individual psychological functioning is properly regarded as one that has been found to hold for each of many individuals, and not merely for the "average individual" (whoever that is) or for an aggregate of individuals. Thus, not only is the study of individuals not antithetical to the search for general principles; it is in fact central to the search for such principles. Nor is any serious conceptual difficulty presented by the fact that in the research the subjects were not required to rate the targets in terms of some common set of attribute dimensions. At issue was the generality of the underlying reasoning *process* by which individuals frame subjective judgments, and not the generality of the substantive attributes in terms of which that process was exercised.

While the weight of the evidence presented clearly favors the view that the underlying reasoning process in question is dialectical and not normative in nature, I am certainly not prepared to assert on the basis of that evidence alone that a general principle of individual psychological functioning has in fact been established. For all the obvious reasons and then some, no one piece of research could ever justify such an assertion, however strong the results. The point here is a logical one: the quest for general principles concerning the processes governing individual psychological functioning is compromised neither by studying individuals nor by doing so in a way that respects their substantive idiosyncracies.

Acknowledging the above, we have yet to specify what implications there might be in all this for the future of basic research in the psychology of personality more broadly conceived. It is to this matter that we turn our attention in chapter 7.

7 Re-Cognizing Basic Personality Research

Neither the conduct of the research reported in the previous chapter nor my discussion of it should be taken as an argument that personality investigators ought now devote themselves exclusively to the study of subjective personality impressions. Indeed, the focus of that research was no more on the subjects' impressions of the targets per se than, for example, the point of Piaget's studies in conservation was the children's perceptions of water levels and arrays of beads. In both instances, a particular line of inquiry was pursued on the belief that it would provide a useful medium within which to learn something of theoretical consequence about the nature of individual psychological functioning. An additional objective of the work discussed in chapter 6 has been to persuade at least some within the field of personality psychology that research that is at once theoretically relevant and methodologically rigorous can be conducted at the level of the individual. For many, however, the relevance of those studies to personality theory will seem rather remote, and it is this matter to which we turn in the present chapter.

Human Cognition as a Focal Subject Matter of Personality Theory

In a recent article, Daryl Bem (1983) described himself as "bemused by how many of our best and brightest get side-tracked into social psychology, substituting the study of what the layperson *thinks* about personality for the study of personality itself" (p. 575). Clearly, Bem does not share the view that the future of personality psychology lies at what Mischel (1979) termed "the interface of cognition and personality." Instead, and as noted in chapter 3, Bem has embraced the modern "interactional" variant of conventional nomotheticism according to which it is insisted that

Our fundamental scientific task is to convert observations of particular persons behaving in particular ways in particular situations into assertions that certain *kinds* of persons will behave in certain *kinds* of ways in certain *kinds* of situations, that is, to construct triple typologies or equivalence classes—of persons, of behaviors, and of situations—and to fashion theories of personality that relate these equivalence classes to one another. (Bem 1983:566)

The echo of generic structuralism reverberates through this passage, and so long as the essential business of personality psychology is defined in this way, the study of cognitive processes is bound to be seen as a digression. For as Bem understands full well, it is at least technically possible for an investigator to engineer a typology of his/her subjects, their behaviors, and the situations in which they behave without ever concerning him/herself with the burdensome matter of what and how the subjects *think*: about themselves, their own actions, one another, etc. All the more reasonable does such an agenda seem to be under the conviction that the job of a theory of personality is to *explain a typology* after it has been duly "discovered." Since my own position is diametrically opposed to any rigid bifurcation of the study of what and how subjects think from the study of "person-

ality itself," our first task here is to consider why without preju-
dice toward any particular theory such a bifurcation is indefensible.

As indicated several times previously—and all continuing resistance to the notion aside—the view that a psychology
of personality must concern itself with the cognitions of persons
is hardly unprecedented. As this is so, the question is not whether
there is any theory of personality that *is* ultimately cognitive in
its focus, but rather whether there is any theory of personality
that *is not* ultimately cognitive in its focus. In the face of this
question, many would undoubtedly assert: "Of course there is."
The thesis I should like to develop here is that *of course there is not.*
Pared to its essentials, my defense of this thesis runs as follows.

As authors too numerous to mention have implied,
but as Levy (1970:19) asserted so crisply, "the concept of personality owes its existence to man's [the human] tendency to seek
meaning in his experience." Now insofar as this view is embraced
(and the implications of rejecting it will be made apparent below)
it follows that any theory of personality must either address itself
to or be held accountable for begging questions concerning how
persons frame or acquire meanings. In the course of addressing
such questions, a theory of *personal knowledge* (see Polanyi 1969)
will inevitably be framed or invoked, and inasmuch as a theory of
personal knowledge is perforce a theory of *cognition* (the term
"cognition" itself being rooted in the Latin *cognoscere*, to know),
the conclusion is inescapable that any theory of personality will
be or invoke and hence rest critically on what by any name is a
theory of cognition.

Lest this argument be taken for something that it is
not, I should stress that it neither contains nor entitles the view
that all theories of personality are essentially "the same" in every
important respect. On the contrary, psychodynamic theories of
personality differ in many ways from cognitive–social learning
theories, which in turn differ substantially from phenomenological, humanistic, and existential theories, and so on. What is implied by the present argument is that, in the final analysis, the

different schools of thought within personality theory are different because they offer or embrace different theories of cognition, and not because some are cognitive while others are not.

If it is obvious that the term "cognitive" can be applied legitimately to theories falling within the cognitive–social learning and phenomenological/humanistic/existential traditions, its applicability to the psychoanalytic tradition might at first blush seem more questionable. Consider, however, the plausibility of describing Freud's theory (the most prominent example of the psychodynamic tradition) as one in which human cognition—the framing of personal knowledge—involves processes whereby psychic energy derived from bodily instincts shapes what are initially unintelligible percepts into meaningful ideas, which are in turn expressed—or not—in overt action, depending upon the degree of resistance with which they are met as they press toward consciousness. Whether or not this is a valid theoretical conception of individual behavior/psychological functioning is not at issue here. What is at issue is whether Freud's theory of personality can properly be regarded as one that is or rests on a particular conception of human cognition.

Undoubtedly, misgivings here would be rooted in the notion that cognition entails awareness, whereas on the Freudian account it is clearly held that the most consequential aspects of psychic activity occur beyond the individual's awareness. However, in the Freudian view knowledge and awareness are not the same thing. "Out of awareness" does not mean "out of mind altogether" within the particular theoretical framework fashioned by Freud, and so it is perfectly sensible under the terms of that framework to say that one "knows" things of which one is unaware. This being the case, and given that the terms "cognition" and its variants are in fact derived from terms that refer to knowledge rather than to awareness, applying the descriptor "cognitive" to Freud's theory violates neither the theory nor etymology (see Cameron and Rychlak 1985).

Accepting all this, one might still doubt that the term "cognitive" can be applied legitimately across the full range of extant theory, and justify skepticism on the grounds that such a view leaves radically behavioral theories unaccounted for. And so it does. But this omission is problematic for the present argument only under the assumption that radically behavioral "theories" (if that is the term) qualify as theories of personality. Fortunately or unfortunately, depending upon one's predilections concerning human nature, that assumption itself is problematic.

Perhaps the clearest and most succinct justification for this view is to be found in the words of I. E. Farber. An avowed behaviorist, Farber defended over two decades ago a psychology of personality conceived as an endeavor "coterminous with the study of behavior," i.e., as a discipline pursued in a manner scrupulously faithful to the central tenets of radical behaviorism. In a most revealing fashion, Farber concluded his discussion:

One may anticipate that as behavior theories become more precise and more comprehensive they will encompass more and more phenomena now referred to under the rubric of "personality." I, for one, look forward to the day, which I do not expect to see myself, when personality theories are regarded as historical curiosities. (Farber 1964:37)

I leave for the reader to judge whether it is personality theory or radical behaviorism that is destined for the niche marked "historical curiosity." But Farber's sagacity was unimpeachable in at least one respect: scientific psychology in the behaviorist view obviates altogether the need for a concept of personality. That is, no agenda for scientific psychology committed from its inception to the exclusion of all concepts referring to mental activity—"consciousness, mental states, mind, content, will, imagery and the like" (Watson 1914:9–10)—requires or even accommodates a concept the very existence of which is linked to the human tendency to seek meaning in one's experience.

Of course, none of this is to deny that within the literature of the field some theories of personality have been *called* "behavioral." But we have seen already that that same literature is replete with loose expressions, and so we are ill-advised to grant uncritically the appropriateness of such labels. Consider, for example, that in at least one well-known textbook (Hjelle and Ziegler 1981), the reader is invited to regard Albert Bandura's cognitive–social learning theory of personality as "behaviorism from the inside" (p. 240). In so doing, the reader must look past the fact that the very expression "behaviorism from the inside" is oxymoronic. Were Bandura's theory truly behavioral in the original—i.e., Watsonian—sense of that term (which it is not), then that theory could not possibly be concerned with the cognitions that presumably transpire "inside" the organism, and so would not be a *cognitive*–social learning theory at all. Conversely, if Bandura's theory is concerned with cognitions "inside" the organism (and it is), then that theory is not behavioral at all. Thus, to describe Bandura's theory as "behaviorism from the inside" is a disservice to both the theory and behaviorism, at least as strict adherents to the latter view (such as there may yet remain) would have themselves understood.

It is only fair to mention here that Bandura has borrowed extensively from the language of behaviorism. Within each framework, for example, one finds the term "reinforcement" being used. However, while Bandura may well have borrowed the term, he also, in so doing, changed its meaning in a way that no card-carrying behaviorist could abide. In Bandura's theory, reinforcement can take place vicariously as well as in consequence of actual behavior. For this and other reasons, "reinforcement" serves Bandura as a referent for knowledge that a person acquires and stores—through verbal encoding and/or mental imagery—concerning the relationships between acts and their consequences. Because this theoretical usage involves a conception of human cognition, it qualifies here as a theory of personality. For the same reason, it qualifies not at all as "behavioral," any superficial similarities notwithstanding.

An argument along these same lines easily could be constructed for any of the other so-called "behavioral" theories of personality. Any theory of personality necessarily invokes a theory of cognition, and because behaviorism as conceived by behaviorists categorically rejects cognition as a legitimate subject matter for a scientific psychology, *there can be no such thing as a "behavioral" theory of personality.*

If it is true that any theory of personality does indeed

invoke a theory of human cognition, then it is also true that in calling for increased empirical research on cognitive processes Mischel and others are not, as some would have it (see Bem 1983) digressing into matters of tangential relevance to personality theory. They are instead moving to reclaim phenomena that, historically, have been of fundamental relevance to personality theorizing all along. The question, then, is not whether theoretically guided personality research should concern itself with cognitive matters but rather *how* theoretically guided personality research should proceed given that it must so concern itself.

Implications for the Conduct of Basic Personality Research

From Individual Differences in Cognitions
to the Cognitions of Individuals

At this point, the direction being suggested departs from currently prevailing trends in the (re-)cognitivization of personality psychology. One reason alluded to before is the fact that cognitive personality psychology is at present being dominated by the logic and methods of individual differences research no less than the trait/type personality psychology that the cognitive movement is supposed to replace. Thus, just as in years past investigators inspired by George A. Kelly's theory of personal constructs focused their attention on individual differences in personal construct systems (see chapter 3), contemporary investigators are focusing their attention on individual differences in scripts (see Cantor and Kihlstrom 1981; Higgins, Kuiper, and Olson 1981; Jones and Pittman 1982), interpersonal construal styles (Golding 1978), cognitive prototypes (Cantor and Mischel 1979; Mischel 1984), and self-schemata (Markus 1977, 1983; Markus et al. 1982; Markus and Sentis 1982; Markus and Smith 1981). In the present view, all such efforts suffer from epistemological problems identical to and no less consequential than those discussed at length in chapter 4. For this reason I would argue that such inquiry cannot, even in principle, yield genuine advances in our understanding of individual psychological functioning.

As a means of crystallizing the issues that are relevant here, consider the following statements with which Markus introduced her discussion of "Self-Knowledge: An Expanded View."

Individuals are assumed to construct self-concepts from the information contained in their unfolding life experiences. As they do so, they gain an impressive base of knowledge, and sometimes a genuine expertise, about their special abilities, achievements, preferences, values, and goals. This construction of the self-concept does not avail itself of information indiscriminately, but is selective, inventive, and creative. (Markus 1983:543)

Now inasmuch as this passage clearly reveals Markus' concern for individuals' conceptions of themselves and their own actions, it reflects commitment to an approach wholly consistent with that being defended here. In the next passage, however, Markus argues as follows:

Variation in the content and organization of self-knowledge reflects significant and enduring differences among people in social histories, perceptions, and actions. The nature of self-knowledge is thus viewed as a critical—perhaps *the* critical—component of personality. (Ibid.)

In this passage, Markus is, in effect, justifying the study of self-knowledge as personality research on the grounds that there are individual differences in self-knowledge. Nor should this rationale surprise us at this point, as it is merely one recent reflection of the long dominant view that where there are no individual differences to investigate empirically (measure, intercorrelate, etc.), there is, finally, nothing for a personality investigator to do.

If I have accomplished nothing else in the preceding chapters of this book, I hope I have made clear the grounds for my conviction that we must abandon this essentially Cronbachian (1957) conception of the role of personality investigators within scientific psychology more broadly defined. Theoretical advances will come, where they do, not through the study of individual differences in scripts but through the study of individual scripting; not through the study of individual differences in schemas, but through the study of individual schematizing; not through the study of individual differences in constructs, but through the study of individual construing.

Putting all this more generally, if inquiry at what Mischel has called "the interface of cognition and personality" is to advance our understanding of personal knowledge and the role that it plays in the production of human behavior, it will do so not by assessing and investigating the correlates of individual differences in personal knowledge, but by revealing the grounds on and reasoning processes by which individuals frame personal knowledge and extend it into action. It was with just this sense in mind that I suggested in chapter 1 that the subject matter of theoretically driven personality research can fruitfully be regarded as personal epistemology.

Although the research discussed in chapter 6 is obviously circumscribed in many respects, it does provide one concrete illustration of the point just made. Of particular relevance here is the fact that while that research most assuredly concerned the cognitions of the subjects, it had nothing whatsoever to do with assessing differences between the subjects. Nor should it have. Cognitions—the processes by which meaningful ideas are framed—take place within the minds or psyches of individuals, and not in the spaces between them. Accordingly, the research was designed and carried out so as to test alternative theoretical conceptions of the reasoning process through which each individual subject framed his/her subjectively meaningful impressions of the targets, and there is simply nothing that could have been learned about that process through *any* analysis of differences between the subjects' impressions. What is more, an analysis of differences would only have deflected attention away from the search for what is common to the subjects' reasoning processes beneath the surface of their substantive differences.

For all this, it remains for us to discuss more fully the sense in which inquiry focused on the cognitions of individuals speaks to questions of fundamental relevance to personality theory. To this end, let us consider the following:

Sometimes mental traits and states are invoked as if they were the causes of behavior while their own antecedents are ignored or forgotten. Unfinished causal sequences are found whenever mental states (cognitions, affects, motives, etc.) are employed as explanations of behavior while the determinants of the mental states themselves are omitted from the analysis. Skinner calls this is the use of mental way stations. . . . Clearly, an adequate analysis must encompass the variables that control the behavior of interest and not merely the hypothetical stops along the route. (Mischel 1968:95).

Since in this passage as well as in many of his subsequent writings, (see Mischel 1973, 1976, 1977, 1979, 1984), Mischel alludes to the importance of identifying the variables that "control" (influence, determine, cause, etc.) behavior, we should perhaps pause here long enough to note that *variables* do not cause, determine, or influence behavior at all. Variables are methodological entities created by investigators for the purpose of systematically investigating the causes of behavior, but those entities are certainly not themselves the causal agents.

Still, Mischel's rather curious metaphysics[1] should not blind us to the validity of his assertion that if explanations for a person's behavior are to invoke the cognitions of the behaving person, then those same explanations must contain some accounting of the cognitions themselves. If Smith's behaving in manner X is to be explained with reference to ideas that Smith had in mind at the time, then the question inevitably arises as to how Smith came by those ideas. Indeed, the question arises as to how Smith comes by any ideas at all. It is in questions of this sort that we find the interface of cognition and personality. Not coincidentally, it is also in the face of such questions that we find the need for theoretical conceptions of cognition, and for adequate means of submitting such conceptions to empirical scrutiny. If such theoretical conceptions, and empirical research per-

1. Not that Mischel is alone in this. On the contrary, Pervin (1985) has averred that "Most personality psychologists would have agreed and would still agree that behavior is influenced by person variables and by situation variables" (p. xxx), and Hyland (1985) has just recently made the theoretical status of person variables the centerpiece of an entire article. The confusion here runs deep indeed.

tinent to them, seem "remote" from the subject matter of a psychology of personality, this is not because their relevance is tangential but because their relevance is so utterly basic. For it is in just those theoretical conceptions that extant notions concerning personhood itself are rooted.

Dialectical Versus Mediational Conceptions of Cognition

Just as any theory of personality contains a theory of human cognition, so also does any theory of cognition contain a theory of the person. It follows that conceptions of personality will prove as central to the coherence of scientific psychology's emergent cognitivism as they were superfluous under the regime of radical behaviorism. That is, since *persons*—not "stimuli," not "responses," and certainly not variables—are the entities that cognize, theoretical conceptions of persons are necessarily basic to any psychology that admits of cognition as relevant subject matter. Here the substantive (as distinct from the purely formal) aspects of the material presented in chapters 5 and 6 become relevant. To clarify, let us consider one construct that has become rather prominent in contemporary accounts of human cognition: the cognitive prototype.

This construct has arisen so as to accommodate the long-standing notion that in order for a person to apply an abstract concept to an object or event in the empirical world and thus frame his/her knowledge of it, one must have some mental reference points against which to evaluate or judge its meaning (see Rosch 1975; Rosch and Mervis 1975). In recent years, Mischel and others (see, e.g., Cantor and Mischel 1979; Higgins, Rholes, and Jones 1977; Mischel 1979, 1984; Wyer and Srull 1981) have suggested that the prototype construct can enhance our understanding of cognition in the interpersonal realm as well as in the realm of nonpersonal objects and events. The essence of this view is that in coming to know oneself or another as, say, "extroverted," one engages a cognitive process whereby salient features of one's conduct are evaluated against an idea corresponding to quintessential extrovertedness. This latter idea would constitute the prototype, and the emerging theoretical view is that as integral parts of the cognitive process, such prototypes are central to the subjective conceptions that persons have of themselves and of one another, and hence to the manner in which individuals act and relate to one another.

But now if we are to take seriously—and I believe that we must—Mischel's (1968) assertion that explanations for behavior invoking the cognitions of behaving individuals are incomplete without some accounting of the cognitions, then in the present context the question inevitably arises: where do cognitive prototypes come from? In Rosch's view, a cognitive prototype is constituted of a *mental average of previously encountered exemplars of the object/event being judged.* Thus, my current idea of the quintessential chair is presumably a kind of composite made up of certain salient features of those chairs which I have experienced in the moments of my life before this one. By a direct extension of this view, the currently prevailing theoretical position among those who employ the prototype construct is that an individual's idea of, say, quintessential extrovertedness is constituted of a mental average of previously encountered displays of that characteristic. For example, in this theoretical tradition Cantor and Mischel (1979) argued that

a categorization scheme [i.e., a set of "person prototypes"] allows one to structure and give coherence to one's general store of knowledge about people, providing expectations about *typical* behavior patterns and the *range of likely variation* between types of people and their characteristic behaviors. Every social experience helps to fill out one's knowledge of the likely behavior and attributes of different types of persons. The resulting expectations, in turn, affect one's impressions of individuals. (1979:6; emphasis added)

The italicized words highlight the fact that Cantor and Mischel's account of cognitive prototypes conforms to what Rychlak (1981a, 1981b) has termed a *mediational* model of human cognition. In this view, endemic to the information processing metaphor that dominates contemporary cognitive psychology, the subjective meaning of "today's inputs" are framed by the individual with reference to the memory traces of "yesterday's inputs" [see Neisser's (1967:281–82) discussion of the "reappearance" hypothesis].

As prevalent as the mediational model of cognition is, I strongly suspect that it is not generally valid. Not least among my reasons for skepticism is the fact that under a purely mediational account of the process by which the subjective meanings of "today's inputs" are framed, at least one vital question goes begging: by what reasoning process does a person identify the first instance of a given cognitive category?

If, for example, my ability to discern the extent to which Smith is extroverted hinges on the existence in my own mind of a cognitive prototype for extrovertedness, and if the existence of that prototype is itself to be explained in terms of the memory traces of my previous encounters with other persons, then there was presumably a time at which I had not yet had any such encounters and hence had no cognitive category corresponding to quintessential extrovertedness. But if such a category did not yet exist for me, then according to the simple mediational view there was no way for me to recognize the first instance of an extroverted person. And if there was no way to recognize the first instance, there was no memory trace available to me for recognizing the second, the third, or any other. All this, of course, would leave me forever with nothing to mentally average and nothing from which to fashion a cognitive prototype.

Clearly, something is wrong. In basic agreement with Rychlak I subscribe to the view that the problem lies not in the construct of cognitive prototypes per se but rather in the mediational conception of cognition to which, implicitly or explicitly, so much of modern cognitive psychology has to date been wed. In the present context, this means that while cognitive prototypes might well be said to play an important role in the psychological process by which persons are able to characterize themselves and others, it does not necessarily follow that those prototypes themselves are best explained in terms of a process of mentally averaging past displays of particular attributes. Instead, it may well be that cognitive prototypes are best understood in terms of a process of *dialectically negating present displays* of particular attributes. Recalling from chapter 6 that in this view the negations need not themselves either "now" or by virtue of memory traces, have independently specifiable referents in the empirical world, it is not difficult to see how a dialectical conception of human reasoning provides at least one plausible answer to the theoretical question posed above.

In connection with this last point, the following remarks by Kosok (1976) are instructive:

> The very act of *affirming* an immediacy, asserting or announcing a given, or recognizing what *is* present, is to set up the *condition* for its negation, since to affirm is to reflect, and allow for the *possibility of its negation*. Both $+e$ and $-e$, or the assertion *of* and negation *of e*, are functions of *e*, which is to say that the *content* or reference-base *e* of assertion and negation is the same, expressed, however, in contrary forms. That which is initially given can be *referred to* positively as that which *is present* (called positive presence) and negatively as that which is *lacking* (called negative presence, since the given makes *itself* evident as a *lack*). The concept of negation viewed dialectically as a type of negative presence is therefore qualitatively different from the standard notion of logical negation. Given a term A, its negation not-A is usually interpreted [i.e., under "the standard notion of logical negation"] to be a positive presence of something other than A, '-A', called, e.g., 'B', such that A and B are not only distinct but *separable* 'truth values'. (1976:328; emphases in original)

Under the traditional mediational conception of human cognition, of course, cognitive prototypes serve as reference points against which to evaluate the meanings of a present "input" in the sense defined by what Kosok calls the standard notion of logical negation. That is, insofar as one speaks at all, under the mediational view, of a cognitive prototype as a negation of some present "input A," one says that the prototype itself is tied to the positive presence of something other than A, either as present "inputs" distinct from A (B, C, D, etc.) or as memory traces thereof. With specific reference to the cognitions underlying characterizations of self and others, however, the research findings presented in chapter 6 strongly suggest that the negations with reference to which the subjects framed their judgments were not of the standard logical sort at all, but were instead dialectical in just that sense of negative presence to which Kosok alludes.

If we can resort briefly to the language of the (highly dubious) computer metaphor for human cognition, we would have to say in discussing those research findings that the subjects somehow managed to "encode" ideas corresponding to the hypothetical activity protocols used to derive the J'_{min} and J'_{max} values of equation (5.3) despite the fact that those activity protocols *were* hypothetical and thus had no distinct empirical referents in the domain of to-be-processed "information." In effect, the evidence suggests that the subjects somehow "saw" activity protocols they were never shown, and that judgments corresponding to those never-shown protocols were integral *psychological* components of the *meanings* being expressed in the ratings of the protocols they *were* shown. Hence, to understand what a subject said in any given instance, i.e., to grasp the meaning of the rating that s/he assigned to a given target with respect to a given attribute, it was necessary to locate the same not within the context of what was said in other instances but within the context of what was not but might otherwise have been said in that instance. The evidence suggests not that this latter context was simply available to the subject in the sense of being "stored" in some memory bank that s/he could "access," but rather that it was *generated by* the subject through the mental activity of negating the given. Just this capacity to conceptualize what is with reference to what is not but might otherwise be would enable a person to *know*—frame the personal meanings of—the objects and events in his/her own life even when the memory traces of prior experiences emphasized under mediational accounts of cognition are irrelevant, inaccesible, or simply nonexistent.

George Kelly once remarked that

the mere prediction of what a person will do . . . . does not demonstrate a full understanding of his behavior. . . , A fuller explanation requires us to be aware of what he might have done. The construct dimension that lends structure to the behavioral event does so by providing contrasting poles. . . . What one does comes into perspective as a contrast to what he might have done. That is to say that human behavior takes on additional meaning when one sees it as a contrast, a denial, an abandonment of alternatives, or as a choice that has left other possibilities unexplored. To see behavior in this perspective one needs reference axes within which he can plot what he actually does in a structured context of what he might possibly do. (quoted in Maher 1969:35)

Beyond Kelly's obvious—and well-founded—disdain for programmatic inquiry geared exclusively to the technical problem of "behavioral prediction," we see in the above passage yet another allusion to the dialectical nature of individual psychological functioning. Nor are such allusions to be found only in the writings of phenomenologically oriented theorists. Within psychoanalytic tradition, for example, dialectical themes are manifest in the work of such as Jung and Erikson, and they are muted only faintly in the work of Freud himself (see, e.g., Rychlak 1981b, esp. chapter 10; see also Ver Eecke 1984). Indeed, the case can be made that among the various schools of thought within personality theory, the cognitive–social learning school—based as it is on a purely mediational conception of human cognition—stands alone in its failure to incorporate such themes (see Bandura 1978; Rychlak 1979). Perhaps, therefore, we have isolated at least one basic issue around which personality theories can, as Feshbach (1984:44) urges, "compete in the marketplace of ideas."

Of Subjects, Scientists, and the Personality of Knowledge

In an important but widely ignored article entitled "Personality Theory: Its Nature, Past, Present, and—Future(?)", Rychlak suggested a broad agenda for the future of theoretically driven personality research:

In his book on *Behaviorism*, John Watson . . . proposed the following principle for all behaviorists to use: "The rule, or measuring rod, which the behaviorist puts in front of him always is: Can I describe this bit of behavior I see in terms of stimulus and response?" I would like to suggest that the personality theorists of the future parallel this with a principle of the sort: "Can I increase my understanding of this bit of behavior I see by presuming the contribution of an identity to the course of events?" (Rychlak 1976a:222)

One important implication of this view is that the conduct of personality research is not best regarded as an activity to be placed alongside the conduct of research on such "other" topics as learning, motivation, emotion, cognition, social inter-action, etc. The former is more a perspective that one brings to bear on any and all of the latter. Personality is not something that one "adds" to other phenomena but that which *centers* the other phenomena and endows them with psychological import.

Now as to what one searches for under the theoretical presumption that some identity contributes to whatever is being observed as one studies learning, motivation, emotion, cognition, social interaction, etc., Rychlak argues that

It is the ability to both have an idea or be doing something and yet at the same time grasp transcendentally that one is thinking and doing these things, to comment on them, *and to know that one could be doing and thinking otherwise*, that leads a personality theorist to postulate the identity factor. (Rychlak 1976a:220; emphasis added)

In chapter 6, an extensive discussion was given over to research focused on "bits of behaviors"—numerical ratings of target activity protocols—that are quite obviously trivial in and of themselves. But its purpose was to adduce, in a rigorous fash-ion, empirical evidence that there were indeed dialectically sen-tient identities contributing to the production of those "bits of behaviors." Insofar as one is sensitive to the dialectical move-ments embedded in human thought, one appreciates in like mea-sure that thought is not merely memorative but *generative*. And while it is the memorative quality of thought that is emphasized under prevailing mediational conceptions of cognition, it is, I believe, in the generative quality of thought that we find the personality of knowledge.

Of course, in speaking of the "personality of knowledge" I am not referring to individual differences in knowledge contents. The personality of Smith's knowledge—about himself, about others, and about the world in which he lives—resides neither in its "uniqueness" to Smith nor in its differences from the knowledge possessed by others. The personality of Smith's knowledge resides in its *individuality*, i.e., in the fact that it is *his own*. Whether it is or is not uniquely his own is a moot point, simply because it remains his own in either case. Moreover, the respects (if any) in which the contents of Smith's knowledge differentiate him from others are equally irrelevant to an understanding of Smith's psychological functioning unless and until those differences are themselves the objects of Smith's reflection. In short, the phrase "personality of knowledge" refers here to the *personal identity* of knowledge in just that sense of identity described by Rychlak. I am arguing, therefore, that it is to questions concerning the nature of personal knowledge, the processes by which it is framed, by which it develops, and by which it relates to action, that basic research should be addressed. Nor do I see that these questions bear any less on our understanding of the scientists then on the subjects of personality psychology, and it is in this context that the relevance of our discussion in chapter 5 of the epistemology of "objective" personality measurement is most clearly seen.

A few years ago, I received from a colleague at another university some correspondence in which I was questioned about the need to invest the scientific study of personality with such theoretical arcana as dialectical reasoning, subjective conceptions of alternative possibilities for action, personal knowledge, etc. Drawing an analogy to the physical sciences, my correspondent asked me (not unfacetiously) if in developing theories about the origin of the universe, the expansion of galaxies from each other, and so on, scientists found it necessary to concern themselves with the interpretation placed by a planet on its own trajectory and velocity. In my reply, I acknowledged astonishment at the inclination to analogize the subjects of our inquiries—persons—to the subjects of inquiry in physical science, rather than to the *inquirers* in physical science. Attempting to provide my correspondent a glimpse at what might emerge were we as personality psychologists more sympathetic to the latter, and surely more apt, analogy, I then offered for his consideration the following passage from William Barrett's *The Illusion of Technique*. As I did for my correspondent, I would note here that Barrett's focus in this passage is not on Galileo's discoveries per se, but on the *kind of thinking* that gave rise to those discoveries.

> The chief theoretical part of the new science was to be mechanics . . . and to establish mechanics mathematically, it was necessary to have a decisive and clear-cut concept of inertia as a fundamental characteristic of moving bodies. What does Galileo do? He does not turn to the "irreducible and stubborn" facts; rather, he sets up a concept that could never be realized in actual fact. Imagine, he says, a perfectly smooth and frictionless plane; set a ball rolling upon this plane, and it will roll on to infinity unless another body and force interpose to stop it. Well, experience never presents us with perfectly frictionless surfaces nor with planes infinite in extension. No matter; these conditions supply us with a concept of inertia more fruitful for theory than any that would be yielded by the "irreducible and stubborn" facts themselves.
> Rationalism does not surrender itself here to the brute facts. Rather, it sets itself over the facts in their haphazard sequence; *it takes the audacious step of positing conditions contrary to fact, and it proceeds to measure the facts in the light of the contrafactual conditions.* Reason becomes legislative of experience—this was the decisive point that Kant's genius perceived as the real revolution of the new science and that he, consequently, proclaimed should become the revolution within future philosophy. (Barrett 1979:200–1; emphasis added)

In this passage, we see Galileo—the scientist but also the person—(a) reasoning away from what is "out there" in the realm of "irreducible and stubborn" facts, and then (b) proceeding to make sense out of—i.e., measure or give meaning to—what is "out there" with reference to what is not out there but conceivable to him nonetheless. In chapter 5, I tried to show how

this same sort of reasoning process is embedded in the epistemology of psychological measurement even when, as has traditionally been the case, the to-be-interpreted measurements are
normative in the technical sense of the term. More specifically,
we saw that while a Z-score (or the area under the normal curve
to which it corresponds) conveys by itself knowledge about the
direction and amount in which an individual deviates from a group
mean with respect to "something," it does not convey any knowledge about what that something is. Thus, the objective of endow-
ing the numerical value with a psychological interpretation—
without which the former bears no interest—cannot be accomplished simply by referring to the "irreducible and stubborn" facts
of other individuals' scores. It can only be accomplished with reference to the alternative possibilities built into the assessment
procedure itself. The latter is in its turn the product of a sentient
investigator's—an identity's—ability to envision alternative possibilities before they are ever instantiated, and indeed whether or
not certain of those possibilities (e.g., the extremes) are ever empirically instantiated at all. Rationalism "surrenders itself to the
brute facts" no more here than for Galileo.

    In all likelihood, the correspondent to whom I alluded
above would object not at all to my suggestion that in his own
efforts as a psychological scientist *he* was reasoning in the style
of Galileo. What is startling, of course, is the preparedness of that
same correspondent to reduce the subjects of his inquiries to the
status of the objects about which Galileo reasoned. Yet like Galileo—and most unlike the objects he studied—the subjects of
the research discussed in chapter 6 seemed to reason away from
the target activity protocols they *were* presented with to ideas about
activity protocols they *were not* presented with, and they seemed
then to "measure" or give meaning to the former with reference
to the latter. It appears, on the evidence, that they took the au-
dacious step of positing conditions contrary to fact, and then proceeded to measure the facts in the light of the contrafactuals. The
"rating behaviors" my subjects gave me to observe and then
quantitatively analyze were thus not mere "responses," but *rational actions*, born of their own capacities as sentient identities to

gain knowledge about "the facts" not with reference to other "facts" (or to the memory traces thereof), but with reference to negations of the facts implicit in the latter's very assertion.

So even as the movement to re-cognize basic research in the psychology of personality continues to unfold, it should do so divested of the assumption that the subjects of our inquiries can safely be analogized to the objects Galileo pondered. In an altogether contrary but most rudimentary sense, we are each of us, as scientists and as subjects, Galileo. In light of its profound theoretical implications, I believe that if a new generation of personality investigators can invest this notion with all the seriousness heretofore reserved for the reliability and validity coefficients generated by individual differences research, the future of this most important subdiscipline of scientific psychology can be bright indeed.

Epilog

Since this discussion has been trained on matters epistemological, there is, of course, much of relevance to the psychology of personality that has gone unsaid. But while the reader is thus burdened to "fill in" various metaphysical, theoretical, and empirical "blanks," either on his/her own with the help of other authors, it is hoped that the arguments developed in the preceding pages will serve to inform such efforts. For if it is true—and it is—that an epistemological inquiry cannot by itself yield a "complete" psychology of personality, it is also true that no viable psychology of personality can issue from faulty epistemology. With this in mind, I conclude by briefly recapitulating the central themes I have sought to develop here. In so doing, I will seek to clarify certain points with respect to which I am wary of being misconstrued.

One question that may be of continuing concern is where the foregoing leaves us with respect to the nomothetic vs. idiographic debate discussed at some length in chapter 1. I would now submit, however, that there is nothing left of this controversy. The grounds for this contention are:

> (a) that individuals are the entities over which the personality theorist seeks generality in his/her quest for nomothetic principles;
> (b) that such principles are thus those found to hold for each of many individuals; and
> (c) that since the empirical findings generated by in-

dividual differences research—i.e., "nomothetic" inquiry in its traditional conception—have no legitimate interpretation whatsoever at the level of the
individual, they cannot possibly constitute knowledge
of what holds for each of many individuals.

The conclusion is inescapable that what has long been
called "nomothetic" inquiry in fact is not, has never been, and
will never be nomothetic in the only sense of that term to which
a personality theorist is logically bound. Moreover, if by the term
"idiographic inquiry" we are simply to mean inquiry conducted
case by case on individual persons, then the conclusion is also
inescapable that idiographic inquiry is the only way to nomothetic principles concerning individual psychological functioning.

Throughout the unfortunate "nomothetic vs. idiographic" controversy, the impediment to progress has always been
the failure of disputants on both sides to grasp the last of the
three assertions listed above. Hence, considerable discussion was
devoted in chapter 2 to the logic and methods of conventional
"nomothetic" inquiry, and in chapter 3 to documenting its legacy
in the various schools of thought that can be identified on the
contemporary scene. These discussions were by way of a prelude
to chapter 4, where it was shown that in all cases except those in
which the aggregate statistical indices generated by individual
differences research are perfect—which is to say in all cases—the
third assertion is both true and, in combination with the first two
assertions (which have never been seriously contested), decisive.
It is for this reason that with respect to very crux of the controversy there is, so far as I can see, nothing more to debate.

Of course, none of this resolves the question of what
we are to study at the level of the individual. The fact that personality theorists differ so dramatically in their conceptions of
individual psychological functioning renders this question all the
more problematic. Still, I have argued that beneath these vast
differences lies a common concern, namely, that of comprehend-
ing individual behavior in terms of its meaning as framed, consciously or otherwise, by the behaving individual. If this is indeed

a central and pantheoretical concern within the psychology of personality, then the most fundamental questions concern the way in which—i.e., the grounds on and reasoning processes through which—persons frame meanings. From here it is but a small step to the realization that human cognition is necessarily a focal subject matter of theoretically driven research. I am persuaded that genuine advances in personality theory await concerted and epistemologically sound efforts of personality investigators in this direction, and I would offer the studies discussed in chapter 6 as one concrete example—illustrative and not definitive—of the manner in which basic personality research should proceed.

One danger in emphasizing as I have the importance of focusing on the cognitive processes of "the actors and the observers, the subjects and the scientists" of personality psychology is that as investigators we eventually leave ourselves and those we study "lost in thought." Out of respect for this hazard I would make the following observations.

First, I do not believe that personality investigators should—or even can—divorce themselves from the study of human action. Indeed, I believe that a considered appraisal of the works of various theorists reveals in every case a commitment to the view that thought and action are intimately interwoven, even as it is true that in the hands of different theorists the fabric of the presumed relationship between thought and action acquires markedly different textures (see, e.g., Leont'ev 1978). Hence, a mature psychology of personality will attend no less to the actions of individuals than to their reasoning processes, an approach implicit in the assertion that the core concern of personality theory is the meaning of behavior as framed by the behaving individual. If in this book I have concentrated on cognition, that is only because I perceive a need to counterbalance the rather curious notion, at large among contemporary personality investigators, that the study of reasoning somehow constitutes a "diversion" from the legitimate concerns of personality theory. In my view, this notion is simply wrong.

A second observation I would make is that in emphasizing the need to study individuals, I am not suggesting that the personality investigator can safely ignore the physical and social milieu in which a person exists. To the best of my knowledge, no personality theorist has ever adopted such a view, for obvious enough reasons. By the same token, however, even those theorists who have often been regarded more as social psychologists in their basic orientations (e.g., Alfred Adler, Harry Stack Sullivan, Kurt Lewin, Julian Rotter, and Albert Bandura, to name just a few) could see that a coherent account of the manner in which the physical and social milieu influences personality and its development would be impossible without an equally coherent conception of individual psychological functioning. Those theorists recognized, in other words, that no viable social psychology, or cognitive psychology, or developmental psychology, or psychology of learning, or psychology of emotion, or psychology of anything can exist without a psychology of person-ality. Unfortunately, far too many intellectual heirs of the above-named theorists have lost sight of this fact, and in so doing fancied (a) that satisfactory explanations for behavior can be fashioned from the study of "causal forces" emanating from the physical and social world, and hence that (b) a coherent theoretical conception of persons is unnecessary. Harré (1981) has commented elegantly on the speciousness of this view:

> It is easy to see how aherence to a degenerate Humean theory of causality leads directly to the mindless empiricism of much psychological experimentation. If there could be causation in the mere juxtaposition of events [e.g., "person variables," "situation variables," and "criterion variables,"; see chapter 7], no role is left for an agent or powerful particular in a theory of production of effects. As a positivist one is counselled to study the confidence levels of correlations between types of treatments and types of effects through examining numbers of cases. By adopting this advice, one can avoid the deep study of the internal processes and activities of agents which bring these effects about. But *causal processes occur only in individual human beings, since mechanisms of actions, even when we act as members of collectives, must be realized in particular persons.* To study causal processes a psychologist would have to adopt an intensive design contrary to the traditional empiricist methodology. (Harre 1981:14; emphasis added)

In many ways, Harré's remarks could serve as a manifesto for the position I am adopting here. For not only has he clearly articulated the need within scientific psychology for a coherent theoretical conception of persons, but in so doing he has also—and not at all coincidentally—found need to conceive of persons as causal agents bringing effects about. While this point broaches a complex metaphysical issue that lies well beyond the scope of the present work, I would offer a few words on the matter here.

In *The Function of Reason*, Whitehead noted that

Many a scientist has patiently designed experiments for the *purpose* of substantiating his belief that animal operations are motivated by no purposes. He has perhaps spent his spare time in writing articles to prove that human beings are as other animals so that "purpose" is a category irrelevant for the explanation of their bodily activities, his own activities included. Scientists animated by the purpose of proving that they are purposeless constitute an interesting subject for study. (Whitehead 1929:16; emphasis in original)

Psychology in general and personality psychology in particular have long been dominated by scientists answering to the description Whitehead offers in this passage. However, at least some contemporaries have endeavored to reintroduce notions such as purposiveness and intentionality into theoretically based explanations for human action. Within personality psychology, one prominent figure in this regard has been Rychlak (e.g., 1976a, 1976b, 1976c, 1977, 1981a, 1981b, 1981c), and it happens that the concept of dialectical reasoning forms the very cornerstone of his theorizing. More specifically, Rychlak argues that if human "mentation"—the framing of personally meaningful ideas—involves the capacity to reason from the world as given to a world not itself given but dialectically implicit as alternative possibilities in what is given, then it is sensible and necessary to incorporate into our theoretical accounts of human action the notion that persons generate both meanings and actions and hence are genuinely causal agents in the production of effects (see also Searle 1983, esp. ch. 4).

I would not wish to be read as an apologist for Rychlak, who is not in need of one, but I do wish to emphasize that, in my own view, the conceptual essence of the material presented in chapters 5 and 6 is quite in line with his view and—again not coincidentally—with that articulated by Whitehead. More specifically, I concur with Rychlak's thesis that the concept of dialectical reasoning or something like it is necessary in order to fashion theories of persons that are at once (a) faithful to the notion that human reasoning involves more than the processing of information "given" by the world of "irreducible and stubborn facts," and hence (b) adequate to the theoretical challenge of capturing the intentionality of human action.

I concur also with Whitehead's thesis that scientists animated by the purpose of proving that they are purposeless constitute an interesting subject for study. Thus did I attempt to show in chapter 5, through a close analysis of a seemingly simple activity that has long constituted the foundation of empirical personality research—the measurement of persons—that the meanings of the products of that activity, i.e., the measurements, cannot be fully articulated without reference to the assessment procedures from which those measurements are derived. Assessment procedures have built into them the alternative possibilities some a priori conception of which must ultimately be invoked in order to endow any given assessment with a psychological interpretation, and those alternatives are themselves fixed by a dialectically reasoning investigator who fashions a particular procedure (selects observational variables, designates weights or "relevance values," etc.) to suit his purposes. I then presented empirical evidence in chapter 6 to the effect that the reasoning process through which the "objects" of the personality investigator's measurement operations—persons—frame their own subjectively meaningful judgments about self and others is similarly dialectical in nature. Hence, just as we are obliged to regard the investigators as causal agents, expressing intended and not merely "processed" meanings via their "objective" measurements of persons, so also, it would seem, must we regard the subjects of personality research as causal agents, capable of expressing intended and not merely "processed" meanings via their subjective ratings of persons.

I should perhaps interject here that I do not offer the model of interactive measurement defined by equation (5.3) as "the" formal representation of dialectical reasoning. Indeed, I am not at all sure that "a" formal expression of dialectical reasoning can be defined. Instead, I have offered that equation as one formal representation of the play of dialectical reasoning within the circumscribed contexts of "objective" and "subjective" person characterization. Stated otherwise, I believe not that interactive measurement "is" dialectical reasoning, but rather that interactive measurement exists as a coherent rationale for the characterization of persons as a result of the human capacity to reason dialectically, i.e., as a consequence of that feature of human judgment whereby the meaning of what is can be framed with reference to a conception of what is not but might be. I further believe, with Cattell, that it is the capacity to calibrate events or entities in this way from which all other rationales for psychological measurement derive. Finally, I believe that if it is possible to discern the play of dialectical reasoning in so simple a context as person characterization, there is every reason to suspect that such reasoning is at play in other human contexts as well. When all is said and done, this is the theoretical point of greatest consequence.

In my view, the difference that seems to exist between the reasoning of personality investigators and the reasoning of the subjects themselves is not a genuine difference at all. It is merely the appearance of a difference, borne of the fact that, having necessarily begun in considerations of a dialectical nature, personality investigators have historically proceeded to obfuscate the epistemological role of those considerations by overlaying them with normative considerations. I would submit that except under conditions where "Smith" is specifically trained or otherwise induced to invoke them, normative considerations are never of more than secondary relevance to his judgments of self and others and, in a great many instances, of no relevance at all.

If the analysis I have offered here is cogent, then there

is indeed a personality of cognition that contemporary cognitive psychology cannot be expected to reveal by itself. Accordingly, there is an important role for personality investigators to play in the further maturation of cognitive psychology. It is my hope that this role will not go begging while those who animate the psychology of personality continue to busy themselves with the assessment and study of individual differences variables. For if through this lengthy and in places difficult treatise I have established nothing else, this much I hope to have made clear: so long as personality investigators remain widely committed to the view that "the study of personality is essentially the study of individual differences," the psychology of personality will never be as well as it is alive.

References

Alker, H. A. 1972. Is personality situationally specific or intrapsychically consistent? *Journal of Personality* 40:1–16.

Allport, G. W. 1937a. *Personality: A Psychological Interpretation*. New York: Holt, Rinehart, and Winston.

Allport, G. W. 1937b. The personalistic psychology of William Stern. *Character and Personality* 5:231–46.

Allport, G. W. 1961. *Pattern and Growth in Personality*. New York: Holt, Rinehart, and Winston.

Allport, G. W. 1962. The general and the unique in psychological science. *Journal of Personality* 30:405–22.

Allport, G. W. 1965. *Letters from Jenny*. New York: Harcourt, Brace, and World.

Allport, G. W. 1966. Traits revisited. *American Psychologist* 21:1–10.

Allport, G. W. 1967. *The Person in Psychology*. Boston: Beacon Press.

Angyal, A. 1941. *Foundations for a Science of Personality*. New York: Commonwealth Fund.

Argyle, M., and B. R. Little. 1972. Do personality traits apply to social behaviour? *Journal for the Theory of Social Behaviour* 2:1–35.

Asch, S. E. 1946. Forming impressions of personality. *Journal of Abnormal and Social Psychology* 41:258–90.

Bakan, D. 1966. The test of significance in psychological research. *Psychological Bulletin* 66:423–37.

Bandura, A. 1978. The self system in reciprocal determinism. *American Psychologist* 33:344–58.

Barrett, W. 1979. *The Illusion of Technique*. Garden City, NY: Anchor Press/Doubleday.

Beck, S. J. 1953. The science of personality: Nomothetic or idiographic? *Psychological Review* 60:353–59.

Bem, D. J. 1972. Constructing cross-situational consistencies in behavior: Some thoughts on Alker's critique of Mischel. *Journal of Personality* 40:17–26.

Bem, D. J. 1982. Toward a response style theory of persons in situations. In R.

A. Dienstbier and M. M. Page, eds., *Nebraska Symposium on Motivation 1982: Personality—Current Theory and Research*, 30:201–31. Lincoln: University of Nebraska Press.

Bem, D. J. 1983. Constructing a theory of the triple typology: Some (second) thoughts on nomothetic and idiographic approaches to personality. *Journal of Personality* 51:566–77.

Bem, D. J., and A. Allen. 1974. On predicting some of the people some of the time: The search for cross-situational consistencies in behavior. *Psychological Review* 81:506–20.

Bem, D. J., and D. C. Funder. 1978. Predicting more of the people more of the time: Assessing the personality of situations. *Psychological Review* 85:485–501.

Block, J. 1957. A comparison between ipsative and normative ratings of personality. *Journal of Abnormal and Social Psychology* 54:50–54.

Block, J. 1977. Advancing the psychology of personality: Paradigmatic shift or improving the quality of research? In D. Magnusson and N. S. Endler, eds., *Personality at the Crossroads: Current Issues in Interactional Psychology*, pp. 37–68. Hillsdale, NJ: Erlbaum.

Bowers, K. S. 1973. Situationism in psychology: An analysis and a critique. *Psychological Review* 80:307–36.

Broughton, R. 1984. A prototype strategy for construction of personality scales. *Journal of Personality and Social Psychology* 47:1334–46.

Bruner, J. S., and R. Tagiuri. 1954. The perception of people. In G. Lindzey, ed., *Handbook of Social Psychology*, pp. 634–54. Cambridge, MA: Addison-Wesley.

Budescu, D. V. 1980. Some new measures of profile dissimilarity. *Applied Psychological Measurement* 4:261–72.

Buss, D. M., and K. H. Craik. 1980. The frequency concept of disposition: Dominance and prototypically dominant acts. *Journal of Personality*, 48:379–92.

Buss, D. M., and K. H. Craik. 1981. The act frequency analysis of interpersonal dispositions: Aloofness, gregariousness, dominance, and submissiveness. *Journal of Personality* 49:174–92.

Buss, D. M., and K. H. Craik. 1983a. The act frequency approach to personality. *Psychological Review* 90:105–26.

Buss, D. M., and K. H. Craik. 1983b. Act prediction and the conceptual analysis of personality scales: Indices of act density, bipolarity, and extensity. *Journal of Personality and Social Psychology* 45:1081–95.

Buss, D. M., and K. H. Craik. 1983c. The dispositional analysis of everyday conduct. *Journal of Personality* 51:393–412.

Buss, D. M., and K. H. Craik. 1984. Acts, dispositions, and personality. In B. A. Maher and W. B. Maher, eds., *Progress in Experimental Personality Research*, 13:241–301. New York: Academic Press.

Buss, D. M., and K. H. Craik. 1985. Why not measure that trait? *Journal of Personality and Social Psychology* 48:934–46.

Buss, D. M., and K. H. Craik. 1986. Acts, dispositions, and clinical assessment:

The psychopathology of everyday conduct. *Clinical Psychology Review* 6:387–406.

Cameron, N., and J. F. Rychlak. 1985. *Personality Development and Psychopathology: A Dynamic Approach*. 2d ed. Boston: Houghton-Mifflin.

Campbell, D. T., and D. W. Fiske. 1959. Convergent and discriminant validation by the multitrait-multimethod matrix. *Psychological Bulletin* 56:81–105.

Cantor, N., and J. F. Kihlstrom, eds. 1981. *Personality, Cognition, and Social Interaction*. Hillsdale, NJ: Erlbaum.

Cantor, N., and W. Mischel. 1979. Prototypes in person perception. In L. Berkowitz, ed., *Advances in Experimental Social Psychology*, 12:3–52. New York: Academic Press.

Carlson, R. 1971. Where is the person in personality research? *Journal of Personality and Social Psychology* 75:203–14.

Cattell, R. B. 1944. Psychological measurement: Normative, ipsative, interactive. *Psychological Review* 51:292–303.

Cattell, R. B. 1950. *Personality*. New York: McGraw-Hill.

Cohen, J. 1968. Multiple regression as a general data analytic system. *Psychological Bulletin* 70:426–43.

Conger, A. J. 1983. Toward a further understanding of the intuitive personologist: Some critical evidence on the diabolical quality of subjective psychometrics. *Journal of Personality* 51:248–58.

Conley, J. J. 1983. Theoretical nihilism in personality psychology. *Personality Forum* 1:8–11.

Crockett, W. H. 1965. Cognitive complexity and impression formation. In B. Maher, ed., *Progress in Experimental Personality Research*, 2:47–90. New York: Academic Press.

Cronbach, L. J. 1957. The two disciplines of scientific psychology. *American Psychologist* 12:671–84.

Cronbach, L. J., and G. Gleser. 1953. Assessing similarity between profiles. *Psychological Bulletin* 50:456–73.

Cronbach, L. J., and P. E. Meehl. 1955. Construct validity in psychological tests. *Psychological Bulletin* 52:281–302.

D'Andrade, R. G. 1965. Trait psychology and componential analysis. *American Psychologist* 67:215–28.

Darlington, R. 1968. Multiple regression in psychological research and practice. *Psychological Bulletin* 69:161–82.

Dawes, R. G. 1986. Representative thinking in clinical judgment. *Clinical Psychology Review* 6:425–41.

DeWaele, J. P. 1985. The significance of action psychology for personality research and assessment. In J. P. Gisburg, M. Brenner, and M. von Cranach, eds., *Discovery Strategies in the Psychology of Action*, pp. 115–70. London: Academic Press.

DeWaele, J. P., and R. Harre. 1974. The personality of individuals. In R. Harre, ed., *Personality*, pp. 189–246. Oxford, England: Basil Blackwell.

Diener, E., R. Larsen, and R. Emmons. 1984. Person x situation interactions: Choice of situations and congruence response models. *Journal of Personality and Social Psychology* 47:580–92.

Ebbesen, E. B. 1979. Cognitive processes in implicit trait inferences. *Journal of Personality and Social Psychology* 37:471–88.

Ebbesen, E. B. 1981. Cognitive processes in inferences about a person's personality. In E. T. Higgins, C. P. Herman, and M. P. Zanna, eds., *Social Cognition: The Ontario Symposium*, pp. 247–76. Hillsdale, NJ: Erlbaum.

Edwards, A. L. 1964. *Experimental Design in Psychological Research.* Rev. ed. New York: Holt.

Ekehammar, B. 1974. Interactionism in personality psychology from a historical perspective. *Psychological Bulletin* 81:1026–48.

Endler, N. S. 1976. The case for person-situation interactions. In N. S. Endler and D. Magnusson, eds., *Interactional Psychology and Personality*, pp. 58–70. Washington, D. C.: Hemisphere.

Endler, N. S., and J. McV. Hunt. 1966. Sources of behavioral variance as measured by the S-R Inventory of Anxiousness. *Psychological Bulletin* 65:336–46.

Endler, N. S., and J. McV. Hunt. 1968. S-R Inventories of Hostilities and comparisons of the proportions of variance from persons, responses, and situations for hostility and anxiousness. *Journal of Personality and Social Psychology* 9:309–15.

Endler, N. S., and D. Magnusson. 1976. Toward an interactional psychology of personality. *Psychological Bulletin* 83:956–74.

Epstein, S. 1977. Traits are alive and well. In D. Magnusson and N. S. Endler, eds., *Personality at the Crossroads: Current Issues in Interactional Psychology*, pp. 83–98. Hillsdale, NJ: Erlbaum.

Epstein, S. 1979. The stability of behavior: I. On predicting most of the people much of the time. *Journal of Personality and Social Psychology* 37:1097–1126.

Epstein, S. 1980. The stability of behavior: II. Implications for psychological research. *American Psychologist* 35:790–806.

Epstein, S. 1983. Aggregation and beyond: Some basic issues in the prediction of behavior. *Journal of Personality* 51:360–92.

Eysenck, H. J. 1954. The science of personality: Nomothetic! *Psychological Review* 61:339–42.

Falk, J. 1956. Issues distinguishing idiographic from nomothetic approaches to personality theory. *Psychological Review* 63:53–62.

Farber, I. E. 1964. A framework for the study of personality as a behavioral science. In P. Worchel and D. Byrne, eds., *Personality Change*, pp. 3–37. New York: Wiley.

Feshbach, S. 1984. The "personality" of personality theory and research. *Personality and Social Psychology Bulletin* 10:446–56.

Fiske, D. W. 1973. Can a personality construct be validated empirically? *Psychological Bulletin* 80:89–92.

Fiske, D. W. 1974. The limits for the conventional science of personality. *Journal of Personality* 42:1–11.

Fiske, D. W. 1978a. *Strategies for Personality Research.* San Francisco: Jossey-Bass.

Fiske, D. W. 1978b. Cosmopolitan constructs and provincial observations: Some prescriptions for a chronically ill specialty. In H. London, ed., *Personality: A New Look at Metatheories*, pp. 21–43. New York: Wiley.

Fiske, D. W. 1979. Two worlds of psychological phenomena. *American Psychologist* 34:733–39.

Forgus, R., and B. H. Shulman. 1979. *Personality: A Cognitive View.* Englewood Cliffs, NJ: Prentice-Hall.

Franck, I. 1982. Psychology as a science: Resolving the idiographic-nomothetic controversy. *Journal for the Theory of Social Behaviour* 12:1–20.

Funder, D. C. 1980. The "trait" of assigning traits: Individual differences in the tendency to trait ascription. *Journal of Research in Personality* 14:376–85.

Gara, M. A., and S. Rosenberg. 1981. Linguistic factors in implicit personality theory. *Journal of Personality and Social Psychology* 41:450–57.

Gergen, K. J. 1982. From self to science: What is there to know? In J. Suls, ed., *Psychological Perspectives on the Self*, 1:129–49. Hillsdale, NJ: Erlbaum.

Giorgi, A. 1970. *Psychology as a Human Science: A Phenomenologically Based Approach.* New York: Harper and Row.

Gleitman, H. 1981. *Psychology.* New York: Norton.

Goldberg, L. R. 1968. Simple models or simple processes? Some research on clinical judgments. *American Psychologist* 23:483–96.

Goldfried, M. R., and R. N. Kent. 1972. Traditional versus behavioral personality assessment: A comparison of methodological and theoretical assumptions. *Psychological Bulletin* 77:409–20.

Golding, S. L. 1975. Flies in the ointment: Methodological problems in the analysis of the percentage of variance due to persons and situations. *Psychological Bulletin* 82:278–88.

Golding, S. L. 1978. Toward a more adequate theory of personality: Psychological organizing principles. In H. London, ed., *Personality: A New Look at Metatheories*, pp. 69–95. New York: Wiley.

Gormly, J. 1984. Correspondence between personality trait ratings and behavioral events. *Journal of Personality* 52:220–32.

Hall, C. S., and G. Lindzey. 1957. *Theories of Personality.* New York: Wiley.

Hall, C. S., and G. Lindzey. 1978. *Theories of Personality.* 3d ed. New York: Wiley.

Hampson, S. E. 1986. Personality traits as cognitive categories. In A. Angleitner, A. Furnham, and G. van Heck, eds., *Personality Psychology in Europe: Current Trends and Controversies*, pp. 103–16. Lisse, The Netherlands: Swets and Zeitlinger.

Harman, H. H. 1967. *Factor Analysis.* 2d ed. Chicago: University of Chicago Press.

Harré, R. 1981. The positivist-empiricist approach and its alternative. In P. Reason and J. Rowan, eds., *Human Inquiry*, pp. 3–17. New York: Wiley.

Harris, J. G., Jr. 1980. Nomovalidation and idiovalidation: A quest for the true personality profile. *American Psychologist* 35:729–44.

Hartshorne, H., M. A. May, and F. K. Shuttleworth. 1930. *Studies in the Organization of Character.* New York: Macmillan.

Hase, H. D., and L. R. Goldberg. 1967. Comparative validity of different strategies of constructing personality inventory scales. *Psychological Bulletin* 67:231–48.

Heilbrun, A. B., Jr. 1963. Evidence regarding the equivalence of ipsative and normative personality scales. *Journal of Consulting Psychology* 27:152–56.

Helson, H. 1964. *Adaptation-level Theory.* New York: Harper and Row.

Higgins, E. T., N. A. Kuiper, and J. M. Olson. 1981. Social cognition: A need to get personal. In E. T. Higgins, C. P. Herman, and M. P. Zanna, eds., *Social Cognition: The Ontario Symposium,* pp. 395–420. Hillsdale, NJ: Erlbaum.

Higgins, E. T., C. R. Rholes, and C. R. Jones. 1977. Category accessibility and impression formation. *Journal of Experimental Social Psychology* 13:141–54.

Hjelle, L. A., and Ziegler, D. J. 1981. *Personality Theories: Basic Assumptions, Research, and Applications.* New York: McGraw-Hill.

Hogan, R. 1983. On publishing in personality psychology: Trends and developments. *Personality Forum* 1:4–5.

Holt, R. 1962. Individuality and generalization in the psychology of personality. *Journal of Personality* 30:377–404.

Hyland, M. E. 1985. Do person variables exist in different ways? *American Psychologist* 40:1003–10.

Jackson, D. N. 1969. The multidimensional nature of human social perception. *Canadian Journal of Behavioral Science* 1:227–62.

Jackson, D. N., and S. Messick. 1963. Individual differences in social perception. *British Journal of Clinical and Social Psychology* 2:1–10.

James, W. 1890. *Principles of Psychology.* New York: Henry Holt.

Jones, E. E., and T. S. Pittman. 1982. Toward a general theory of strategic self-presentation. In J. Suls, ed., *Psychological Perspectives on the Self,* 1:231–62. Hillsdale, NJ: Erlbaum.

Jones, L., and F. W. Young. 1972. Structure of a social environment. Longitudinal individual differences scaling of an intact group. *Journal of Personality and Social Psychology* 24:108–21.

Kelly, G. A. 1955. *The Psychology of Personal Constructs.* New York: Norton.

Kenrick, D. T., and D. O. Stringfield. 1980. Personality traits and the eye of the beholder: Crossing some traditional philosophical boundaries in the search for consistency in all of the people. *Psychological Review* 87:88–104.

Kerlinger, F. N., and E. J. Pedhazur. 1974. *Multiple Regression in Behavioral Research.* New York: Holt, Rinehart, and Winston.

Kim, M. P., and S. Rosenberg. 1980. Comparison of two structural models of implicit personality theory. *Journal of Personality and Social Psychology* 38:375–89.

Kleinmuntz, B. 1967. *Personality Measurement: An Introduction.* Homewood, IL: Dorsey Press.

Kosok, M. 1976. The systematization of dialectical logic for the study of development and change. *Human Development* 19:325–50.

Krauskopf, C. J. 1978. Comment on Endler and Magnusson's attempt to redefine personality. *Psychological Bulletin* 85:280–83.

Lamiell, J. T. 1980. On the utility of looking in the "wrong" direction. *Journal of Personality* 48:82–88.

Lamiell, J. T. 1981. Toward an idiothetic psychology of personality. *American Psychologist* 36:276–89.

Lamiell, J. T. 1982. The case for an idiothetic psychology of personality: A conceptual and empirical foundation. In B. A. Maher and W. B. Maher, eds., *Progress In Experimental Personality Research*, 11:1–64. New York: Academic Press.

Lamiell, J. T. 1984. Personality: The individual in a scientific psychology. In W. N. Dember, J. J. Jenkins, and T. J. Teyler, *General Psychology*, 2d ed., pp. 635–77. Hillsdale, NJ: Erlbaum.

Lamiell, J. T. 1986. Epistemological tenets of an idiothetic psychology of personality. In A. Angleitner, A. Furnham, and G. van Heck, eds., *Personality Psychology in Europe: Current Issues and Controversies*, pp. 3–22. Lisse, The Netherlands: Swets and Zeitlinger.

Lamiell, J. T., M. A. Foss, and P. Cavenee. 1980. On the relationship between conceptual schemes and behavior reports: A closer look. *Journal of Personality* 48:54–73.

Lamiell, J. T., M. A. Foss, R. J. Larsen, and A. Hempel. 1983. Studies in intuitive personology from an idiothetic point of view: Implications for personality theory. *Journal of Personality* 51:438–67.

Lamiell, J. T., M. A. Foss, S. J. Trierweiler, and G. M. Leffel. 1983. Toward a further understanding of the intuitive personologist: Some preliminary evidence for the dialectical quality of subjective personality impressions. *Journal of Personality* 53:213–35.

Lamiell, J. T., and S. J. Trierweiler. 1986a. Personality measurement and intuitive personality judgments from an idiothetic point of view. *Clinical Psychology Review* 6:471–91.

Lamiell, J. T., and S. J. Trierweiler. 1986b. Idiothetic inquiry and the challenge to conventional "nomotheticism." *Journal of Personality* 54:460–69.

Lamiell, J. T., S. J. Trierweiler, and M. A. Foss. 1983a. Detecting (in)consistencies in personality: Reconciling intuitions and empirical evidence. *Journal of Personality Assessment* 47:380–89.

Lamiell, J. T., S. J. Trierweiler, and M. A. Foss. 1983b. Theoretical vs. actuarial analyses of personality ratings, and other rudimentary distinctions. *Journal of Personality* 51:259–74.

Landfield, A. W. 1976. Interpretive man: The enlarged self-image. In J. K. Cole and A. W. Landfield, eds., *Nebraska Symposium on Motivation*, 24:127–77. Lincoln: University of Nebraska Press.

Lay, C., and D. N. Jackson. 1969. Analysis of the generality of trait-inferential relationships. *Journal of Personality and Social Psychology* 12:12–21.

208   References

Lehman, H. C., and P. A. Witty. 1934. Faculty psychology and personality traits. *American Journal of Psychology* 44:490.

Leont'ev, A. N. 1978. *Activity, Consciousness, and Personality.* Englewood Cliffs, NJ: Prentice-Hall. (Translated from the Russian by Marie J. Hall.)

Levy, L. 1970. *Conceptions of Personality: Theories and Research.* New York: Random House.

Loevinger, J. 1966. Psychological tests in the conceptual framework of psychology. In K. R. Hammond, ed., *The Psychology of Egon Brunswik,* pp. 107–48. New York: Holt, Rinehart, and Winston.

McClelland, D. C. 1951. *Personality.* New York: Sloane.

McGowan, J., and J. Gormly. 1976. Validation of personality traits: A multicriteria approach. *Journal of Personality and Social Psychology* 34:791–95.

Magnusson, D., and B. Ekehammar. 1975. Perceptions of and reactions to stressful situations. *Journal of Personality and Social Psychology* 31:1147–54.

Magnusson, D., and N. S. Endler. 1977. *Personality at the Crossroads: Current Issues in Interactional Psychology.* Hillsdale, NJ: Erlbaum.

Maher, B. A., ed. 1969. *Clinical Psychology and Personality: The Selected Papers of George Kelly.* New York: Wiley.

Mancuso, J. C., and J. R. Adams-Webber, eds., 1982. *The Construing Person.* New York: Praeger.

Markus, H. 1977. Self-schemas and processing information about the self. *Journal of Personality and Social Psychology* 35:63–78.

Markus, H. 1983. Self-knowledge: An expanded view. *Journal of Personality* 51:541–65.

Markus, H., M. Crane, S. Bernstein, and M. Siladi. 1982. Self-schemas and gender. *Journal of Personality and Social Psychology* 42:38–50.

Markus, H., and K. Sentis. 1982. The self in social information processing. In J. Suls, ed., *Social Psychological Perspectives on the Self,* 1:41–70. Hillsdale, NJ: Erlbaum.

Markus, H., and J. Smith. 1981. The influence of self-schemata on the perception of others. In N. Cantor and J. Kihlstrom, eds., *Personality, Cognition, and Social Interaction,* pp. 233–62. Hillsdale, NJ: Erlbaum.

Mehrabian, A., and E. O'Reilly. 1980. Analysis of personality measures in terms of basic dimensions of temperment. *Journal of Personality and Social Psychology* 38:492–503.

Mischel, W. 1968. *Personality and Assessment.* New York: Wiley.

Mischel, W. 1969. On continuity and change in personality. *American Psychologist* 24:1112–18.

Mischel, W. 1973. Toward a cognitive social learning reconceptualization of personality. *Psychological Review* 80:252–83.

Mischel, W. 1976. The self as the person: A cognitive social learning view. In A. Wandersman, P. Poppen, and D. Ricks, eds., *Humanism and Behaviorism: Dialogue and Growth,* pp. 145–56. New York: Pergamon Press.

Mischel, W. 1977. On the future of personality measurement. *American Psychologist* 32:246–54.

Mischel, W. 1979. On the interface of cognition and personality. *American Psychologist* 34:740–54.

Mischel, W. 1984. Convergences and challenges in the search for consistency. *American Psychologist* 39:351–64.

Mulaik, S. A. 1964. Are personality factors raters' conceptual factors? *Journal of Consulting Psychology* 28:506–11.

Murray, H. A. 1938. *Explorations in Personality*. London: Oxford University Press.

Neisser, U. 1967. *Cognitive Psychology*. New York: Appleton-Century-Crofts.

Nicholls, J. G., B. G. Licht, and R. A. Pearl. 1982. Some dangers of using personality questionnaires to study personality. *Psychological Bulletin* 92:572–80.

Norman, W. T. 1967. On estimating psychological relationships: Social desirability and self report. *Psychological Bulletin* 67:273–93.

Norman, W. T. and L. R. Goldberg. 1966. Raters, ratees, and randomness in personality structure. *Journal of Personality and Social Psychology* 4:681–91.

Nunnally, J. C. 1967. *Psychometric Theory*. New York: McGraw-Hill.

Ostrom, T. M., and D. Davis. 1979. Idiosyncratic weighting of trait information in impression formation. *Journal of Personality and Social Psychology* 37:2025–43.

Passini, F. T., and W. T. Norman. 1966. A universal conception of personality structure? *Journal of Personality and Social Psychology* 4:44–49.

Paunonen, S. V., and D. N. Jackson. 1986a. Nomothetic and idiothetic measurement in personality. *Journal of Personality* 54:447–59.

Paunonen, S. V., and D. N. Jackson. 1986b. Idiothetic inquiry and the toil of Sisyphus. *Journal of Personality* 54:470–77.

Pervin, L. A. 1985. Personality: Current controversies, issues, and directions. In M. R. Rosenzweig and L. W. Porter, eds., *Annual Review of Psychology*, 36:83–114. Palo Alto, CA: Annual Reviews.

Peterson, D. R. 1968. *The Clinical Study of Social Behavior*. New York: Appleton-Century-Crofts.

Phares, E. J. 1976. *Locus of Control in Personality*. Morristown, NJ: General Learning Press.

Polanyi, M. 1969. *Personal Knowledge*. London: Routledge and Kegan-Paul.

Rorer, L. G., and T. A. Widiger. 1983. Personality structure and assessment. In M. R. Rosenzweig and L. W. Porter, eds., *Annual Review of Psychology*, 34:431–63. Palo Alto, CA: Annual Reviews.

Rosch, E. 1975. Cognitive reference points. *Cognitive Psychology* 7:532–47.

Rosch, E., and C. Mervis. 1975. Family resemblances: Studies in the internal structure of categories. *Cognitive Psychology* 7:573–605.

Rosenberg, S., C. Nelson and P. S. Vivekananthan. 1968. A multidimensional approach to the structure of personality impressions. *Journal of Personality and Social Psychology* 9:283–94.

Royce, J. R. 1978. How can we best advance the construction of theory in psychology? *Canadian Psychological Review* 19:259–76.

Runyan, W. M. 1982. *Life Histories and Psychobiography: Explorations in Theory and Method*. New York: Oxford University Press.

Rychlak, J. F. 1976a. Personality theory: Its nature, past, present and—future? *Personality and Social Psychology Bulletin* 2:209–24.

Rychlak, J. F., ed. 1976b. *Dialectic: Humanistic Rationale for Behavior and Development.* Basel, Switzerland: Karger.

Rychlak, J. F. 1976c. Is a concept of self necessary in psychological theory, and if so why? A humanistic perspective. In A. Wandersman, P. Poppen, and D. Ricks, eds., *Humanism and Behaviorism: Dialogue and Growth*, pp. 121–43. New York: Pergamon Press.

Rychlak, J. F. 1977. *The Psychology of Rigorous Humanism.* New York: Wiley.

Rychlak, J. F. 1979. A non-telic teleology? *American Psychologist* 34:435–38. (Comment)

Rychlak, J. F. 1981a. *Introduction to Personality and Psychotherapy.* 2d ed. Boston: Houghton-Mifflin.

Rychlak, J. F. 1981b. *A Philosophy of Science for Personality Theory.* 2d ed. Malabar, FL: Kreiger.

Rychlak, J. F. 1981c. Logical learning theory: Propositions, corollaries, and research evidence. *Journal of Personality and Social Psychology* 40:731–49.

Sanford, N. 1963. Personality: Its place in psychology. In S. Koch, ed., *Psychology: A Study of a Science*, 5:488–592. New York: McGraw-Hill.

Schneider, D. J. 1973. Implicit personality theory: A review. *Psychological Review* 79:294–309.

Searle, J. R. 1983. *Intentionality: An Essay in the Philosophy of Mind.* Cambridge: Cambridge University Press.

Sears, R. R. 1963. Dependency motivation. In M. R. Jones, ed., *Nebraska Symposium on Motivation*, pp. 25–64. Lincoln: University of Nebraska Press.

Sechrest, L. 1976. Personality. In M. R. Rosenzweig and L. W. Porter, eds., *Annual Review of Psychology*, 27:1–27. Palo Alto, CA: Annual Reviews.

Sechrest, L. 1983. Personal constructs theory. In R. J. Corsini and A. J. Marsella, eds., *Personality Theories, Research, and Assessment*, pp. 229–85. Itasca, IL: F. E. Peacock.

Shaver, P. 1985. Self, situations, and social behavior. *Review of Personality and Social Psychology*, vol. 6. Beverly Hills, CA: Sage.

Shweder, R. A. 1975. How relevant is an individual differences theory of personality? *Journal of Personality* 43:455–84.

Shweder, R. A. 1977a. Illusory correlation and the M.M.P.I. controversy. *Journal of Consulting and Clinical Psychology* 45:917–24.

Shweder, R. A. 1977b. Likeness and likelihood in everyday thought: Magical thinking in judgments about personality. *Current Anthropology* 18:637–48.

Shweder, R. A. 1980. Factors and fictions in person perception: A reply to Lamiell, Foss, & Cavenee. *Journal of Personality* 48:54–73.

Shweder, R. A. 1982. Fact and artifact in trait perception: The systematic distortion hypothesis. In B. A. Maher and W. B. Maher, eds., *Progress in Experimental Personality Research*, 11:65–100. New York: Academic Press.

Shweder, R. A., and R. G. D'Andrade. 1979. Accurate reflection or systematic distortion: A reply to Block, Weiss, and Thorne. *Journal of Personality and Social Psychology* 37:1075–84.

Shweder, R. A., and R. G. D'Andrade. 1980. The systematic distortion hypothesis. In R. A. Shweder, ed., Fallible judgment in behavioral research. *New Directions for Methodology of Social and Behavioral Science,* 4:37–58. San Francisco: Jossey-Bass

Symonds, P. M. 1931. *Diagnosing Personality and Conduct.* New York: Appleton-Century-Crofts.

Tyler, L. 1978. *Individuality: Human Possibilities and Personal Choice in the Psychological Development of Men and Women.* San Francisco: Jossey-Bass.

Ver Eecke, W. 1984. *Saying "No": Its Meaning in Child Development, Psychoanalysis, Linguistics, and Hegel.* Pittsburgh: Duquesne University Press.

Watson, J. B. 1914. *Behavior: An Introduction to Comparative Psychology.* New York: Holt.

Wegner, D. M., and R. R. Vallacher. 1977. *Implicit Psychology: An Introduction to Social Cognition.* New York: Oxford University Press.

White, R. W. 1972. *The Enterprise of Living: Growth and Organization in Personality.* New York: Holt, Rinehart, and Winston.

White, R. W. 1975. *Lives in Progress: A Study of the Natural Growth of Personality.* New York: Holt, Rinehart, and Winston.

Whitehead, A. N. 1929. *The Function of Reason.* Boston: Beacon Press.

Wiggins, J. S. 1973. *Personality and Prediction: Principles of Personality Assessment.* Reading, MA: Addison-Wesley.

Wiggins, J. S. 1979. A psychological taxonomy of trait descriptive terms: The interpersonal domain. *Journal of Personality and Social Psychology* 37:395–412.

Wiggins, J. S. 1980. Clinical and statistical prediction: Where are we and where do we go from here? *Clinical Psychology Review* 1:3–18.

Wiggins, J. S., K. E. Renner, G. L. Clore, and R. J. Rose. 1976. *Principles of Personality.* 2d ed. Reading, MA: Addison-Wesley.

Wiggins, N. 1973. Individual differences in human judgments: A multivariate approach. In L. Rappoport and D. A. Summers, eds., *Human Judgment and Social Interaction,* pp. 110–42. New York: Holt.

Windelband, W. 1921. *An Introduction to Philosophy* London: Unwin. (Translated by J. McCabe.)

Woodworth, R. S. 1918. *Dynamic Psychology.* New York: Columbia University Press.

Woody, E. Z. 1983. The intuitive personologist revisited. A critique of dialectical person perception. *Journal of Personality* 51:236–58.

Wyer, R. S., and T. K. Srull. 1981. Category accessibility: Some theoretical and empirical issues concerning the processing of social stimulus information. In E. T. Higgins, C. P. Herman, and M. P. Zanna, eds., *Social Cognition: The Ontario Symposium on Personality and Social Psychology,* pp. 161–97. Hillsdale, NJ: Erlbaum.

Index